Doing History

Research and Writing in the Digital Age

SECOND EDITION

MICHAEL J. GALGANO
James Madison University

J. CHRIS ARNDT
James Madison University

RAYMOND M. HYSER
James Madison University

WADSWORTH
CENGAGE Learning

Australia • Brazil • Japan • Korea • Mexico • Singapore • Spain • United Kingdom • United States

WADSWORTH
CENGAGE Learning·

Doing History: Research and Writing in the Digital Age, Second Edition
Michael J. Galgano, J. Chris Arndt, and Raymond M. Hyser

Senior Publisher: Suzanne Jeans

Senior Sponsoring Editor: Ann West

Assistant Editor: Megan Chrisman

Editorial Assistant: Patrick Roach

Media Editor: Lisa Ciccolo

Marketing Program Manager: Caitlin Green

Design Direction, Production Management, and Composition: PreMediaGlobal

Manufacturing Planner: Sandee Milewski

Rights Acquisition Specialist: Jennifer Meyer Dare

Cover Image:
 PC Tablet: © vm/iStockphoto
 Statue of Herodotus:
 © Hemera/Thinkstock

For product information and technology assistance, contact us at **Cengage Learning Customer & Sales Support, 1-800-354-9706**

For permission to use material from this text or product, submit all requests online at **www.cengage.com/permissions**
Further permissions questions can be e-mailed to **permissionrequest@cengage.com**

Library of Congress Control Number: 2012931473

ISBN-13: 978-1-133-58788-0

ISBN-10: 1-133-58788-7

Wadsworth
20 Channel Center Street
Boston, MA 02210
USA

Cengage Learning is a leading provider of customized learning solutions with office locations around the globe, including Singapore, the United Kingdom, Australia, Mexico, Brazil, and Japan. Locate your local office at **international.cengage.com/region**

Cengage Learning products are represented in Canada by Nelson Education, Ltd.

For your course and learning solutions, visit **www.cengage.com**

Purchase any of our products at your local college store or at our preferred online store **www.cengagebrain.com**

Instructors: Please visit **login.cengage.com** and log in to access instructor-specific resources.

Printed in the United States of America
1 2 3 4 5 6 7 16 15 14 13 12

✸

To our students—past, present, and to come

Contents

Preface and
Acknowledgements

For more than 20 years, the three of us have taught undergraduate historical methods from a common syllabus. During this period, we have worked closely together to present a coherent, "nuts and bolts" introduction to historical methodology, which emphasizes identifying all available evidence, weighing and selecting this evidence, analyzing and interpreting it, and presenting coherent history in both oral and written formats. The course has been enormously successful in teaching students how to "do history." Many of those who prepared papers in our Historical Methods course have successfully presented their findings at state, regional, and national undergraduate and professional conferences. Several have won prizes for the best paper in their respective categories. Some of these papers have also been published as abstracts, articles, and in one case, a short book. Whether or not they have continued the formal study of history, most students who completed the course have indicated its lasting influence on their lives as critical readers, thinkers, and citizens.

Our goal in teaching this class—and in writing the first edition of *Doing History: Reading and Writing in the Digital Age*—has been to cover the basics of what a beginning researcher needs to know about how historians think about the past, how they locate and collect evidence, how they analyze and synthesize their sources, and what the writing and presentation processes entail. We have been gratified to discover that both instructors and students who have used the first edition have appreciated our systematic introduction to historical methods. In the second edition, we have kept the same approach, while expanding some topics and adding others to address the needs of today's history students.

Two new chapters have been added to this second edition. Chapter 6 on "Writing the Short Essay" walks students through the process of writing different kinds of short essays, including summaries, five-paragraph essays, and article reviews. Chapter 6 also covers short writing assignments that will be helpful to students in the future – such as grant-writing and preparing résumés. A new final chapter (8), "Sharing Scholarship," extends the discussion of writing and presentation to presenting research at conferences, including how to prepare oral presentations, posters, and possible publication.

Doing History is filled with writing exercises and examples of student writing. Many of the writing examples come from one student and culminate in a final paper, which appears in full in Appendix B. We have also added a new Appendix C, "CourseReader Assignments," which contains additional assignments referred to in Chapter 6 and linked to an online primary source supplement available with *Doing History*. In addition to the specific sources tied to these assignments, *CourseReader for Doing History* provides other key primary and secondary sources that can serve as prompts for further writing exercises. Go to Cengage.com/coursereader for more information.

This text will teach beginners to research, think, and write like historians. Those who use the text will learn to:

- think like a historian in selecting a topic
- master a thorough and sophisticated approach to using a library with particular emphasis on the most recent applications of technology
- refine a research topic based upon extant and available materials
- develop critical thinking skills needed for the analysis of both primary and secondary sources
- understand the importance of historical context, historiography, argument, use of sources, and conclusions
- prepare a polished written presentation of their findings through the process of drafting, editing, conducting further research, and rewriting to prepare more effective short essays and reviews for various audiences
- evaluate their own writing and that of their peers
- deliver a sound oral presentation of their findings
- prepare a finished presentation for conference presentation
- review online materials for research and peering
- cite source material appropriately

We are indebted to our colleagues in the James Madison University Department of History for their contributions and inspiration. Their high standards of teaching excellence coupled with their strong sense of collegiality and professionalism provide the perfect atmosphere for excellent instruction. We extend a special thanks to Christian Davis, T.J. Fitzgerald, Steve Reich and Emily Westkaemper for their suggestions on the text.

We wish to thank Patricia Hardesty, reference librarian at James Madison University and friend to students of history, for providing her guide to reference works (Appendix A). Our undergraduate students have contributed greatly by showing us that beginning researchers can indeed "do history." We are especially grateful to Paul McDowell, Sean Crowley, Lelia Harrison Tinsley Smith and Jillian Viar for their examples of student writing.

The thoughtful observations, criticisms, and suggestions of reviewers did much to improve this book, enabling us to refocus our attention in some areas and clarify our thinking in others. We are indebted to the following:

Mark Beasley, Hardin-Simmons University

Kevin Gannon, Grand View College

Marcus Hall, University of Utah

Carolyn Knefely, University of West Florida

Karen Miller, Oakland University

Jessamyn Neuhaus, State University of New York, Plattsburgh

Oliver Pollak, University of Nebraska

Brooks Simpson, Arizona State University

Dan Snell, University of Oklahoma

Eric Strahom, Florida Gulf Coast University

Claire Strom, North Dakota State University

Leslie Tuttle, University of Kansas

Sally West, Truman State University

Any remaining errors are our own.

Special thanks go to our friends at Cengage Publishing who have been most supportive from the inception of this project. It could not have been completed without their professionalism and support. Ann West is a terrific editor who patiently guided us through the final stages of the writing and editing process. Her keen insights and steadfast support made this a much better book than it would have been otherwise. Finally, we thank our wives, V. M., Andi, and Pamela, for their love, support, and tolerance.

We are eager to hear from readers of this book. Please feel free to offer your comments about *Doing History* by contacting us at the Department of History, 58 Bluestone Drive, MSC 2001, James Madison University, Harrisonburg, VA 22807, or through our e-mail addresses: Michael J. Galgano, galganmj@jmu.edu; J. Chris Arndt, arndtjc@jmu.edu; Raymond M. Hyser, hyserrm@jmu.edu.

About the Authors

Michael J. Galgano   is a professor of history at James Madison University in Harrisonburg, Virginia, where he teaches courses in European, World, and family histories, and historical methods. He focuses his research interests on the family, religion, and gender in the Early Modern period.

J. Chris Arndt   is a professor of history at James Madison University in Harrison-burg, Virginia, where he teaches courses in U.S. history, the early Republic, and historical methods. He focuses his research interests on the study of states' rights and economic change in antebellum America.

Raymond M. Hyser   is a professor of history at James Madison University in Harrisonburg, Virginia, where he teaches courses in U.S. history, U.S. business history, Gilded Age America, and historical methods. He focuses his research interests on business and agriculture in the Gilded Age.

Introduction

The active examination of the past is best achieved through research and writing. In this way, historians employ critical thinking skills and imagination to blend their questions about the subject with existing scholarship to produce their own interpretations. Simply put, the best way to learn history is to research and write it. This book is intended as a "nuts and bolts" introduction for beginning researchers in choosing a topic, identifying all available evidence, analyzing and interpreting this evidence, then presenting their findings in an organized and clear manner. In this way, beginning researchers take responsibility for their own learning.

Undergraduates can perform serious, reflective scholarship if they follow the process outlined in subsequent chapters. In an era when undergraduate research has increasingly become the hallmark of an excellent college education, this text will provide beginning historians with the skills to practice history. The research, critical thinking, writing, and speaking skills will also prepare them to be informed citizens and consumers. In addition, since they live in a digital age, the text includes numerous examples of how to employ the Internet and other forms of modern digital technology. This book was written with each of these ends in mind.

This text is designed to provide an introduction to researching and writing history, with the primary goal being the production of an essay modeled after the scholarly journal article. In order to reinforce fundamental skills and elements, there is some replication in its pages. The opening chapter responds to the question "What is history?" It goes beyond simply describing the discipline and the tools necessary to practice it by offering an overview of the rich variety of approaches historians use to study the past. An appreciation of this variety will enable the beginning researcher to better understand the role of analysis and historical context necessary for the writing of history. It also helps readers develop a sense of their own approach to understanding the past.

The second chapter guides researchers through the vicissitudes of selecting a topic and conducting historical research. Through the "research trail," they learn an exhaustive approach to collecting information in a systematic manner that includes an examination of the basic reference works in the discipline. By examining each in detail, beginning researchers start to develop an understanding of the significant role that readily available reference materials play in successfully completing a research project.

Chapters 3 and 4 discuss the analysis of secondary and primary sources, respectively. Secondary sources introduce beginning researchers to historical context, historiographical interpretations, and methodological approaches. By understanding these works, beginning researchers learn the importance of context as well as the concept that not all sources are of equal quality. Knowledge of secondary sources enables them to better engage the essence of history—primary sources. The chapter on primary sources examines the different types of primary evidence and the tools used by historians to evaluate them.

The fifth chapter offers an overview of writing a research paper. Its particular emphasis is on the importance of drafting, peer reviewing, editing and revising, proofreading, presenting orally, and producing a final written essay.

The sixth chapter examines a wide range of short essay writing types, many of which complement and supplement researching and writing the type of paper described in Chapter 5. It includes explanations and examples of writing effective summaries, analyses, syntheses, and book and article reviews, among many others. The chapter also considers grant writing, writing an effective letter of application, and assembling a curriculum vitae or résumé.

The seventh chapter discusses how and why historians cite evidence and offers numerous examples of how to acknowledge sources for notes and bibliographic purposes in standard form.

Finally, the eighth chapter explains how to continue the conversations started with the initial research project by applying to present the finished work at a conference. The appendices contain a guide to historical reference works found in many academic libraries, a set of source analysis assignments, and an example of writing by an undergraduate researcher, Paul McDowell. Throughout this book, McDowell's paper serves as an example of a beginning historian's research and writing. Some chapters in the text are followed by a brief list of suggested readings. For other chapters, the reader is directed to the extended reference guide found in Appendix A. Most chapters also include specific exercises to underscore the main points presented.

1

✴

What Is History?

Every semester in undergraduate historical methods classes across the country, students are asked, "What is history?" Students respond in a variety of ways. "History is everything that has happened in the past." "History is our interpretation of the past." "I saw a movie about the American Revolution last night, but it certainly wasn't historical." "If you understand the past, you can predict the future." Each answer may contain some kernel of truth, but none seems to describe precisely what history is. Further reading and class discussion sometimes clarify, but occasionally muddle, the issue. Perhaps the better question would be to ask, "What is history and why do we seem to care so much about it?" In short, what is history, why is understanding history important, and how has our understanding of the past evolved over time?

Throughout the ages, various cultures have told stories about their past. Part entertainment, part chronicle of events, part myth and popular memory, history might offer knowledge about important traditions or teach a moral lesson, but little more. It was not until the nineteenth century that scholars began to recognize the study of the past as a discipline that could provide a perspective for understanding the world in which one lives. As such, **history is not a collection of facts about the past whose primary value is to improve one's skills while playing trivia games; it is an interpretation of the past based on the weight of the available evidence**. Despite the controversy between those who see history as a science that uncovers universal laws and those who see it as a humanity that engages a combination of reason and imagination to recreate the past, large numbers of well-educated individuals—from political leaders, to businessmen, to lawyers—turn to history for the sense of perspective it provides. Popular claims aside, history cannot predict the future (if it could, professional historians would spend less time in archives and more time at the racetrack),

1

but it can convey a sense of what is deeply rooted in a culture and what is ephemeral, and by extension what is important and what is not. Historical understanding provides one with a powerful tool for critically thinking about the world in which one lives. And historical interpretations are subject to change. Fifty years ago most American historians believed that the overwhelming majority of colonial Americans were liberal, meaning that they embraced individual rights and participated in early forms of capitalism prior to the American Revolution. More recent research on early America has shown that many colonists placed community values before those of the individual and had only a rudimentary stake in early capitalist enterprises. This reinterpretation challenges Americans armed with an understanding of the past to reconsider a belief that America was born democratic and capitalist. The informed public has a need to understand how past events gave direction to the historical trajectory leading to the present. Only then can one make sense of the factors that give rise to and influence the way people think and act in the contemporary world. History conveys a perspective that enables individuals to understand how a culture or society arrived at the particular historical moment, how it views itself, how it sees its place in the world, and by extension, the likely range of reactions of a society or culture to future events.

THE MISUSE OF HISTORY

Unfortunately, many seek to misuse historical understanding of the past for their own purposes. In some cases, those pursuing pet ideological—particularly political—agendas seek to twist history to suit their own ends. This often is achieved by a variety of means, including tendentious selection and use of evidence (or cherry-picking the facts), choosing myths that suit the argument, or distorting the evidence to achieve the desired end. Such an approach to history may involve imagination, but it is anything but historical, lacking a reasoned or even reputable examination of the evidence. One of the most common misuses of history results from popularly held views about the past. Such views of the past are **popular memory**. Popular memory in Germany, for example, maintains that the German people were not enthusiastic in their support of Nazism, while historical knowledge shows considerable public support for the Nazis in the 1930s. But because of history's powerful ability to legitimize activities or policies, totalitarian regimes such as the Nazis and Soviets sought to abuse history to serve certain political ends. History, which by definition implies historical consciousness, is based on the careful evaluation of available evidence that must be understood within the context of the time it was produced. Such analysis may lead to divergent views from other historians who simply interpret the evidence differently, but it remains an interpretation based on the weight of the evidence.

HOW MUCH CAN WE KNOW OF THE PAST?

In the centuries before the Enlightenment, Western intellectuals conceived of the past as shaped primarily by God's intervention. The late seventeenth and eighteenth centuries witnessed a growing awareness of the distinctiveness of the historical past and the process of change over time. The period also embraced a sense of progress characterized by a rejection of the distant past. Since the emergence of a modern historical consciousness in the nineteenth century, the question of how much can be known about the past has challenged those interested in the important lessons history can suggest. Historical knowledge is limited in two ways: by the available sources and by the approach taken by individual historians.

The primary limitation on what can be known of the past is relative to the quantity and quality of available evidence. For some events, particularly those that are more recent, there is a profusion of evidence that can at times be too much for even the most experienced historian to master. For example, anyone studying the role of the Catholic Church in World War II would be overwhelmed by the volume of available primary sources housed in the Vatican Library. But the paucity of evidence often places limits on historians' ability to understand the past. When dealing with the distant past or with groups that left few or no records, it becomes necessary to examine the scarce written evidence in new ways or to use evidence other than the written word. For example, there is an abundance of evidence on President Lyndon Johnson's decision to expand United States involvement in Vietnam, but there is far less material discussing the life of a Chinese peasant during the eighth century CE[1] Tang dynasty in China. Limitations in the quality of evidence, even when there is a relative abundance, may still leave some questions unanswered. But as much as historians might like to establish a sequence of events and motives beyond a shadow of doubt, the threshold for making historical claims is not quite this high. Historians often have to infer from the evidence and make guarded assertions about the past of which they can never be absolutely certain. To make such assertions requires a thorough knowledge of the evidence as well as the ability to imagine some details that may not be directly supported by the existing evidence but that are suggested. Chapter 4 will examine how the historian analyzes such primary sources.

A long-standing philosophical dispute within the profession further limits knowledge of the past. Historians have occasionally made bold proclamations about their discipline, claiming that by employing the scientific method and avoiding personal biases they could uncover historical truths and laws. Still, others dissent, saying that the past has too many variables that allow for little more than the historian's informed impression of the past. Generally, historians fall somewhere on a continuum between these dialectical approaches. At one end of the spectrum are **positivists**, who see history as a scientific endeavor. The positivist approach to history argues that the historian can maintain some semblance of

---

1. *CE* refers to the "common era" and is the preferred method of indicating the period traditionally referred to as *AD*. *BCE* refers to "before the common era" and has replaced *BC* in use among historians.

objectivity when evaluating evidence to produce a truthful account of the past that meets a standard for accuracy similar to the hard sciences. Such historians would assert that history is a social science. The second approach to understanding history is known as **historicism**, which derives from the idealist school of philosophy and takes a humanistic approach to the discipline. Historicist-minded historians believe that human societies are too complex, with far too many variables, to be studied like a natural science and that historians' points of view make objectivity difficult. Instead, historicists recognize the distinctiveness of the past and offer an interpretation based on available evidence and the interpretive imagination to offer a carefully reasoned vision of the past based on the weight of the evidence. Such historians see the discipline as a humanity.

Historians from either end of the continuum would agree that an understanding of the **historical context** of a particular time period is imperative. This context, which might be seen as the setting of a period, involves the social, cultural, political, economic, and technological milieu of the day. Among the questions historians should ask are:

- What were the values and beliefs of the time period?
- What type of economy existed; how was wealth distributed?
- What type of political system existed; what did the social structure look like; what was the relationship between genders or differing classes or different ethnicities?
- What were the religious values and mentality of the studied time period?
- What was the basic technological level?

Historical consciousness must be firmly rooted in an understanding of historical context. For example, some Civil War enthusiasts muse that if Confederate military leaders had followed Thomas "Stonewall" Jackson's advice to pursue retreating Union forces following the Battle of Manassas in 1861, Southern armies could have taken Washington, D.C. While such reasoning seems plausible today with the battlefield only a 30-minute drive from the U.S. capital (except during rush hour traffic), such assertions ignore the mid-nineteenth century reality that reaching Washington would have required battle-weary troops to run the equivalent of a marathon after a hard day of fighting—something few inexperienced soldiers (and even fewer Civil War buffs) could accomplish. Only through the establishment of such a context can a historian make sound and fair judgments about the historical past.

THE PROBLEMS OF HISTORICAL INQUIRY

The failure to place events in their appropriate historical context is one of the greatest causes of an **ahistorical** or nonhistorical perspective. Popular conceptions of history are often rife with such ahistorical perspectives. One of the greatest threats to historical understanding is **presentism**, where one assumes that present attitudes and beliefs were the same as those in the past. Such approaches to history are common, but they misread the past by denying what is different or unique about it. Present-minded approaches to history also assume that the circumstances available to historical characters were similar to those of today and that people in past ages would have reacted to these conditions much as a contemporary person would. England's King Richard the Lionheart should be condemned for his massacre of 2,700 Muslim prisoners in 1191. But one should avoid charging him with a violation of human rights since such concepts did not emerge in Europe until the Enlightenment. Instead, one must remember that in the eyes of contemporaries Richard's participation in the Third Crusade actually provided some legitimacy for his actions. One might still condemn the behavior, primarily as a violation of the Christian virtues Richard swore to defend, but it needs to be done with respect to the historical context.

Another problem for historians relates to **point of view.** A point of view might be something as benign as a mild preference or what one tends to find more believable, or it may be a preference that is closer to a prejudice that influences how one collects and weighs evidence. For example, a historian of American Indians in the modern period would likely possess a very different point of view about Custer's Last Stand than a historian who lived in the late nineteenth century. But can historians balance a point of view with an honest and thorough handling of the evidence? If not, should a historian be allowed to let personal views run amok, interpreting a narrowly selected body of evidence in ways that result in little more than a reflection of the author's own prejudices and self-absorption? Certainly not. But conversely, the holy grail of objectivity is an impossible one to grasp and difficult even to envision. The conflict between subjectivity and objectivity is one of the central debates among historians and one not easily resolved. Historians will always have a point of view that may deeply influence the way they collect and interpret evidence. Whereas historians might find it impossible to eschew their own points of view, they must be aware of their prejudices and guard against letting these intrude into their approach to historical study. Scholars must also be aware of the point of view of particular sources they read. Just because an author of a particular source has certain prejudices does not mean that the source is invalid; it simply means that it must be analyzed with knowledge of the particular point of view and how it may influence the source produced. The tension between objectivity and subjectivity, and the related question of point of view, is best resolved by conducting as exhaustive a search for materials as possible and then offering a critical but fair evaluation of that evidence. The evidence might be tested against a **hypothesis**, or **theory**, but one should avoid simply looking for convenient facts to support a pet idea. Historical research and writing requires hard work, self-knowledge and self-restraint, an understanding of historical context, rigorous analysis of sources, and constant writing, editing, and rewriting before any evidence of historical understanding may be attempted.

THE STUFF OF HISTORY

The methods used by historians to learn about the past are nearly as varied as the number of historians. All historians make use of two general categories of sources. Most students are already familiar with **secondary sources**, which are chronicles or interpretations of events written after the fact. Books (often referred to as **monographs** because they comprise an extended essay written around a central theme), biographies, and **scholarly journal articles** are perhaps the types of secondary sources that students are familiar with, but the list of secondary sources also includes historical dictionaries and encyclopedias, websites, lectures, and reviews. Secondary sources provide historians, both experienced and beginning, with two very important types of information:

- Secondary sources are useful in providing background information about a topic.
- Secondary sources help to provide **historical context**.

Reading a secondary source can convey a strong sense of a time period and the individual, theme, or event discussed—information that is essential for developing a historical understanding of the period. Because no secondary source is perfect in capturing the essence of a moment, it is essential to read several of the best secondary sources on a subject to begin to capture the flavor and feel of a period. Chapter 3 will explore the identification and evaluation of secondary sources.

Secondary sources also provide a sense of historiographical context. **Historiography**, or the study of the history and methodology of historical interpretation, is of great interest to historians. A careful reading of several secondary sources can convey a sense of how the important questions that preoccupy historians and their resulting interpretations have evolved over time. Evolving methodologies, coupled with changing values and beliefs, affect the types of questions historians ask of the past. An understanding of historiography demonstrates what questions have received considerable or scanty attention and reveals aspects of the past that demand scrutiny. For example, prevailing views toward the institution of apartheid in South Africa came under global attack during the era of decolonization. Possessing a different mindset than their predecessors and armed with new methodologies that enabled them to go beyond the accounts of white South Africans, a generation of historians revolutionized our understanding of the institution.

In addition to developing a mastery of the secondary sources, a historian must conduct an exhaustive search for **primary sources** that can be carefully analyzed. Primary sources are the forms of evidence contemporary to the event or process described. Although secondary evidence is essential to the historian, primary sources are the stuff from which history is written. Historians have traditionally used written primary sources, some of which are published, and others that are in manuscript form. These include diaries, official records, private correspondence, newspapers, memoirs, autobiographies, tax records, census materials, and wills. More recently, historians have begun to expand this list of sources to include cartoons, movies, fiction, architecture, art, and cultural artifacts. Historians use primary sources to piece together an interpretation of the past that can be supported by the weight of available evidence. It might be best to think of secondary sources as serving as a guide and introduction to a particular topic, but the primary evidence is the actual material from which one can make generalizations and assertions.

THE HISTORY OF HISTORICAL WRITING:
AN OVERVIEW

Although the public generally conceives of history as a nonfiction **narrative** largely devoid of interpretation, historical study requires interpretation. Because of this, historical interpretation has changed over the years. Historical understanding as currently conceived began in the early nineteenth century with the Romantic Movement and the associated rise of romantic nationalism. At a time when German philosopher Georg Wilhelm Friedrich Hegel offered the concept of the *volkgeist* (loosely translated as "spirit of the people"), it became important to discern what that spirit was. History, with its emphasis on the common experience that bonded a people together, became a pillar of this new ideology. In some nineteenth century countries, historians played important roles in fashioning how a culture thought about itself, nowhere more so than in Czechoslovakia, where the historian František Palacký became the father of Czech nationalism.

It was also during the nineteenth century that a modern way of thinking about the past and writing history was born. While the roots of this approach can be found in the ideas of eighteenth and early nineteenth century philosophers, the first to offer an approach to the study of history was Leopold von Ranke, a German scholar. While Ranke was more interested in looking to the past to discover the handiwork of a Christian god, his sense that each past age was distinct (a concept known as **historicism**) and that past events shaped what came later brought about the first understanding of history's significance. Ranke argued that while the historian could attempt to understand the past on its own terms, it required a certain leap of imagination. More important than Ranke's philosophical position was his methodology, both as a historian and an instructor. Ranke's method, which in turn became the standard for the profession, rested on rigorous examination and critical evaluation of written primary sources synthesized into a scholarly presentation for a research seminar. This seminar enabled students to more fully engage the sources and deconstruct the weaknesses of one another's ideas in order to produce a more accurate representation of the past.

Ranke's method survived, but his philosophical approach to history came under attack by the late nineteenth century. In an era when science seemed capable of unlocking all of the universe's secrets, historians enlisted scientific approaches in a quest for truth. For example, Karl Marx developed a universal theory for understanding the past based on its relationship to the means of production and class struggle, while Henry Adams applied the Second Law of Thermodynamics to understanding the Jefferson and Madison administrations. The seminar survived, but the earlier historicism of Ranke had yielded to a **positivist** interpretation of history. **Positivism** claimed to be objective and, in the extreme, argued that by using the scientific method historians could efface themselves of their biases, report what had occurred, and ultimately uncover laws of human behavior. By claiming to be scientific, historians could confidently make truthful claims about the past.

If the positivists were right, ultimately all historians would come to the same conclusions because they sought objective universal laws. But such a claim would be hard to support. The first serious attacks against positivist-minded historians came from the **Progressive** school. The Progressives included important philosophers such as John Dewey; the most important progressive historians were Charles Beard, Carl Becker, and James Harvey Robinson. Progressive historians, reacting against the certitudes of late nineteenth century thought, sought to examine the historical roots of social problems. They shifted attention from the study of politics and the state to the study of society. In addition, the methodologies of the emerging social sciences were especially attractive to the Progressives. This increasingly interdisciplinary approach, coupled with a shift of focus, led to controversial findings. Beard's *An Economic Interpretation of the Constitution of the United States* replaced the historical orthodoxy that viewed America's founders as great men who disinterestedly implemented the American system of government with an interpretation that the founders pursued a stronger central government as a means to secure their own financial interests. Robinson's efforts led to the creation of the "new history," which sought to more carefully examine society. By the 1920s, studies of everyday life appeared in both U.S. and European history. The Progressives' skepticism about the scientific claims of earlier historians ultimately led Carl Becker to claim in his 1932 presidential address to the American Historical Association, entitled "Everyman His Own Historian," that history is "an imaginative creation" derived from individual experience. Such statements reveal the growing relativism embraced by historians who believed that the author's point of view often colored the final interpretation.[2]

Historical writing took a decidedly different turn following World War II. The effort required to defeat the Axis powers caused historians to reflect on the common values that united Americans rather than the differences that divided them, so they began to look for that common thread of unity. The events of the Cold War reinforced this theme. The so-called **consensus** historians would assert that despite some differences, Americans had throughout their history been united around the concept of liberal democracy. Louis Hartz's *The Liberal Tradition in America* and many of Richard Hofstadter's works emphasized the basic agreement on core liberal (individual political and economic rights) principles from America's founding to the present. The consensus historians were challenged on a variety of fronts during the 1960s. The growth and democratization of the academy

---

2. Charles A. Beard, *An Economic Interpretation of the Constitution of the United States* (New York: Macmillan Co., 1913); James Harvey Robinson, *The New History: Essays Illustrating the Modern Historical Outlook* (New York: Macmillan Co., 1912); This essay appeared as Carl L. Becker, "Everyman His Own Historian," *The American Historical Review* 37, no. 2 (January 1932): 221–236; Arthur M. Schlesinger and Dixon Ryan Fox, series eds., *History of American Life*, 12 vols., (New York: Macmillan Co., 1927–1944).

(community of professional historians) generated far more scholarship than in previous generations, and the types of questions being asked changed dramatically as well.[3]

Several schools of thought emerged during the 1960s that transformed how historians saw the past. One of the most important of these was Marxism. Although always evident in historical study, Marxist approaches to history had been something of an intellectual backwater in Great Britain and the United States before World War II. But the splintering of the British Communist Party in 1956 enabled new forms of Marxism and Marxist historiography to flourish. Most important among the early British Marxists was Edward P. Thompson. His study, *The Making of the English Working Class,* carefully chronicled the rise of the English working class unified by a class consciousness, persuasively arguing that it was tied to the greater structure of production. The importance of this work rested both with its subject matter, which shifted attention from rulers to the less articulate members of society, as well as its dynamic presentation of class relationships in nineteenth century Britain. The work is also distinguished by the kinds of evidence used to present its historical argument. Thompson's work deeply influenced the study of labor in postcolonial societies throughout the world. The emergence of Marxism in British historical writing also clearly influenced a second, somewhat related intellectual movement in the United States, the New Left.[4]

New Left historians in the United States drew inspiration from the Students for a Democratic Society's (SDS) call for the rejection of impersonal corporate society and sought a similarly inclusive, democratic interpretation of the American past. The New Left view of history saw more conflict than consensus in studies that broke new ground in the examination of slavery, race, ethnicity, class, and later gender. Many New Left historians embraced the methods of social scientists, believing that such approaches offered greater certainty for historical claims than could be made by previous generations of historians. In particular, the use of statistics and mathematical models held out the promise of realizing the positivist dream of uncovering historical truths.[5]

A third approach to history that challenged tradition was the Annales school. The Annales approach to history began with French historians Lucien Febvre and Marc Bloch in 1929. Rebelling against the focus on politics and

---

3. Louis Hartz, *The Liberal Tradition in America: An Interpretation of American Political Thought since the Revolution* (New York: Harcourt, Brace, 1955); Hofstadter's two most important works that set the stage for the consensus school are Richard Hofstadter, *The American Political Tradition and the Men Who Made It* (New York: Alfred A. Knopf, 1948); *The Age of Reform: From Bryan to F. D .R.* (New York: Vintage Books, 1955).

4. Edward P. Thompson, *The Making of the English Working Class* (New York: Vintage Books, 1963).

5. The term *New Left* became popular during the 1960s to categorize an emerging generation of historians who criticized the consensus school of the previous decade. These revisionists ran the gamut from disillusioned liberals to Marxists. Some of the more prominent New Left historians are Eugene Genovese, *The Political Economy of Slavery: Studies in the Society and Economy of the Slave South* (New York: Vintage Books, 1965); Herbert Gutman, *The Black Family in Slavery and Freedom, 1750–1925* (New York: Pantheon Books, 1976); Gabriel Kolko, *The Triumph of American Conservatism: A Reinterpretation of American History, 1900–1916* (New York: Free Press of Glencoe, 1963); and William A. Williams, *The Tragedy of American Diplomacy* (New York: Dell Publishers, 1962).

government, Annales historians sought to write "total history" that examined history over *la longue durée* (the long term). Their interest in studying the rhythms of everyday life and recapturing the *mentalité* of an era is perhaps best captured in the works of Febvre's student Fernand Braudel. The Annales approach to history influenced a growing number of British and American historians. The focus on change over the long term was particularly congenial to those whose focus was on the history of previously inarticulate groups such as slaves, women, and workers using a new array of sources such as diaries, wills, and census data.[6]

The simultaneous emergence and overlapping interests (and conclusions) of these three schools (Marxist, New Left, and Annales) led historians of one approach to borrow promiscuously from the others. Combined, these trends helped give rise to a wave of the new histories. Perhaps most significant was the "new social history." What characterized the new social history, whatever the approach, was the interest in previously inarticulate groups as a means to both democratize and flesh out the historical understanding of the past as well as the identification of new methods for reconstructing the past. Social historians sought to reconstruct lives previously unrepresented but also to uncover historical social structures as well. Each of these trends that emerged in the 1960s and 1970s made varying claims to recreate the past in an objective manner. But the variability of their findings undermined such claims.

The social scientific approach borrowed by all three schools, and the claims of scientific objectivity made in particular by Marxists and New Left American historians soon came under attack. The book that questioned historians' claims of objectivity and truth-seeking was Thomas Kuhn's *On the Structure of Scientific Revolutions*. Kuhn showed that scientific explanations of how the universe works, such as Sir Isaac Newton's theory of gravity, were not immutable truths but instead the best interpretations that could be made based on the available evidence. Kuhn demonstrated that, over time, scientists uncovered information that challenged important theories of how the universe worked, but the theory would hold with some qualifications until the weight of dissenting evidence forced a reinterpretation. According to Kuhn, the truth was merely what appeared to be true relative to one's point of observation based on the available evidence. In challenging the truth claims of the hard sciences, Kuhn created doubt for those making similar claims in history and the social sciences. Such relativism and skepticism opened the door for **postmodern theory** that came into vogue in recent years.[7]

---

6. The Annales school emerged with the establishment of the journal *Annales d'histoire économique et sociale* (*Annals of Economic and Social History*) in 1929. The Annales school is closely associated with founders Marc Bloch, *Feudal Society*, trans. L. A. Manyon (Chicago: University of Chicago Press, 1961); *The Historian's Craft*, trans. Peter Putnam (New York: Vintage Books, 1953); Lucien Febrve, *The Problem of Unbelief in the Sixteenth Century: The Religion of Rabelais*, trans. Beatrice Gottlieb (Cambridge: Harvard University Press, 1982); and Febvre's student, Fernand Braudel, *The Mediterranean and the Mediterranean World in the Age of Philip II*, 3 vols., trans. Siân Reynolds (New York: Harper and Row, 1972) and *Civilization and Capitalism: 15th to 18th Century*, 3 vols., trans. Siân Reynolds (New York: Harper and Row, 1982–1984).

7. Thomas S. Kuhn, *The Structure of Scientific Revolutions* (Chicago: University of Chicago Press, 1962).

HYPOTHESIS AND THEORY

The public's image of what constitutes history might actually be closer to nonfiction literature than what most historians do for a living. While nonfiction narratives of the past will always be popular with the reading public, few professional historians today approach history in such a manner. Nonfiction literature alone, while highly informative and entertaining, often falls short of the discipline's claims of offering a critical perspective of the past. The modern historian must do more than merely recite the facts and recount tales of past events. But how does one discern patterns from the complex, convoluted mix of evidence about the past? One of the most common ways in which historians attempt to make sense of this jumble is through the use of a **hypothesis**. Much as a scientist makes preliminary observations and develops a hypothesis to test in a laboratory, the historian should begin to develop a hypothesis after preliminary reading of important secondary sources. **This hypothesis, or central question, must then be tested against the primary evidence. It should not become an end to be proven by a careful selection of only that evidence that fits a preconceived notion or pet argument.** For example, some preliminary reading about the causes of the American Revolution might suggest that a hypothesis focusing on ideological conflicts between Parliament and colonial elites was a key factor in the Revolution. But if an examination of the evidence points in other directions, it may be necessary to modify the developing argument or change it altogether. Ultimately, a hypothesis will evolve into a **historical argument** (sometimes called a **thesis**) that is based on the weight of the evidence. But how does one develop a hypothesis? Many historians find theory a useful tool to develop central questions to test against the evidence.

Theory is useful in that it helps to give form to the questions asked of the past and imposes some discipline on the historians' approach to the evidence. The use of theory remains controversial to some, who assert that it is often imposed on the past, resulting in selective cherry-picking of evidence to suit the theory. If used responsibly with a full examination of all evidence, however, such an approach can result in new ways to understand various aspects of the past. Indeed, even historians who eschew the use of theory and prefer to provide a narrative that stands alone often espouse views that are vaguely informed by theory. As such, theory is a tool for understanding, not a replacement for critical analysis and synthesis of the evidence.

The varieties of theory are numerous. Although this text will not carefully review each theory or privilege one approach above another, it is important that beginning scholars have some appreciation of major theoretical approaches. Some of the most important theories traditionally employed by historians are rooted in the works of Karl Marx, Max Weber, and Émile Durkheim.

Karl Marx's ideas are often dismissed today because of the economic and political failures of communism in the late twentieth century, but as a tool for understanding the past, Marx has been highly influential. According to Marx, a society could only be understood through examining its means of production. His scientific view of history held that all elements within a society—its values, ideology, politics, social structure—resulted from the means of economic production. Such an approach may seem rigidly determinist, but it does provide a metatheory for understanding the dynamics of a past society. Max Weber was a German sociologist writing in the early twentieth century. His most famous work, *The Protestant Ethic and the Spirit of Capitalism* (1904–1905), responds to Marxist claims of economic materialism by pointing out the ideological factors that contributed to early capitalism as a rational form of modernization. Weber's ideas contributed to the emergence of modernization theory, which looked at social upheaval and dislocation as part of the modernization process. Émile Durkheim, also a contemporary of Weber, responded to problems he saw in Marxist analysis. Writing in late nineteenth century France, Durkheim's emphasis on changing long-term processes and their impact on individuals and communities provided inspiration for the Annales school.[8]

More recently, historians have turned in other directions for theories to aid the process of historical understanding. Anthropology has made important contributions. Clifford Geertz disagreed with the scientific claims of his own and other disciplines. Rather than uncovering laws of a culture through careful observation of methodology, Geertz argued that one can uncover meaning (rather than causation) through "thick description" that set behavior in a context that made it understandable to an outsider. Victor Turner's studies of symbols and rituals provided yet another approach for understanding culture. These ideas provided historians with greater interpretive freedom and helped to popularize the study of cultural history. These approaches also led some historians to shift their efforts from uncovering cause and effect to a search for meaning.[9]

One of the most controversial theoretical approaches is **postmodernism**. Postmodern theory was largely a French creation most closely identified with the philosophers Jacques Derrida and sometimes Michel Foucault. Emerging in post–World War II (and soon to be postcolonial) France, it challenged widely held assumptions about the ability to reason. Amorphous in nature and difficult to characterize, postmodernism often rejects historians' ability to produce accurate truth claims about the past. For postmodernists, fragmentary evidence and the inability of an observer to escape his or her point of view makes the past unknowable. Instead, they believe that history is little more than an aesthetic representation of the past that reveals more about the author than the period discussed. At face value, such claims appear to question the very legitimacy of historical inquiry as traditionally practiced and imply that the doctrine of rational inquiry rooted in the Enlightenment is something of a dead letter. One of the most common applications of the postmodern approach is seen in the linguistic turn, most often associated with American literary historian Hayden White. First

8. Karl Marx, *Capital: A Critique of Political Economy*, ed. Friedrich Engels, trans. Samuel Moore, Edward Aveling, Marie Sachey, and Herbert Lamm (Chicago: Encyclopedia Britannica, 1952); Émile Durkheim, *The Division of Labor in Society*, trans. George Simpson (Glencoe, IL: The Free Press, 1949); Max Weber, *The Protestant Ethic and the Spirit of Capitalism*, trans. Talcott Parsons, with a foreword by R. H. Tawney (New York: Scribner's, 1930).

9. Clifford Geertz, "Thick Description: Toward an Interpretive Theory of Culture," "Deep Play: Notes on a Balinese Cockfight," *The Interpretation of Cultures: Selected Essays,* comp. Clifford Geertz (New York: Basic Books, 1973); Victor Turner, *Dramas, Fields, and Metaphors: Symbolic Action in Human Society* (Ithaca, NY: Cornell University Press, 1974).

emerging with the new literary historians during the 1970s and 1980s, proponents of the linguistic turn argue that the instability and fluidity of language hides more about the past than it reveals and that interpretation of narratives reveals more about the author than about the narratives in question. Proponents of this approach ultimately deem the past unknowable from the perspective of scientific truth and instead deconstruct texts to recover multiple, often obscure meanings. From their perspective, there is no historical truth.

Although extreme applications of such ideas might seem ahistorical and even illogical, the implications of postmodern theory have actually been important to historians. For example, postmodernists have pointed out the elasticity of meaning for categories of analysis such as gender, race, class, and ethnicity. Many historians influenced by postmodern ideas have begun to more carefully examine the meaning of these culturally defined concepts and the context that defines them, greatly enriching historical understanding.[10]

THE HISTORICAL ARGUMENT

History then, is clearly the search for a usable past that can help us make sense of the world in which we live. And given the numerous theoretical and methodological approaches employed by historians, a cursory review of historical writing on any period will reveal a wide variety of historical interpretations. Ultimately historians develop what some might call a thesis or hypothesis about how and why events transpired as they did. We prefer to use the term *historical argument*. By *historical argument*, we do not imply that historians spend a good portion of their time shouting at one another (although this does occur at the occasional professional conference). Instead, a historical argument is simply a historian's explanation of cause and effect or the meaning of an event that is based upon the weight of the evidence. While it may seem as if the discipline of the evidence would drive most arguments in the same direction, the differing ways in which individual historians weigh that evidence allows for a wide array of interpretations.

THE VARIETIES OF HISTORY

Because educated people believe that history provides a sense of perspective to understand the present and how society arrived at a particular point in time, there are many different types of history. Traditionally, the dominant area of

10. Jacques Derrida is often called the "father of postmodernism." His major works include Jacques Derrida, *Of Grammatology,* trans. Gayatri Chakravorty Spivak (Johns Hopkins University Press, 1976); *Writing and Difference,* trans. Alan Bass (Chicago: University of Chicago Press, 1978); *Speech and Phenomena, and Other Essays on Husserl's Theory of Signs,* trans. David B. Allison (Evanston, IL: Northwestern University Press, 1973); Michel Foucault, *The Order of Things* (New York: Pantheon Books, 1970); *The Archaeology of Knowledge*; trans. A. M. Sheridan Smith (New York: Pantheon Books, 1972); Hayden White, *Metahistory: The Historical Imagination in Nineteenth Century Europe* (Baltimore: Johns Hopkins University Press, 1975); *Topics of Discourse: Essays in Cultural Criticism* (Baltimore: Johns Hopkins University Press, 1978); Keith Jenkins, *Refiguring History: New Thoughts on an Old Discipline* (London: Routledge, 2003).

historical inquiry has been **political history**. Believing that important questions in a society were ultimately determined in the political arena, political historians tend to examine the great statesmen and their impact in shaping events or to look at the rise of political parties or ideologies. Political history practiced in such a way relies on readily available forms of evidence such as state papers, autobiographies, memoirs, and newspapers chronicling the leading figures of a particular period. **Military history, diplomatic history**, and the **history of empire and colonialism** were in many ways derived from political history, with a focus shifted from great political leaders to generals, foreign policy leaders, or colonial officials. Another traditional approach employed by historians is to examine the great ideas that influenced a culture or nation. **Intellectual history** examines the great philosophers to understand the ideas that they contributed. In some ways, the early study of **religious history** fused these approaches in the examination of leading clerical figures, religious institutions, and beliefs.

Each of these approaches offers important insights into the topics they examine, but they suffer from what some would later refer to as a "top down bias." The problem with focusing on leading figures of society is that often many groups are left out of the story. Historians eager to understand the conditions that shaped past lives often look to **economic history**. This approach not only sheds light on past economic trends and conditions, but borrowing methodology from economists offers a higher threshold of certainty in the claims one could make about the past. In some ways, economic history opened the door to **social history**. Although initially written as a narrative to describe the everyday lives of people, in the last 40 years social historians have sought to understand history from the bottom up as well as trying to understand the demography, social structures, and *mentalités* within a society. Social history eventually wrote many groups into history, including racial and ethnic minorities, immigrants, African Americans, women, the family, workers, and more recently gays and lesbians. Many of these oppositional histories have, as their opponents often claim, a political agenda that seeks to use history to advance a present-day issue, but similar claims could easily be made of the elite-centered history practiced by earlier generations of historians. Simply put, if history helps to provide perspective, then the types of questions raised will always have political overtones. Social historians have made immense contributions to fleshing out the historical record and in offering a deeper and richer context to what is known of the past. They have helped answer the question, "Whose history?"

While the emergence of social history has greatly enriched the understanding of past societies, its main contribution may have been methodological. In order to uncover the history of the inarticulate, social historians turned to nontraditional forms of evidence such as demographic data (census and tax records), wills, and oral history, and employed methodologies from the social sciences to reconstruct the past lives of these groups. The emphasis of many of these monographs has been on group or collective biography.[11] While more traditional branches of history may have criticized the use of such forms of evidence, it was not long before political historians were looking at voting records to determine mass political behavior, military historians were examining the cultural aspects of a nation's approach to war, intellectual historians were carefully setting important thinkers in their social and cultural milieu, historians of colonialism were examining the response of the colonized, and religious historians were trying to discern the faith of the common people. **Cultural history**, as practiced by followers of the Annales school and more recently by proponents of postmodernism, has emerged as an important approach to understanding the past. The interpretation of cultural artifacts carefully placed within a historical context has offered profound new insights into the historical past.

Finally, the areas that historians focus on are virtually unlimited in scope. Some historians carefully examine an event or a specific cultural setting in an effort to better understand the past. Such studies tend to focus intently on the local and the particular and extrapolate from there. Other historians may focus on a narrow subject but look at change or persistence over an extended period of time. Yet other historians look broadly at trends within a society that are part of a larger regional or even global perspective.

THE PUBLIC AND HISTORY

Given the important role that history plays in helping people understand their place in the world, the search for a usable past cannot be confined to the walls of the academy. Historians must be evangelical with their discoveries. Besides, the public has a real thirst for historical knowledge. Nothing proves this point more than the popularity of the History Channel. The History Channel shows both the problems and promise of historians' effort to reach a mass audience. Some shows offer speculative (and in some cases crackpot) approaches to important historical events, spinning highly questionable arguments supported with questionable use of evidence; others offer well-researched and carefully reasoned arguments presented in a visual format. As a consumer of historical knowledge, it is important to use the same techniques of historical criticism (outlined in Chapters 3 and 4) as one would use when reading secondary or primary sources.

The implications of social and cultural history have helped fuel the proliferation of living history museums and historical buildings that carefully reconstruct past lives for present consumption. This has contributed to the rise of **public history** as yet another field of historical inquiry. But again, not all museums and interpretations are created equal; some are supported by the

---

11. The technical term for collective biography used by historians is *prosopography*.

force of deep research and historical reasoning, thereby enriching the public, while a handful of others offer little more than flimsy opinions that merely stoke popular memory rather than offering anything resembling historical understanding.

THE INTEGRITY OF HISTORY

Historians continuously seek as accurate an understanding of the past as they can find. Given the important role that history plays within a society, few things are more paramount than the level of integrity involved in this search. Certainly, historical arguments will differ, but one must be scrupulous in citing the sources. And one cannot select from those sources the ones that support a pet notion or belief, but instead the historian must consider all of the evidence that is available. One of the ways in which historians can demonstrate such scrupulousness is through the citation of sources. Careful and detailed citing of sources not only underscores this integrity but also provides a roadmap for other historians to re-trace. The antithesis of this integrity can be found in the age-old problem of **plagiarism**. Plagiarism is act of presenting someone else's work or ideas as one's own. As such, it is a fundamentally dishonest act that strikes at the heart of intellectual honesty and integrity. Often, plagiarism results from cutting and pasting from websites, books, or periodicals in which a dishonest student pieces together the work and ideas of others as his or her own. Such efforts in the age of the Internet are foolhardy, however, given the proliferation of computer pro-grams such as TurnitinSafely or Viper that enable one to easily discover what is original and what is "borrowed." So how does one avoid plagiarizing? Taking good notes that clearly show what is quoted from a source and what is para-phrased is helpful, but the best piece of advice is to carefully cite from the sources consulted.

THE WORLD OF HISTORY

The approaches employed by historians and the types of questions that historians ask about the past are numerous and varied. Most historians' inquiry into the past focuses on some combination of place (such as a region, nation, or subcontinent), time period, or theme. Most historical writing began by focusing on the nation-state. Although **national history** may not be as popular as it once was, in many areas, particularly the United States, it remains a staple of the profession. **Regional and local history** is in many ways a subgenre of national history. Some historians have moved past the boundaries of the nation-state to examine historical events from a continental or global perspective. **World or global his-tory** has increasingly displaced the traditional study of **Western civilization** as an undergraduate staple while simultaneously redefining how historians of all types think about their area of study. Focus on global regions such as the Atlantic world or the Islamic world offers historians the opportunity to see a larger picture. The practice of using a particular theme to discern a larger picture has contributed to the growing popularity of **comparative history**.

Historians often categorize themselves by their periods of expertise. Traditionally, historical periodization was pegged to political movements or dynasties or, in the case of premodern periods, broad expanses of time characterized by similar institutions that reflected the idiosyncrasies of a particular place. In the United States, historians claimed to be experts on the Colonial Period or the Gilded Age; in Britain, there are Tudor–Stuart specialists, and in both could be found ancient and medieval scholars. Increasingly, social and cultural historians—with their interest in looking at change over time—have stretched, redefined, and in some cases shattered traditional periodization. Thus, the Age of Jackson has increasingly given way to the Market Revolution, and the Victorian Era has been supplanted by the Industrial Revolution. Many historians refuse identification with a time period. Instead, their primary approach is thematic, leading them to identify themselves as scholars of gender history, economic history, or religious history. Regardless of field or approach, all historians are united in their efforts to add to knowledge of the past through a rigorous approach to historical research, analysis, and writing.

THE HARD WORK OF HISTORY:
RESEARCH, ANALYSIS, WRITING

No introduction to the study of history would be complete without a discussion of the requirements of producing a historical essay. Even after carefully reading and rereading the secondary literature; after hours and hours of painstaking research in libraries, archives, museums, government offices, and online; after consideration of the historiography, methodology, and theory; the historian's work has only begun. No serious actor appears on stage after one rehearsal, no serious athlete competes for a championship after one practice, and no serious historian presents his or her conclusions after one draft. The process of producing history is, as the old aphorism claims, "1 percent inspiration and 99 percent perspiration."

Writing history should be thought of as a conversation with both the secondary and primary sources, and indeed with yourself and what you think about the event in question. The only way to make sense of what one really believes and what can be legitimately asserted about the past is to work these ideas out critically. For the seeds of an idea about the past to bloom into a full-blown interpretation, it will be necessary to commit one's ideas to paper in a preliminary way, to constantly test these ideas against the evidence, to subject one's developing argument to other historians who can point out strengths and weaknesses, and to constantly respond to this ongoing conversation through more drafting and editing. But remember, no essay is perfect—at some point, either because of a deadline or perhaps your own weariness, you will have to complete it. However, if you follow the advice found in the ensuing chapters, you will be rewarded with a sense of self-satisfaction that results from a demonstration of acute skills of research, analysis, and synthesis and from mastery of the subject matter.

SUGGESTED READINGS

Appleby, Joyce, Lynn Hunt, and Margaret Jacob. *Telling the Truth about History*. New York: W.W. Norton, 1994.

Brown, Callum. *Postmodernism for Historians*. New York: Pearson/Longman 2005.

Himmelfarb, Gertrude. *The New History and the Old: Critical Essays and Reappraisals*. Cambridge, MA: Harvard University Press, 1987.

Iggers, George G. *Historiography in the Twentieth Century: From Scientific Objectivity to the Postmodern Challenge*. Middletown, CT: Wesleyan University Press, 2005.

Molho, Anthony and Gordon Wood, eds. *Imagined Histories: American Historians Interpret Their Past*. Princeton, NJ: Princeton University Press, 1998.

Novick, Peter. *That Noble Dream: The "Objectivity Question" and the American Historical Profession*. Cambridge: Cambridge University Press, 1988.

Wilson, Norman J. *History in Crisis?: Recent Directions in Historiography*, 2nd ed. Upper Saddle River, NJ: Prentice Hall, 1999.

2

✳

Locating the Sources

Successful historical research blends imagination and a methodical exploration of the sources. Historians seek to understand what happened to people, societies and cultures, and places in the past. Then they explain their conclusions in a clear, organized, and well-written manner. They are always curious to find more sources while maintaining a healthy skepticism of the sources they do find. One of the first tasks in conducting any research project is fusing historical imagination and rigorous method to define a topic and to locate the necessary sources. This chapter examines the selection of a topic, the development of a prospectus, and the stages involved in conducting a systematic, thorough search for primary and secondary materials, also called a research trail. The process is similar for all types of written research from a short essay to an extended research project.

CHOOSING A TOPIC

One way to think about the process of historical research is as a series of ongoing conversations: conversations with yourself, with peers, and especially with the evidence. Whenever possible, researchers should select a topic of their own choosing that interests and excites them, that has sufficient evidence to complete an effective research project, and that is appropriate to the assignment. Frequently, in the case of a paper assignment for a course, students are asked to conduct research in an unfamiliar area and may struggle to define a topic that will actively engage their interest. It is critical therefore to consider carefully what actually interests you. For example, if you have a passion for the environment and are engaged in research in a course in early Chinese or Native American history, you might think about the environmental issues faced in these societies. What were some of the environmental issues in Ming China or in southwestern North America at the point of contact? Were those living in these societies aware of environmental issues? If they were, did they propose solutions? It is important to recognize that many contemporary concerns had their counterparts in past times. Limiting the scope of a topic is often conducted during the research process as the researcher learns more about the available sources. Thus, the first questions seek to determine an individual's research interests.

The process of deciding upon an appropriate topic usually takes one of two forms: researchers either begin with a series of questions that interest them about a subject, or they read carefully in a body of primary evidence and allow topics to emerge. The first approach, **problem-driven**, is the more common as scholars are most often drawn to study the past to seek answers to their own specific questions. With ready access to so many digital resources, however, even beginning researchers may have occasion to immerse themselves in one or more primary source collections, reading until topics suggest themselves. This second approach is **source-driven**. Each approach has particular strengths and limitations, and most historians actually combine elements of both as they define and advance their research projects.

Problem-driven research projects start with particular questions connected to what a scholar wants to learn about a topic. What arouses my curiosity about this subject? Why do I want to know about it? What are some of the problems connected to studying this topic? Who are the people and personalities involved? Where did the events occur? Have other historians writing about the topic sufficiently answered my questions? What new questions do I bring to what is already known? Has new information come to light since scholars last studied the topic? What can a particular source or piece of evidence tell me? Is there anything missing from the extant evidence about the topic? Is the topic important? Can I look at the same evidence in new or different ways? Is the topic likely to hold my interest?

Some of these and similar kinds of questions suggest building upon what the historian may have already read about the topic. They imply a certain contextual understanding of the broad area under study. They also provide a hint of what the historian might expect to discover among the various source collections. While such questions may help the researcher focus on particular things to look for among secondary and primary materials, they suggest an important caveat. They may prevent identifying fresh areas for development or lead the scholar to overlook something obvious in the evidence. They may also tempt the researcher to pursue the questions already examined in one or more of the books or articles about the topic. Finally, they may also guide the reading of sources in unproductive or even reductionist directions. Thus, researchers employing this approach must take special care to continually review and critique early questions, adjusting them as the evidence uncovered dictates. Despite these cautions, the problem-driven research project remains the more common and comfortable for most beginning researchers.

Source-driven research begins by immersing yourself in one or more major resource collections. (Primary source collections and archives are discussed fully in Chapter 4.) For beginning researchers this approach is the more daunting. It may be compared to being dropped into the middle of a deep lake and told to swim since few beginning researchers have any prior knowledge of source collections or their contents. The collections themselves, unless they are printed and edited, offer little direct guidance. There is, however, one benefit to source-driven research: it imposes a boundary on the scope of the project from the outset since the questions emerge from reading the evidence. By contrast, limiting the scope of the topic is potentially more difficult if the problem-driven approach is followed because the questions brought to the sources are based upon background reading in more general accounts.

When using source-driven approach, the researcher begins by reading deeply in a collection, trying to understand what the documents reveal. Next, the researcher proceeds to the secondary accounts to establish historical context and to acquire a sense of what other scholars have written about the topic. Having closely read one or more source collections, the historian is more conscious of what is actually present among the primary sources and what questions may reasonably be studied. Of greater significance, beginning with the raw evidence of a source collection adds the critical element of individual discovery to the research process. It is possible to identify some fresh dimension or idea that will make the research project genuinely original.

There are some disadvantages as well. Researchers delving into any source collection, even one focused on the recent past, must understand the nature of the materials they are examining. What is the collection? What were the reasons it was gathered and preserved? Who compiled it? Is it complete, or have some materials been removed? If documents are missing, do we know why they were removed? Was the collection intended to be read and studied by later researchers? Is the collection manuscript or typescript? Is it visual? If it is in manuscript format, is the writing clear and legible? Is the script standard to a particular time? (There are guides to manuscript alphabets, and these should be consulted from the very beginning of any study). If the collection survives in typescript, was it edited? Who was the editor? Is the language used familiar to a modern reader? Do the words or terms found among the documents have the same meaning today? Without sufficient context, can the researcher really understand the topics discussed in the collection?

Similar questions to those outlined in the discussion of the problem-driven approach should also emerge. What can a particular source or piece of evidence tell me? Is the subject really important? Can I look at the same evidence that others have examined in new or different ways? Is the topic likely to hold my interest over time?

Using either approach or a combination of them will ultimately result in limiting the scope of the topic as the researcher learns more about the subject and the sources needed to support the research. Thus, the first set of questions will inevitably seek to determine an individual's research interest and the likelihood of its leading to a successful research project. Ultimately, though posing thoughtful initial questions is crucial, it is even more important to consider the possible answers in a full and open manner as the initial idea becomes transformed.

- Factors to consider when deciding on a manageable research topic:

  Curiosity—Beginning researchers often draw their first ideas from a curiosity aroused by their readings, coursework, television, or the movies. For example, the civil rights movement in the United States triggered many historians to not merely examine slavery but to research the history of slave resistance, organization, and nationalism in ways never previously imagined. Students should rely on their own experiences in thinking about a topic. The experience of decolonization looks very different to an official in London than to a young boy living in West Africa. The student researchers' curiosity will help keep them intellectually engaged. Less attractive topics will probably be abandoned, faced with less than full vigor, and yield predictably poor results. In examining source collections, it is equally important to be curious about the collection being read. Its contents must hold your attention and engage your intellect. With either approach, there must be an openness to extend the chronological boundaries of individual curiosity.

  Historical interest—Closely related to curiosity is historical interest. What kinds of history interest you? When you read history, what time period, themes, personalities, or ideas attract you? Do you find more fascination in reading the private correspondence or the diaries of a particular individual, public records from a time period, newspapers, or other forms of primary evidence found in archival collections? The answers to these kinds of questions are the starting point in selecting a research topic. Having a topic of interest is essential since the research process is lengthy, involved, and occasionally tedious.

  Imagination—Curiosity and historical interest must be coupled with imagination. The historian's imagination shapes the questions about a topic, the way in which the sources are perceived, and the possible interpretations of that evidence. All that limits imagination are the facts of history. The historian must be particularly cautious not to read anything into the sources that is not actually there by allowing free reign to the imagination.

  Narrowing the topic—Students' curiosity, historical interest, and imagination often lead them to broad topics such as World War II, the communist takeover in China, or the collapse of the Roman Empire. While such topics are interesting, they are too broad to be viable. However, a carefully limited idea that examines a narrower aspect of these larger themes enables the researcher to satisfy his or her curiosity and engage the imagination while studying a more manageable topic. But how does one do this?

- Thinking about the potential topic:
  After the initial steps in selecting a topic, it is wise to discuss the ideas with others. These conversations sharpen thinking by forcing researchers to articulate what they want to find out about a subject and encourage new questions about the subject and the sources. If researchers can explain what they plan to study to someone else, they are more likely to understand the topic

themselves. None of these preliminary discussions needs to be particularly polished because their purpose is to establish potential interest, build a scholarly vocabulary, and identify questions for study.

The first conversations are often an informal **brainstorming** exercise during which historians begin to shape a topic. Starting with one or two fairly open-ended questions or ideas, these conversations are likely to be initially vague and roughly defined. The more common questions may relate to changes, causes, consequences, meanings, or connections. To learn some fundamentals about a topic, examine a general introduction to the subject found in a historical encyclopedia, a biographical dictionary, or a textbook. From this preliminary reading, the historian gains a broad understanding of the personalities, places, and events associated with the topic. Such preliminary reading allows historians to generate more refined questions and ideas. Historians are well served if they jot down these initial thoughts for future reference.

PROSPECTUS

As researchers begin to record ideas and questions about a topic, or as topics emerge from a reading in a source collection, they are prepared to produce a somewhat more structured **prospectus**. The prospectus is an informed conversation in which the researcher proposes a topic and writes focused questions and ideas to initiate the research process. These early questions help the researcher develop an argument around which the research topic will later be constructed. The argument introduces the questions that define the topic, provides its context, and organizes each part of the paper. Thus, the argument at this stage initiates the process of forming more precise questions and setting the project's direction. The argument will likely be modified as the historian locates, examines, reads, and analyzes the evidence. The prospectus is a written exercise; the questions will change once the researcher becomes better informed through careful reading and thinking. The prospectus is a natural extension of the brainstorming exercise.

The following is student historian Paul McDowell's problem-driven prospectus concerning the murder of New Orleans Police Chief David Hennessey:

> After some deliberation, I have decided to focus my research on the Hennessy murder in New Orleans and the ensuing lynching of eleven Sicilian immigrants. Not only was this the largest mass lynching in United States history, but it also marked the first time that the term 'mafia' was used in the United States. My goal is to explore this event and discover what events or cultural mindsets led up to the murder. Why would the white Americans in New Orleans have been so incredibly upset when some of the Sicilian suspects were acquitted, and what would have driven them to a mass lynching? What did the actual Sicilians in New Orleans and the rest of the country think about all of these events? Did the anti-immigrant societies throughout the United States use this event as leverage, arguing that it emphasized how undesirable the new immigrants were to

their country? I think I will be able to find some primary sources from letters or notes of contemporary Italians and whites in New Orleans, as well as government or anti-immigrant society officials during the trial and days following the lynching.[1]

Several points stand out in this first conversation:

- The prospectus is informal. It reflects the author's interests in urban, cultural, and immigrant history.

- The prospectus identifies some very specific questions or topic areas the author plans to explore. The author is less concerned with the event itself and more interested in its causes and consequences. What were some of the responses to the incident in New Orleans and beyond? The researcher offers some indication regarding the kinds of primary evidence he thinks will form the basis for his argument. He suggests they will be a combination of private "letters or notes of contemporary Italians and whites in New Orleans" and public documents from "government or anti-immigrant society officials." The prospectus offers sufficient information to guide initial thinking as the researcher begins to search for more specific primary and secondary sources. It is important to have a peer or colleague review the prospectus and provide constructive suggestions about possible future directions of the topic. As the researcher began to search for sources, he learned that he did not have access to the first-person accounts he had hoped to use and altered his focus to consider contemporary responses and reactions.

By reviewing one's own work and incorporating the suggestions of others, the topic can be further refined. Such conversations should immediately precede a comprehensive search for sources because they provide researchers with a basic vocabulary about the topic and some insights into the kinds of materials necessary. If the prospectus was source-driven, it would begin with an immersion in trial records and other public documents or personal accounts with topics following from that reading.

The prospectus and the resulting conversations are comparable to studying a road map before beginning a journey. The prospectus provides a general idea of direction. As these questions become more refined, it is possible to begin a careful, systematic search for sources to find as many materials as possible about the topic. This literature search is the research trail.

RESEARCH TRAIL

A **research trail** is the systematic identification and collection of all relevant materials available in print and online necessary to conduct scholarly research on a particular topic. The research trail not only involves an exhaustive search

---

1. Paul McDowell, "Prospectus," e-mail, January 21, 2009. His paper will be followed through the research and writing process. Other examples of student work will also be used to illustrate specific points.

for sources, it offers knowledge and awareness of the topic that is fundamental in shaping it. Since historical accuracy depends upon corroboration of evidence, locating every potential source that might shed light on the topic is important. To avoid embarrassing omissions, successful researchers should follow a careful research trail and list all potential resources. Some of the materials listed in an original trail may be subsequently discarded once particular items are evaluated and compared, yet the first examination of the literature should be as full as the careful researcher can make it. Since new sources of information appear regularly, the trail is not a static search. Successful historians check for more updated materials to add to their lists as the project unfolds. Appendix A contains a guide that annotates the basic resources used to conduct a research trail. The materials can be found in most academic libraries or online, but, of course, some libraries house larger collections than others. While online resources are rapidly supplanting print materials, they must still be supplemented with a careful review of specific printed resources only found in a library. In 2010, Google estimated that there were about 130 million unique books in the world (129,864,880 to be exact) and that it intends to scan all of them by the end of the decade. On 14 October 2010. Google announced that the number of scanned books was over 15 million. Though most scanned books are either no longer in print or commercially available, more than 100 million are found only in print.

The research trail is a multistep process that proceeds from locating the most general guides to historical materials to the more specific works that lead to the identification of primary and secondary sources pertaining to the paper topic. The research trail has four purposes:

- It helps the historian become familiar with the major reference works in history.
- It enables researchers to compile lists of materials for the specific research project. This is especially important since it helps researchers to better understand what has already been written about a topic and how their own work might consider new questions or add nuances.
- It provides a working list of materials to be read and analyzed for the project and a rationale for their selection over others.
- It offers information that helps narrow the research topic and frame new questions.

The steps in the research trail are comparable to a toolbox that includes all of the necessary research tools. Some "tools" may never be explicitly used; however, researchers never know what tools they may need. Like a useful toolbox, the organized and systematic research trail simplifies the entire project. Familiarity with research tools is essential to completing the project.

Preparing for the Research Trail

Throughout the research trail process, beginning historians should record information about each source—such as author, title, city of publication, publisher, and year of publication—as well as how the particular reference works are organized. In addition, a comment about what materials they provide and some assessment of their value will be useful as the research proceeds. It is also wise to list the source and page or URL (uniform resource locator) for online materials as well as the date you accessed the site. This information may be recorded in a note-taking program or in a standard word processing program, by downloading citations from library catalogs or other online sources, or by writing the information on note cards. Researchers should develop a single method for collecting information and stick with it. While this habit may seem tedious at first, it helps reinforce the researcher's citation skills and facilitates constructing the final bibliography. It also simplifies the process of locating the work again among the myriad of citations and accumulated information that result from any serious project. (For an expanded discussion of note taking, see Chapter 3.) Through repetition, the process becomes ingrained and is done more or less mechanically.

Doing the Research Trail

The following steps outline the basic research trail. While it may be abbreviated to suit individual needs or as researchers become more knowledgeable about the contents of individual resources, it is also worthwhile to know something about the basic resource tools of history in order to become more self-reliant and confident that you have found the most useful sources. The research trail is the most detailed model for conducting exhaustive research. During the stages of the process, any researcher will have a better idea of whether there are sufficient sources to complete a proposed project, where to begin reading, and which materials to select.

Review a standard guide   For beginning historians the trail should commence with a close review of a published guide that can be found online at many libraries. Currently, the standard is Ronald H. Fritze, Brian E. Coutts, Louis A. Vyhnanek, *Reference Sources in History: An Introductory Guide.*[2] This volume includes fourteen sections that explain the basic reference types that all researchers should know as they tackle any research project. Specific sections describe bibliographies, book review indexes, periodical guides, guides to newspapers, government publications, geographical and statistical sources (among others), and how to use them. Perusing a good guide will provide insights into resources vital to support any project. After browsing a guide, beginning historians should poke around in the reference section of their local library to become familiar with its organization and to locate its specific types of holdings. Even a basic knowledge of the library's reference section will later save time and can facilitate research.

---

2. Ronald H. Fritze, Brian E. Coutts, Louis A. Vyhnanek, *Reference Sources in History: An Introductory Guide* (Santa Barbara, CA, and Oxford: ABC-CLIO, 2004).

Review basic guides to reference books and bibliographies of bibliography Armed with this introductory information, historians are ready to begin a close examination of three important reference sets available in many college libraries:

- Robert Balay, ed., *Guide to Reference Books*. The 11th edition was the last printed version. It has been superseded by the online subscription database, *Guide to Reference*, edited by Bob Kieft and published by the American Library Association. The online resource is updated regularly and includes entries on both print and online reference sources.

- Theodore Besterman, *A World Bibliography of Bibliographies and of Bibliographical Catalogues, Calendars, Abstracts, Digests, Indexes, and the Like*.

- *Bibliographic Index: A Cumulative Bibliography of Bibliographies*.[3] A WorldCat search indicates 2,109 libraries include Balay in their collection, while Besterman is held by 703 and the *Bibliographic Index* by 949. Thus, most students should have access to some of these standard works. These numbers have actually dropped in recent years as more libraries have shifted to online resources. Balay may be accessed online.

While there are certainly others that might be used fruitfully, these three are the most comprehensive. All beginning researchers should work through each reference for their specific subject areas. After becoming familiar with their organization and contents, researchers may later employ shortcuts; however, the first review should be meticulous.

Balay's *Guide,* the 11th edition of a volume first published by the American Library Association in 1907, is the basic reference for libraries and librarians. Although many libraries will subscribe to the online *Guide to Reference Books*, the print version is still valuable for browsing. It covers works and collections throughout North America. Among its more than 15,000 **annotated** entries, the largest single group, under classification (D), is for history and area studies. (An annotation is a brief description of the contents and nature of a particular work and provides researchers with very basic information.)

Although dated, Besterman's five volumes should also be examined. Global in scope and coverage, this monumental work—the fullest bibliography of bibliographies ever printed—lists more than 117,000 titles by subject and by country and includes works in all languages.

The *Bibliographic Index* complements Balay and Besterman by listing titles that have appeared since they were last published. By using these resources together and reading them intelligently, the beginning student will likely identify all of the possible bibliographies and reference works that potentially include information about a given topic. As researchers become more familiar with a particular area of scholarship, they will learn which bibliographies to consult

---

3. Robert Balay, ed., *Guide to Reference Books*, 11th ed. (Chicago and London: American Library Association, 1996); Theodore Besterman, *A World Bibliography of Bibliographies and of Bibliographical Catalogues, Calendars, Abstracts, Digests, Indexes, and the Like*, 4th ed. (Lausanne, Switzerland: Societas Bibliographica, 1965–1966), 5 vols; *Bibliographic Index: A Cumulative Bibliography of Bibliographies* (New York: H. W. Wilson, 2011).

first, but newcomers must know where these volumes are located in their library or online and examine each systematically.

Paul McDowell's paper, found in Appendix B, began with a review of the three standard bibliographies. This first step in the research trail identified the following: Henry P. Beers, *Bibliographies in American History, 1942–1978: Guide to Materials for Research; Writings on American History; Blackwell Reference Online; America's Historical Newspapers, 1690–1922; and 19th Century U.S. Newspapers.*[4] These bibliographies led the researcher to basic primary and secondary sources about the topic.

Search standard subject bibliographies and databases   Having reviewed the three Bs (Balay, Besterman, and the *Bibliographic Index*), the historian next examines more specific subject bibliographies and databases. The number of subject bibliographies in history is daunting; researchers must avoid becoming overwhelmed or discouraged by the sheer quantity.

One of the most important subject bibliographies is the American Historical Association's (AHA) *Guide to Historical Literature*; it should be reviewed closely early in the search of the literature.[5] The third edition (1995) of this richly annotated survey of the most important modern secondary scholarship covers all periods and all countries. Though somewhat dated, this edition remains valuable for many topics. The two volumes are divided into topical and chronological sections; each opens with a brief and useful essay outlining recent scholarly interests, issues, and questions. For many topics, particularly in political, diplomatic, or military histories, it may also be helpful to consult the earlier editions (1931, 1961). The second and third editions are online through ACLS Humanities E-Book and many libraries lease access to this reference work. Researchers should continue conversations similar to those noted earlier in this chapter about the kinds of sources that will be most useful in light of the themes or questions they plan to pursue. These conversations should evolve throughout the literature search, becoming gradually more detailed and more substantive. At this juncture, researchers begin to recognize specific authors of secondary studies whose publications tend to appear more frequently than others.

The next choice of subject bibliography depends upon the particular area or topic under study. Some bibliographies are regional or national in coverage; others focus on specific topics, themes, or source types. In more recent years, some of the very best subject bibliographies may be accessed online. To increase the probability of locating the fullest number of potential sources, more than one subject bibliography should be consulted. Some examples of standard print and

4. Henry P. Beers, *Bibliographies in American History, 1942–1978: Guide to Materials for Research* (Woodbridge, CT: Research Publications, 1982), 2 vols.; *Writings on American History* (Washington, DC: American Historical Association, 1902–1961); and *Blackwell Online Reference* http://www.blackwellreference.com; *America's Historical Newspapers, 1690–1922*, http://www.newsbank.com; and *19th Century U.S. Newspapers*, http://gdc.gale.com.

5. Mary Beth Norton, ed., *Guide to Historical Literature*, 3rd ed. (New York and Oxford: Oxford University Press, 1995), 2 vols. Students should also consult the earlier editions for many topics. George Matthew Dutcher, ed., *A Guide to Historical Literature, prepared by the Committee on Bibliography of the American Historical Association* (New York: The Macmillan Company, 1931); George Frederick Howe, ed., *A Guide to Historical Literature*, 2nd ed. (New York: Macmillan, 1961).

online subject bibliographies for various geographical regions include the following:

Africa

Asamani, J. O. *Index Africanus. Stanford, CA: Hoover Institution, 1975.*

Africa Bibliography. Manchester, England, Dover, New Hampshire: Manchester University Press, 1985–2010. The bibliography is now available online. Beginning in 2011, it is published as the International African Institute. Cambridge: Cambridge University Press.

Africa since 1914: A Historical Bibliography. Santa Barbara, CA: ABC-Clio Information Services, 1985.

Asia

Bibliography of Asian Studies. Ann Arbor, MI: Association of Asian Studies, on going series.

Cumulative Bibliography of Asian Studies, 1941–1965. Boston: G. K. Hall, 1970.

Bibliography of Asian Studies. Ann Arbor, MI: Association for Asian Studies. The bibliography began as *The Far Eastern Bibliography*, published in *The Far Eastern Quarterly* (1946–1955). It continued in *The Journal of Asian Studies* as the September issue until 1968. It was published as a separate annual volume (1965–1991) and is available online at http://bmc.lib.umich.edu/bas/. The subscription database includes citations from 1971 onward.

Europe

Modern European History: A Research Guide. http://legacy.www.nypl.org/research/chss/grd/resguides/eurhist/. New York: New York Public Library, 1996.

International Bibliography of the Historical Sciences. Internationale Bibliographie der Geschichtswissenschaften. Paris: Librarie Armand Colin, on going series.

Roach, John, ed. *Bibliography of Modern History.* Cambridge, England: Cambridge University Press, 1968.

Latin America

Handbook of Latin American Studies. Gainesville: University of Florida Press, on going series.

HAPI, Hispanic American Periodicals Index. Los Angeles: Latin American Center, University of California, on going series.

Modern Middle East

Selected Middle East Reference Works at Columbia University Libraries, prepared by Frank H. Unlandher, Middle East Studies Librarian. http://www.columbia.edu/cu/lweb/indiv/mideast/cuvlm/CulBib.html.

Index Islamicus, subscription database, ProQuest CSA, on going series. http://search.proquest.com/indexislamicus.

United States

Writings on American History. Millwood, NY: KTO Press, 1902–1990. Some volumes
    published by the American Historical Association; others by the Library of Congress;
    annual, irregular.

Merriam, Louise A., and James Warren Oberly, eds. *United States History: A Bibliography
    of New Writings on American History*. Manchester, England, and New York:
    Manchester University Press, 1995.

The AHA's *Guide* and other subject bibliographies will thus provide a reliable
preliminary list of secondary works on most topics. Many also include primary
sources.

Beginning researchers should review the standard printed bibliographies of
bibliography and guides before proceeding to online searches. Numerous online
search engines allow access to websites that include subject bibliographies to
supplement what is available and appropriate in print. Using such broad search
engines must be done with the greatest of caution since anyone can create a
website and there is no professional review process for them. One of the better
online bibliographies is **The Witchcraft Bibliography Project** at http://www
.hist.unt.edu/web_resources/witchcraft_bib.pdf, housed at the University of
North Texas Department of History website. It is a treasure of primary and
secondary sources in multiple languages for witchcraft in early modern Europe.
Beginning researchers may profitably consult this site as a model.

Search WorldCat, LibDex, other research databases, and online catalogs   A
review of the subject bibliographies is followed by a search of important online
catalogs: the researcher's institutional library, the catalog of the nearest major
research library, WorldCat, and, if appropriate, LibDex and other online catalogs.[6]

Each online library catalog has its own idiosyncrasies; however, there are
some general guidelines for searching them to produce satisfactory results. It is
important to become familiar with the guidelines of a particular library's search
engine before conducting a search for sources. Most library catalogs can be
searched by keyword, subject, author, and title. Researchers should examine
the various online search engines and seek to identify the broadest number of
sources. Both beginning and experienced historians may fruitfully begin their
searches with **keyword** queries. Such keywords result from the earlier readings
on the subject. Many libraries allow for the combination of keywords with
AND, OR, IN, or NOT (a Boolean search) to help identify potential materials.
The beginning historian's prospectus centered on the Hennessy murder in New
Orleans and the subsequent lynching of a group of Sicilian immigrants. Some
possible Boolean combinations include the following: New Orleans AND Italians, New Orleans AND lynching, New Orleans lynching AND responses.
Using the first combination at James Madison University's Carrier Library, for
instance, yielded over 1,600 entries; the second combination yielded 60; the
third 2. Totals, of course, will vary significantly among libraries. More varied

---

6. The URL for WorldCat is http://www.worldcat.org/. For LibDex it is http://www.libdex.com/.

and creative keyword mixtures will result in a more fruitful search. Some library catalogs also include a browsing function that enables the researcher to highlight the call number for a particular work and then search for those items that appear on the same or adjacent shelves. Another useful strategy is to take note of the subject headings that have been applied to the books that appear to be most useful. Most academic libraries in the United States use the Library of Congress Subject Headings. These authorized words and phrases offer librarians a controlled vocabulary to gather together similar concepts under one term. If initial combinations fail to produce the desired result, vary the terms or try other keywords. If the resulting combinations are not especially fruitful, then consult a reference librarian and specify what searches have been conducted, what keywords were used, and what the results were.

As the systematic search of subject bibliographies and the local library catalog take shape, the researcher's conversations and questions should begin to relate more specifically to the viability of the projected topic. Do there appear to be enough secondary source materials on the topic to write this paper? Are the available monographs and journal articles sufficient to support further inquiry into this subject? Did the same author write most of the books and articles on a given topic? Do most of my initial questions appear to have been answered in the pages of the available secondary literature? These questions and others like them help determine whether or not the original topic idea needs to be modified or changed.

The remaining vital online catalog searches include those of the best research library in the region and of WorldCat or other appropriate online catalogs. The former should be searched with an eye to what volumes are not available in the researcher's own library and might reasonably be obtained either through interlibrary loan or by a visit to the research library itself. While conducting this search, historians should also learn how to use their own library's interlibrary loan services. This service provides access to books, articles, and other materials not found in the local library.

WorldCat includes the catalogs of libraries primarily from the United States, Canada, and the United Kingdom, offering scholars access to millions of book titles from more than 10,000 participating libraries and institutions. It is linked to a variety of online resources, including digital manuscripts and books, web resources, and computer files. It may be examined using the same types of searches used to identify records in a local library. Another useful feature of WorldCat is that it lists the libraries that hold particular volumes in their collections. This information facilitates ordering titles through interlibrary loan and thereby accelerates research. In addition, individual WorldCat records include a wealth of critical information to assist both beginning and experienced researchers. Individual records may be marked to simplify identifying only those items the searcher wishes to save, download, or copy. Finally, WorldCat is a useful source to identify the most recently published materials on a topic. LibDex is a useful web resource for locating library websites and online catalogs of libraries around the world.

The searches done to this point should identify most books and some articles necessary to complete any research project. The source type most commonly ignored by beginning historians—scholarly journal articles—must, however, receive the same careful scrutiny. Journal articles provide ready access to a rich variety of interpretations about a topic and often represent a scholar's initial public discussion of a new idea. Beginning historians would be well served to have a strong grasp of journal articles, which can provide a better understanding of major interpretations than books. At the same time, searching online journal article databases helps familiarize beginning researchers with the most important scholarly journals for the various history subfields. In fact, beginning researchers should probably begin their review of scholarly journals using online databases and then proceed to what is in print or available through interlibrary loan.

There are five principal online databases to locate scholarly journal articles: *PIO (Periodic Index Online)*, *Humanities Index*, *Social Sciences Index*, *America: History and Life*, and *Historical Abstracts*. The principal advantages of the online versions, if available, are ease of searching and completeness.

- *PIO (Periodicals Index Online)* is probably the fullest electronic index to scholarly periodicals for the study of history currently available. The database includes almost 7,000 periodicals in the humanities and social sciences and indexes full runs of periodicals published continuously since the eighteenth century. It also covers all chronological periods and includes journals published in about forty languages. *PIO* is also an essential resource for researchers seeking scholarly book reviews of works published before 1960. Like most online databases, *PIO* is searchable by keyword, title, subject, or author. Some libraries provide direct access to full text versions of these articles through *Periodicals Archive Online (PAO)*; others only subscribe to the index. Because of its lengthy chronological coverage and the rich variety of scholarly periodicals included, *PIO* is particularly helpful in identifying journal articles not found in a researcher's local library, thereby facilitating the processing of interlibrary loan requests.

- *Humanities Index* and *Social Sciences Index* include articles from many disciplines. *Humanities Index* provides citation access to 500 English-language periodicals and is searchable by author, title, or keyword. Updated monthly, it also includes scholarly book reviews. *Social Sciences Index* functions in the same manner. These databases include articles and reviews from several disciplines and from all chronological periods. All researchers should become familiar with both of these databases and use them on a regular basis to locate scholarly articles and reviews on any subject. Many libraries will provide access to the backfile of these two indexes through Wilson Web's *Humanities* and *Social Sciences Retro* (1907–1984).

  Paul McDowell, the student researcher whose paper is referenced throughout the text, examined *Humanities Index* and *Social Sciences Index* to identify several articles used in the paper to enhance the context of the discussion and provide crucial evidence supporting the conclusions. Scholarly articles led to materials not found in the books cited and helped define the topic in new ways. They provided the student researcher with good information about specific issues relating to perceptions of immigrants, especially in New Orleans, and the reaction to the lynching of the eleven Sicilians.

■ *America: History and Life* and *Historical Abstracts*, although narrower in scope, are equally valuable. The former includes journal articles and reviews for United States and Canadian history, while the latter does the same for world history since 1453; thus, both are restricted geographically and chronologically. Both, however, provide researchers with abstracts of articles and reviews to help make choices among potential secondary sources. Like most other online databases, records located in *America: History and Life* or *Historical Abstracts* may be saved to a researcher's flash drive, downloaded directly to a laptop or other computer, or emailed. Online book reviews, especially of more recent publications, may also be accessed through H-NET online. H-NET is an international interdisciplinary organization of scholars and teachers. There is a direct link to reviews from its homepage.

Scholarly journal articles identified in any of these online databases may sometimes be read in full text online through a "link resolver" that makes the link between the index entry and the full text of the article transparent. Some have a "Check for Full Text" link in the online catalog to help the researcher locate the article and determine availability in an online or a print version. There are three major online full-text journal databases for history: *PAO* (which has already been described), *JSTOR*, and *Project Muse*. *JSTOR* (Journal Storage Project) began in 1995 with assistance from the Andrew W. Mellon Foundation. It has digitized runs of select scholarly periodicals and made them available online in full-text versions. *Project Muse* offers similar networked access to full texts. If a researcher finds a particular title in *America: History and Life*, for instance, it is possible to click and be directly linked to the actual article in full text from one of these databases. If there is no direct link to any of these or other services, the researcher records the citation and locates the journal among the library holdings in hard copy or in microform, or secures it through interlibrary loan. *PAO, JSTOR,* and *Project Muse* are also searchable using the online search strategies outlined earlier. They differ from the indexes in that a search will typically examine the entire full text of articles, not only the key fields such as title, abstract, and subject headings. They provide researchers with ready access to a wealth of scholarly articles and book reviews. A librarian at the researcher's institution will explain how to check if specific periodical articles are available at their institution, either online, in print, or in microform.

Search and evaluate relevant websites and digitized databases for primary and secondary sources   The examination of printed subject bibliographies and the online search of printed materials are fundamental in identifying appropriate primary and secondary sources. This ever-growing list must be augmented by a search for online materials, the availability of which has increased exponentially with the Internet. Beginning historians now more easily link to manuscripts and documents once only accessible in archives, other repositories, or in microform. The holdings of many national and international archives may be searched via the Internet. Online primary sources are now so voluminous that no discussion can reasonably identify them all; what follows is merely a sampling to suggest some possibilities. The ability to search and locate these collections has already transformed research, and the future is even more promising.

For historians of the United States, the major online resource to locate and identify primary sources is the American Memory website sponsored by the Library of Congress: http://memory.loc.gov/ammem/amhome.html. It offers direct access to millions of digitized records from both the Library of Congress and other libraries. Its homepage is clearly marked with links to the collections and explanations of how to use them most effectively. The Library of Congress American Memory collection includes written materials, photographic records, motion pictures, and sound recordings. The holdings may be searched by key-word, and the system is simple enough for beginners to navigate comfortably. For any topic in United States history requiring primary sources, a virtual visit to the American Memory website is mandatory. Its holdings are regularly supple-mented, and researchers should check periodically to see what new resources have been added to existing files.

Complementing the holdings of the Library of Congress are the collections of the National Archives and Records Administration (NARA) at http://www .archives.gov/. NARA's homepage is also easy to navigate and has many direct links to online documentary records. NARA also links directly to the various presidential libraries, which contain a wealth of digitized information. Although the volume of online records is less than the number digitized by the Library of Congress, the site allows sophisticated searches for manuscripts and other records found among its holdings.

National archives outside the United States may be similarly searched. Many nations and institutions around the globe have established online cata-logs or homepages that link to indexes of documents or digitized images. They sometimes include information about ordering hard copies of their holdings or ordering materials through interlibrary loan, though some actually have full-text records online. For instance, the National Archives of Canada/Archives nationales du Canada, http://www.collectionscanada.gc.ca/, with links in English and French, explains how to order copies or request microfilm items from its collections through interlibrary loan. Such materials may even be bor-rowed through libraries and institutions outside Canada. Like many others, the Canadian National Archives offers information for beginning researchers explaining how to consult its holdings. Some document categories may be accessed and consulted online. For example, the diaries of former prime minister William Lyon Mackenzie King may be searched by date, word, or phrase. The *Colonial Archives* database offers online access to more than 70,000 documents found in the Canadian National Archives. These materials document the British and French colonial periods in Canada, as well as the Catholic Church.

In addition to state archives worldwide, researchers should consult online holdings. Many universities, colleges, departments, organizations, corporations, and individuals have pioneered efforts to digitize primary sources (often, though not exclusively, those found in their own collections). Others have gathered resources to make them more available. A quick Google search (http://google .com) can help identify myriads of fascinating materials readily accessible to any scholar. Copyright laws, however, govern all such digitized sources, and researchers should make certain they understand and follow all regulations. The proper citation of these and all other records will be discussed in Chapter 7.

Seven examples illustrate the range of source possibilities currently available:

- *History Matters*, http://historymatters.gmu.edu/, is an excellent site for various materials on United States history. Maintained by George Mason University, it includes numerous primary sources, guides to analyzing various kinds of primary sources, as well as reviewed and annotated links to other websites pertaining to United States history.

- *Eurodocs*: Online Sources for European History, http://eurodocs.lib.byu .edu/, is a rich collection of transcriptions, facsimiles, and translated documents for all of the European states from prehistoric to modern times. The site is easy to navigate.

- *Documenting the American South*, http://docsouth.unc.edu/, a project sponsored by the University Library at the University of North Carolina at Chapel Hill, is a comprehensive digital archive organized into fourteen thematic collections. It is an outstanding collection of materials relating to Southern history from colonial times through the first decades of the twentieth century. There are more than 1,000 books and manuscripts in the collection, and it continues to grow.

- *The Records of Earls Colne*, http://linux02.lib.cam.ac.uk/earlscolne/intro/ project.htm, is a comprehensive compilation of materials on an English village spanning from the late medieval period to the mid-nineteenth century. It includes all estate, ecclesiastical, and state records for the village.

- *The Valley of the Shadow: Two Communities in the American Civil War*, http:// www.iath.virginia.edu/vshadow2/, contains a variety of public and private sources on Franklin County, Pennsylvania, and Augusta County, Virginia.

- *World Digital Library*, http://www.wdl.org/en/, is an international digital library developed jointly by UNESCO and the Library to Congress. In particular, it is an attempt to increase the number of non-English language and non-Western sources available electronically and includes documents, manuscripts, maps, rare books, and other materials worldwide.

- *Google Books*, http://books.google.com/, is a massive undertaking to digitize approximately 130 million unique books by the end of the decade. The project includes books, magazines, and other out-of-print materials. The collection is becoming richer and deeper daily. It will soon be essential to any research project.

The research topic certainly determines the primary sources that should be consulted, and historians should now consider the types available through the Internet when completing a research trail. Student Paul McDowell located many printed primary sources through his research trail. In particular, he found a large array of contemporary newspapers that led him to shift the focus of his research to focus on perceptions and responses. These newspapers verified other evidence and enhanced the final product.

In the search for primary sources, researchers also make extensive use of **microform** collections. Microform was done before full-text scanning and is the filming on reel or card of large sets of materials. These materials can be read using a special microform reader found in most libraries. Most libraries list their microform holdings in the online catalog. These collections allow researchers direct access to vast quantities of material, and many libraries now provide either photocopying or digitizing services. Perhaps the clearest examples of microforms are newspapers, printed books, and popular magazines. In recent years, many of these sources have been digitized and placed on the Internet to provide easier access. One of the features of microforms is that most can be obtained through interlibrary loan.

Identify available reference sources for use throughout the research project   At some point in the research process, it is essential to identify a group of reference tools that can be used to answer questions that emerge from the reading and analysis of individual sources. While the permutations are limitless, these questions are often about people, places, events, even terminology, and require clarification if the research is to proceed smoothly. All researchers should become familiar with the reference works essential to successful scholarship in their subfields of inquiry. Knowing the best dictionaries for terms, biographical sketches, or background information, and having them readily available will save hours, avoid embarrassing mistakes, and help keep research focused on more significant issues. Some of these reference materials may apply to issues of writing and scholarly citation. Having a copy of Turabian or *The Chicago Manual of Style* will allow citation and other questions to be answered promptly and correctly.[7] The *Chicago Manual of Style* is now available online. (A full discussion of citation form can be found in Chapter 7). A guide to writing can help with issues of grammar, organization, and style. In addition, every historian should own a dictionary and thesaurus. Among the best dictionaries is the *Oxford English Dictionary (OED)*, which is available online, in CD format, and in print. A descriptive, historical dictionary of usage throughout the English-speaking world, the *OED* provides definitions for many different time periods with examples of how a word was used in the past. If it is not possible to gain access to this dictionary, researchers should consult basic guides to reference works or reference sections of the local library to find the best substitute. The same process should be followed for encyclopedias and atlases.

If the topic under examination requires knowledge of a different calendar or the cost and value of specific items, the researcher should anticipate these kinds of needs as early as possible and identify necessary references in print or online. Understanding the distinctions between the Gregorian, Julian, or other calendars may be important, and those students considering global topics must make

7. Kate L. Turabian, *A Manual for Writers of Research Papers, Theses, and Dissertations*, 7th ed. (Chicago: University of Chicago Press, 2007); *The Chicago Manual of Style*, 16th ed. (Chicago: University of Chicago Press, 2010).

certain they know the calendar used in a particular region or how to quickly find such information. Similarly, researchers often need to know the modern value of goods, services, or monies found in the historical evidence. A useful website for comparing the value of American and British money since the seventeenth century is http://www.eh.net/ehresources/howmuch/sourcenote. As new questions occur during the process of assembling and interpreting evidence, compiling a list of reference sources will help resolve these potentially thorny matters.

Know the scholarly journals that print articles in the area of the research   Finally, as part of the search for journal articles, historians should become familiar with journals that include articles on their research topic. One purpose is to have an idea of the most logical journals to search for book reviews once the actual process of examining the secondary sources begins. In examining these journals, keep in mind how long it takes after a book is published for a review to appear. This is particularly important if the researcher lacks access to online book review services. Those with Internet access should consult H-Net Online Reviews, http://www2.h-net.msu.edu/reviews/, which is a part of H-Net, a collaborative organization of scholars. H-Net Online Reviews also include listservs in many subfields that can help beginning researchers better understand current debates and discussions among scholars.

A more significant reason to become familiar with the journals in a historical field is to know the most important ones and to read them regularly. Even if the research topic is a classroom assignment, knowing the basic journal sources is a good idea because it helps beginning researchers learn from good scholarly models and improves their understanding of a basic disciplinary tool.

The comprehensive search for primary, secondary, and reference materials is now concluded, and research turns to examining the sources identified. If each step has been followed systematically and all the sources discussed have been exploited fully, researchers can be confident that they have not overlooked anything major and are now ready to initiate conversations to decide which of the many works they have found are essential and which are less important. Although the process of locating resources is labor intensive and there may be a temptation to omit several steps or ignore certain guides, bibliographies, or other potential resources, the consequences of such an approach may create problems, especially for the beginning researcher. Being aware of all the major secondary and primary sources on a topic, especially if the references have been annotated in the work consulted, allows researchers to make informed decisions as they decide which sources are most important to their study. Having identified the secondary and primary sources through the research trail, the researcher begins the process of critical reading and analysis.

EXERCISES

List each of the following resources identified for your individual research project. Explain each of your choices briefly.

1. The best general reference work for your topic
2. The most useful bibliography
3. The most useful two monographs
4. The most useful two scholarly journals
5. The most useful four primary sources
6. The most useful part of the research trail

3

✳

Tools for Analysis— Secondary Sources

The identification and selection of evidence described in the research trail is only the first step in the process of writing history. After locating the sources, historians review and evaluate the secondary literature on a topic. While some historians prefer to immerse themselves in primary sources from the beginning of their research, beginning historians are often better served to begin scholarly analysis with the secondary sources. Starting with the secondary literature offers researchers a basic vocabulary about the topic, a good sense of historical context, and an appreciation of the contributions of earlier historians. The questions posed by these historians, their interpretations of the sources, and the ways in which they supported their arguments provide a framework for approaching a topic. Once this information is examined, the researcher is better equipped to add to the body of historical knowledge with new analyses and interpretations.

Reading the secondary sources begins the exciting search for historical knowledge. A generation ago, immersion in the secondary literature required a trip to one or more libraries to locate books, journal articles, dissertations, reviews, and other materials that offered scholarly interpretations of a past event, as well as a visit to the interlibrary loan desk to request those materials not readily available. The advent of the Internet has made a wide and growing array of secondary sources available at the click of the mouse. Historians still must visit libraries and use the resources of interlibrary loan to find some necessary secondary materials, but this may now be accomplished in conjunction with searching the vast quantities of secondary literature available online.

A careful review of the secondary literature is essential to historical research and writing on several levels. As the first part of the research process, it will shape how a historian begins to think about a topic and the historical context. More subtle and perhaps more important, the final result of the historian's efforts is a contribution to the existing secondary literature. Historians must therefore approach secondary works critically from the outset, questioning what they read through a conversation with the secondary literature and, by extension, with the historians who wrote it. This chapter will examine the critical reading of secondary sources.

WHAT IS A SECONDARY SOURCE?

Often, a textbook, or a section of a textbook, piques the researcher's interest. This can lead to consulting a historical dictionary or encyclopedia to learn more about the topic. If the subject proves interesting enough, it may become a topic for research. Most historians proceed from this point, beginning with a careful collection of the secondary literature discovered on the research trail. A **secondary source** is a summary or interpretation of an event based on primary sources contemporary to the event. Unlike a novel, secondary historical works are nonfiction. Secondary works include **monographs**,[1] **biographies**, and **scholarly articles**, which offer scholarly interpretations of cause, effect, implication, and meaning. Researchers should also be familiar with scholarly reference materials and consult them when necessary. These may include **textbooks**, **historical dictionaries**, **encyclopedias**, **lectures**, and **other printed online materials**.

Reading secondary sources should be an active process that involves critical review of all the material. Initially, historians may seek answers to the basic questions of who, what, where, when, and why. Eventually the inquiry should become more sophisticated. A review of the secondary works has three important purposes:

- To provide background material on a topic
- To provide historical context
- To provide historiographical context, including the theoretical and methodological approaches employed by historians.

The concepts of historical context and historiographical context need some explanation.

HISTORICAL CONTEXT

One of the most important intellectual contributions historians make is their ability to place people, ideas, and events in a **historical context**. Historical context can be described as the forces that shaped people's lives, or the beliefs and mindsets people possessed during a particular time. For example, it would

---

1. An argument-centered, extended essay that nonhistorians simply call a book.

be difficult to understand 1950s America without knowing about the Cold War, challenges to existing racial relations, or the impact of television and the automobile. Similarly, one could not understand much about the modern Middle East without a detailed knowledge of Islam and European colonialism. Such context yields valuable perspective by conveying a sense of what has changed and what has persisted over time. The old adages that "people never change" and that "history repeats itself" could not be further from the truth. Historians recognize that technology, wealth, values, religious beliefs, language, and a host of other factors can vary greatly even within a generation. Such changes render much of the past a foreign country. In much the same way that one must learn a foreign language to begin to communicate with and understand that culture, so too must the historian understand the historical context of a particular time and place.

Secondary sources provide excellent access to these different worlds by providing the historian with an examination of a particular event, issue, or trend during a time period or a description of everyday life in a particular historical era. An understanding of historical context enables the historian to better understand a period on its terms rather than impose present values and points of view on the past. Without an understanding of historical context, it is impossible to understand and appreciate the differences between past and present, as well as to discern that which has changed little or not at all.

HISTORIOGRAPHICAL CONTEXT

Secondary sources are also invaluable in helping one understand the **historiography** of a period or theme. **Historiography** is the study of what historians have written on a topic, particularly pertaining to how interpretations and methodologies regarding a specific topic have changed over time. Some of this change is generational; historians often reflect many of the values, biases, and perspectives of their own time. Other differences may result from differing values or beliefs that can vary from one historian to another. Certainly, individuals of different religions, genders, political outlooks, and ethnic backgrounds are likely to view the past through different lenses.

The discovery of new primary sources, as well as new approaches to the use of existing primary sources, also influences historiographic trends. For example, the opening of Soviet archives following the collapse of communism shed new light on many important events in twentieth century global history. That said, it is more difficult to ascertain historiographical context than historical context. But a familiarity with the types of questions historians have asked about a topic, their approaches to a subject, their use of sources and, in particular, the dominant interpretations of a historical period or theme provide all historians with a sense of how to frame and approach their own questions. A close search through the standard bibliographies and other reference sources provides access to the historiographical context of a subject.

WHICH SECONDARY SOURCES ARE BEST?

Historians must be able to determine which of their secondary sources are most useful. The research trail, discussed in Chapter 2, serves two purposes when considering secondary sources:

- To familiarize students with the most useful guides and bibliographies
- To enable researchers to locate and conduct a preliminary evaluation of specific sources

By reading guides, bibliographies, abstracts, and book reviews, researchers can save time in determining which secondary sources are best. In a perfect world where time is not a problem and where deadlines do not exist, researchers could take the time to review all of the extant secondary literature turned up by the research trail. However, such a world does not exist.

The research trail enables the historian to identify the most important sources for consultation. Most beginning researchers will have examined the American Historical Association's *Guide to Historical Literature* as well as located subject bibliographies as part of the research trail. In addition, **abstracts** of books and articles, annotated bibliographies, and bibliographic essays are useful for this purpose. These reference works often identify the best scholarship on a particular topic. Abstracts and annotations offer fairly simple synopses of a book or article, providing a brief summary and little else.

Beginning historians are well advised to consult comprehensive abstracts. The best collections of abstracts are described in Chapter 2. For North American (U.S. and Canadian) history since 1492, researchers begin with *America: History and Life*. This database provides brief abstracts of scholarly journal articles and bibliographic entries for doctoral dissertations and book reviews. The non–North American equivalent is *Historical Abstracts*, which includes journal article and book review abstracts on world history subjects since 1453, as well as bibliographic information on monographs and doctoral dissertations.

One of the most useful sources of information on scholarship is **book reviews**. They differ from abstracts and book reports by going beyond a summary to offer analysis of a book's strengths, weaknesses, approach, use of sources, and appropriate audience. Scholars frequently make use of reviews to better understand a monograph's content and place in the literature. Historians of the United States and Canada can locate relatively recent reviews by using such resources as *America: History and Life*; non–North American historians must examine *Historical Abstracts*. *Book Review Digest* also provides access to book reviews. A fuller resource for earlier scholarship is the *Combined Retrospective Index to Journals in History, 1838–1974*. The first three are available as online databases. The fourth, printed in eleven volumes, is found in many libraries. Beginning scholars should avoid relying on solely on abstracts and book reviews when making final selections about which journal articles, monographs, and dissertations to consult, but they can use these guides effectively to eliminate sources.

THE PRELIMINARY REVIEW

Despite the usefulness of bibliographies, guides, abstracts, and book reviews, students will ultimately have to make choices about secondary sources on their own. Some monographs and articles may be too recent to appear in the reference works listed above. It is not always possible to determine if a book, article, or website is worthwhile; therefore, it is helpful to understand how to conduct a preliminary review of a secondary source. The beginning historian should ask several questions of a secondary source before determining its usefulness.

- *Who is the author?* Many monographs offer brief biographical information about the author, and some journal articles and websites do as well. A quick consultation of the Internet or the *Directory of American Scholars* or *Contemporary Authors* in the library reference section can generally provide more information. *Historical Abstracts* goes so far as to provide the author's institution in its book review abstracts. Focus on the author's qualifications. For example, does he or she possess professional training, such as a PhD? While one need not be a professionally trained historian, such qualifications generally mean one has been carefully vetted by other historians and usually guarantees a more scholarly approach to a topic. Regardless of the author's qualifications, one should determine if the author has written on this topic previously. If not, has the author written other reputable historical works on the time period or the theme?

- *Who is the audience for this work?* Knowing the audience can often tell much about the work itself. The inclusion of footnotes and a bibliography suggests a scholarly audience. Is it written for a popular audience? For children? Often, the publisher indicates the anticipated audience. In addition, the tone of a secondary source may yield clues about the audience. For example, essays aimed at a popular audience are likely to be well written but may lack depth of analysis.

- *When was the source written?* Although some might insist that only the most recent scholarship is worthwhile, knowledgeable historians understand that a number of fine monographs, articles, and lectures appeared in years past. The most recent scholarship offers the advantage of being able to reflect upon and incorporate earlier interpretations. In addition, the values and beliefs of a particular time may influence the historian's interpretation, but older scholarship is often of great use.

- *Who published the secondary work?* Knowing who published a monograph or scholarly article is also important. University presses and scholarly journals tend to produce monographs and articles for academic audiences, and some trade presses also have a history of publishing academic works. Such scholarship undergoes a **peer review process**. This process begins with an editor, or members of an editorial staff, reviewing a book or essay to see if it meets scholarly standards. If the internal review is positive, the essay is often sent to two or three leading academic experts in the field, who offer a critique of the work, recommendations for revision, as well as a final recommendation as to whether the work should be published by the press or journal.

Some scholarly presses and journals carry more prestige than others, although one should not assume a rigid hierarchy of publishers. Many excellent works have been produced in unusual venues, so it is important to examine a book or article carefully on its own merits. Regardless of where they are published, most of the best monographs and articles have gone through a lengthy peer review process and may be accepted as reliable.

- *Does the secondary source include footnotes and a bibliography?* If so, how complete are the footnotes? Footnotes indicate that the author can substantiate the claims made in a book or article. Conversely, a lack of footnotes might mean that the book has been produced for a less-than-scholarly audience or that the author's reputation is so great that footnotes are deemed unnecessary by the publisher.

  Bibliographies are especially useful if they are annotated or appear as a bibliographical essay. A researcher should examine the sources in the bibliography. Are primary sources included? Is the collection diverse? Do most of the sources that appear in the bibliography also appear in the footnotes? Inexperienced scholars might cite a number of sources in their bibliography, but if few actually appear in the footnotes, this is likely a disingenuous attempt to "pad" the bibliography.

THE INTERNET—OPPORTUNITY AND PROBLEM

The selection of secondary sources has become more problematic with the emergence of the Internet and the proliferation of websites. Although the Internet has democratized publication by providing an unprecedented number of venues for publishing one's ideas and has made an abundance of information available with a few clicks of the mouse, it has also introduced a number of problems for the researcher. The egalitarianism of the Internet, one of its great strengths, can also be a weakness because there is no peer-review process. On the web, all authors may appear equal. So how does the researcher discern the quality of what is found at a website or determine what is reliable and what is not? While many sites are reputable and offer easy access to useful information, the web is full of sites containing half-truths, lies, conspiracy theories, and distortions conjured by individuals and groups who possess little more than an agenda and an active imagination. Most of these sites might be useful for conducting a study of modern psychopathologies but are of little use to the historian. With monographs and scholarly articles, a well-established peer-review process enables scholars to know with reasonable certainty that a secondary source is reputable. The lack of similar vetting for many websites requires that scholars carefully scrutinize web-based sources. The following offers a series of questions necessary in reviewing a website.

Who Is the Author of the Website?

Sites run by scholars, scholarly organizations, universities, libraries, and archives are likely to be reputable. Since Internet sites generally indicate who maintains, produces, or edits the site, discerning this information should be relatively easy.

Many of these have the added benefit of providing links to other websites. In many ways, these online guides provide a preliminary version of the more traditional guides available in print. An example of a first-rate website is the American Council of Learned Societies History E-Book Project, located at http://historyebook.org/titlelist.html. Information made available through links at the site clearly demonstrates its reliability. Another highly regarded website is the American Memory website, http://memory.loc.gov/ammem/index.html, maintained by the Library of Congress.

Conversely, sites run by individuals or groups with an avowed agenda will have little regard for anything other than advancing their own agenda. A keyword search of "Holocaust" will turn up over one million hits, a small percentage of which will deny the Nazis' well-documented extermination of European Jews and others. For example, the Committee for Open Debate on the Holocaust (CODOH)'s archive of historical revisionism maintains a website at http://www.codoh.com/. A perusal of the website will reveal that its author does not believe that the Nazis engaged in the systematic extermination of the Jews during World War II. While the title might convey a sense of legitimacy, the site does not allow researchers to test the credentials of those who maintain the website. Perhaps a more important way to check a website is to compare known facts with information contained within the website. Where significant discrepancies exist, beware.

A second, and perhaps more common, problem with websites is their seductiveness. It requires less effort to sit at home in front of a computer at any convenient time rather than to make the trip to a library or archive. Despite the vast and growing quantity of material available on the web, numerous sources still cannot be found online.

A third issue with websites is their permanence. One of the reasons it is necessary to list the URL and the date one accessed a website when referencing online information is that sites may be put up and taken down by the individual or institution that established them without regard for anyone else. Generally speaking, the more reputable sites tend to remain accessible on a more or less permanent basis.

READING THE SECONDARY SOURCE

Historians review secondary sources on a variety of levels. They begin by trying to learn more about the specific topic they are studying, but they are also interested in understanding historical context and are eager to discern historiographical nuance and scholarly approach. The reading that often begins a research process is basic and informational. In some cases, a researcher will discover that much has been written on a topic. For example, a student interested in writing a paper on the rise of Nazism in Germany would quickly discover that a mountain of information exists. However, the existing scholarship might provide suitable context for the exploration of a more limited topic, which might still address the larger question.

Another aspect of reading secondary sources is to determine the historio-graphical landscape. There are two major ways to do this. First, a researcher may read several works that interpret the same topic in different ways. From this reading, the beginning researcher develops an appreciation for the various interpretations of the topic and the evidence used to construct and support the arguments. Second, a researcher can read a historiographical essay that outlines the various scholarly interpretations.[2] Secondary sources may also demonstrate what historians have not yet discovered.

READING CRITICALLY

Historical reading must go beyond gaining a general understanding of a topic. One of the most important historical skills is reading critically. This is different from simply knowing the basic mechanics of how to read. Many beginning historians complain that they cannot remember what they read. This is not sur-prising, as the investigation of a new topic often presents a profusion of new and unfamiliar information. One of the best approaches to reading is **not** to simply open to page 1 and begin reading. If the researcher wants to retain background and contextual material and understand the author's argument, other approaches must be employed. The initial examination of a topic might begin with some general reading about a topic of interest. By doing so, the historian can begin to learn the "who, what, and where" of the event in ques-tion. The beginning researcher should also consider taking cursory notes about these questions. Early selective reading should also include a perusal of the index, table of contents, footnotes, and bibliography. But to understand the process more deeply, it is essential to go beyond an understanding of the basic events and to interpret what is significant about them. This requires a more critical reading of the material.

Many inexperienced historians also need to learn how to read critically. To fully grasp the argument offered in a several-hundred-page monograph, or even in a thirty-page journal article, a careful reading of the prefatory and introductory materials is essential. While those uninitiated to the standards of critical reading often skip these sections as extraneous, the preface and intro-duction are full of important information. Most modern secondary sources will offer the reader a fairly clear statement of their **historical argument** early in the essay or in the preface of the monograph. The thesis is the central argument around which the monograph, journal article, or lecture is devel-oped. Knowing the thesis of a secondary source is requisite to understanding the reading, as most authors use the central argument as a "spine" that holds together the body of their narrative.

2. There is a fuller discussion of historiography later in this chapter.

An examination of Paul McDowell's paper provides the reader with a clear statement of his argument at the bottom of his first page:

> Newspapers around the United States quickly seized the opportunity, using the event to display anti-immigrant sentiments. Many newspapers favored the extreme measure to which the upper-class New Orleans residents had carried out justice upon the devious Sicilians, and only a few factions of the American press condemned such rash action. Despite different political and social reasoning, most newspapers from all around the United States shared the same underlying anti-Italian sentiment in their reports of the 1891 lynching of eleven Sicilians in New Orleans.

Like many journal article length studies, Mr. McDowell uses his introductory paragraph to set the stage for the paper, enticing the reader to read more. The paragraph ends with a summary statement of his historical argument.

Reading the **conclusion** can further enhance the understanding of a scholarly work. The conclusion does more than summarize the contents of a monograph or scholarly article. Most recent historical scholarship contains an elaborate restatement of the argument as well as drawing subsidiary and related conclusions from the study. Again, refer to Paul McDowell's conclusion:

> Italians all around the country quickly denounced any relations to the Mafia in a variety of public ways. Secrecy and a code of silence trademarked the Italian Mafia throughout its history, so any open denouncement of the Mafia clearly went against the common Mafia principles. From New York to California, hundreds of thousands of Italians publicly denied any connections with the Mafia, making the existence of such an apparently widespread organization implausible at best.
>
> While not all newspapers openly celebrated the 1891 lynching of eleven Sicilians in New Orleans, every single one exhibited anti-Italian prejudice in one way or another. From San Francisco to New York, the entire country believed that the victims were guilty. Even the newspapers that eased up on the eleven lynched Sicilians demonstrated clear prejudice against the Italian people. The same anti-Italian fervor that plagued the Hennessy case lasted well into the twentieth century, and the belief in the Mafia's existence in the United States never disappeared. The trial of those accused of David Hennessy's murder and the subsequent lynching of eleven Sicilians soon became lost in history, but the event nevertheless altered the American outlook toward Italians for many years afterward.

The concluding paragraphs not only offer a restatement and elaboration of Paul McDowell's historical argument, but they examine the legacy of the case, including how the case affected Italian American perceptions of the Mafia. Knowing the argument and conclusion of a monograph, biography, dissertation, or scholarly article can provide important clues about the main points of a work.

In addition, a review of citation materials, and, if available, a table of contents and index can provide additional clues about a work.

THE PAST IS A FOREIGN COUNTRY—READING
FOR HISTORICAL CONTEXT

"The past is a foreign country,"[3] and one cannot make accurate historical assertions without an understanding of historical context. Because of the unique nature of the historical past, historians must read beyond the narrow confines of their chosen topic to develop a better understanding of a time period. Only by understanding this broader setting can one begin to understand and interpret an event or trend.

Reading for historical context involves looking at an event from a number of vantage points, some close to the event in question, others more distant. A historian who sets out to write a story about a figure in the Mexican Revolution might provide an exciting narrative of events, but without some understanding of conditions during the period of the *Porfiriato* before the Revolution, the impact of global capitalism in late nineteenth century Mexico, the concerns of traditional Indian communities in preserving access to traditionally held lands, and the relationship between the United States and Mexico, the historian could not begin to provide a satisfactory interpretation of what transpired in early twentieth century Mexico or comment effectively on its significance.

A list of questions that beginning researchers should keep in mind while reading for historical context might include the following:

- Who are the important participants in a particular event? How did they respond to events?
- What factors seem to have conditioned this response?
- What are the participants' values? Beliefs? Are they at odds with others of the time period? In what ways?
- What is the economic system like? Political system? Social structure? Culture? How do these function? To what extent are issues such as ethnicity, class, and gender important? Are these changing?
- What seem to be the major historical forces at work during the time? How do these effect different groups?

Without such grounding in context, the uninitiated are likely to make judgments that are **ahistorical**—that is, without historical basis. Often, this comes in the guise of **presentism**, where an individual with little regard for historical context either reads the present into past events or more commonly assumes

---

3. English writer L. P. Hartley used this phrase to open his award-winning novel *The Go-Between* (London: Hamish Hamilton, 1953).

that present points of view, assumptions, and even word usage were the same as in past generations. Writers employing such methods often grotesquely distort the past, sometimes out of ignorance but often to advance some sort of present political agenda. For example, many partisan writers have credited President Ronald Reagan with single-handedly "winning" the Cold War. Although President Reagan played an important role in the demise of Soviet-style communism, to argue that the achievement was his alone would ignore the significant contributions of many others—two generations of American presidents whose policies he followed; Pope John Paul II, Mikhail Gorbachev, and Lech Walesa in challenging communist orthodoxy; as well as the millions of people living in communist countries who ultimately had to face down these regimes. A usable past is important to understand the present and how it came to be; it is absolutely essential that the reconstruction and interpretation of past events take place within the discipline of historical context. Anything less is ahistorical and, indeed, intellectually dishonest.

READING FOR HISTORIOGRAPHICAL CONTEXT

Historians read secondary sources to develop a sense of background, historical context, and historiographical context and to understand the author's central argument and use of sources. Beginning researchers may have little trouble grasping background material or the concept of historical context but have less familiarity with historiographical context or even how to identify the central argument of an essay. Having a sense of historiography can help the reader understand why interpretations, methodology, and scholarly approaches have evolved. Although the uninitiated may believe that history is simply an arranging of facts into a narrative, history is really an interpretation based on the weight of available evidence. This allows historians wide, but not unlimited, latitude in interpreting the past. In addition, the questions asked by historians and the approaches—both theoretical and methodological—employed by historians have varied greatly over time. It is necessary that the researcher have some sense of the types of theory and methodology historians have employed in the past, and which of those have held up over time and which have not.

Some historiographical change is quite stark. For example, historians of the American frontier traditionally followed Frederick Jackson Turner's thesis as a key to understanding the significance of the frontier in U.S. history. Writing during the 1890s at the end of the Indian Wars and following the Census Bureau's announcement that the unbroken line of frontier in the West no longer existed, Turner sought to explain what the end of this era meant to Americans. According to Turner, the frontier process could be explained as the unfolding of "superior" Western culture across the continent where it displaced more "backward" peoples, plants, animals, and landscapes. Turner believed that the frontier experience gave America its unique character, including democracy, and helped to explain America's exceptional nature. Writing in the late nineteenth and early twentieth centuries deeply affected Turner's perspective, giving him strongly nationalist views and stridently ethnocentric beliefs that led him to laud the west-ward movement of American culture as a sign of progress. Today, most histor-ians describe the process as one of conquest, dispossession, and genocide. Patricia Nelson Limerick, writing in the more multiculturally spirited milieu of the late twentieth century, argues in her work, *Legacy of Conquest: The Unbroken Past of the American West*, that the conquest of the West was incomplete and that the so-called conquered groups were reasserting their cultures.[4]

Often, historiographical fashions are not such binary opposites. The scholar-ship of the American Revolution has evolved over time, but for the past 100 years two major approaches have dominated with only a few challenges: A Whig (and later neo-Whig) thesis has argued that the Revolution was ideo-logical in nature, while Progressives (and more recently neo-Progressives) believe that social conflict was the main cause of the Revolution. Here, each side has subsumed some of the other's argument while relying on increasingly sophisti-cated methodologies to make their case. Only through understanding the histo-riographical context can a student test a prevailing thesis against the evidence and argue, pro or con, with the existing interpretations.[5]

But how do historians read for historiographical context? How do they con-fidently determine an author's central argument? A careful examination of book reviews appearing in scholarly journals offers an excellent means to quickly dis-cover much about a monograph's historiographical context. But what if the reviews are less than helpful, or if the monograph is too recent to have been reviewed, or if the beginning researcher is dealing with a journal article or a dis-sertation, which generally are not reviewed?

Many important clues about a secondary work may be found in the prefa-tory or introductory materials. Here, historians can find fairly clear assertions of thesis. The preface and introduction provide hints about the author's **point of view**, **use of sources**, and **theoretical approach**. For scholars who are evalu-ating a secondary source, it is essential that they understand the author's **point of view**. Often, authors simply state their point of view, but even if they do not, there are numerous clues. Footnotes, historiographical footnotes, and bib-liographical essays often include references to favored works, historians, or philo-sophers, offering clear clues to an author's preferences. But to fully understand the author's point of view, beginning researchers must know who the author is, when he or she lived, what his or her values are, under what conditions the secondary work was written, and the author's relationship to the topic.

4. Frederick Jackson Turner, "The Significance of the Frontier in American History," *The Frontier in American History* (New York: Henry Holt and Co., 1920); Patricia Nelson Limerick, *The Legacy of Conquest: The Unbroken Past of the American West* (New York: W. W. Norton, 1987).

5. An excellent and brief introduction to the major schools of thought on the American Revolution can be found in Richard D. Brown's introduction to "Chapter 1: Interpreting the American Revolution," in *Major Problems in the Era of the American Revolution, 1760–1791: Documents and Essays*, 2nd ed., ed. Richard D. Brown (Boston: Houghton Mifflin, 2000). Alfred F. Young offers a more detailed discussion with a decidedly neo-Progressive slant in his introduction to *Beyond the American Revolution: Explorations in the History of American Radicalism*, ed. Alfred F. Young (DeKalb: Northern Illinois University Press, 1993). For a detailed but somewhat dated bibliographic essay, see Edward Countryman, *The American Revolution* (New York: Hill and Wang, 1985), 246–274.

Researchers can learn much about the author through reviews of his or her works, online searches, and by consulting guides such as *The Dictionary of Literary Biography*. For example, a search of "Eric J. Hobsbawm," one of the most important historians writing in the English language, would provide a clear hint as to his approach with the following statement:

> Eric Hobsbawm remains one of the great figures of twentieth-century cultural and economic history, a thinker distinguished less by his articulation and defense of a distinctive historiographical style or method than by his exceedingly broad conceptual and thematic ranges of reference, and by the originality, topicality, and suppleness of his Marxist cultural-critical analyses.[6]

Working-class issues and revolution are major themes throughout Hobsbawm's work. Here, one can clearly see that Professor Hobsbawm's use of Marxist theory influences his point of view.

One of the most important influences on an author's approach to history is the use of **theory**. Those who acclaim the use of theory argue that it helps historians consider new types of evidence or consider old types of evidence in new ways. They claim that theory can shape new questions to be tested against the evidence and provide a structure for understanding an event or trend in a new way. Indeed, theory can bring a different perspective to a theme or subject, ultimately enhancing historians' understanding of the past. For example, Marxist theory—with its emphasis on economic structures and their impact on society, culture, and ideology—led both Marxist and non–Marxist historians to a clearer understanding of the interplay between these factors. The linguistic turn, employed by historians informed by postmodern theory, has carefully analyzed language as a cultural artifact that yields important clues about past societies. This development has led historians to more carefully examine the nuanced meaning of words and phrases used in the past, since such words and phrases often had different meaning. An etymological dictionary that examines the origin and historical development of words and phrases can be useful, but more often only a thorough knowledge of the historical context will enable the researcher to truly understand the meaning. Historians of gender have used theory to illuminate key aspects of how men and women have related to power and to one another. Generally, gender historians have examined the past by looking at how the expectations and limits of gender roles during a certain period affected historical actors. These findings have opened up a world of structure, thought, and culture that has greatly enriched historians' understanding of the past.

Despite the effective use of theory, many historians remain bitterly critical of its application to historical study. Arguing that the selection of a particular theory often determines the final conclusion, they see theory as driving the selection of facts to fit a preconceived agenda. Still, a familiarity with theory and its

---

6. Information on Eric J. Hobsbawm can be found at *The Dictionary of Literary Biography: Complete Online*, http://galenet.galegroup.com/servlet/DLBC_Online?locID=viva_jmu (accessed October 11, 2011).

application can greatly enhance the historian's understanding of monographs and journal articles and can help to shape his or her own approach to research.

It is important to remember that theories should be tested against the evidence, but the evidence should not be made to conform to the theory. Marxist theory might seem the likely key to understanding working-class unrest in a society, but such an approach might exclude the roles that religion and ethnicity or other factors play. Theory can yield great benefits to an understanding of the past, but it should be employed with caution since using evidence to fit a preconceived structure only obscures the understanding of the past while relieving the author of the difficult burden of thinking for himself or herself.

READING FOR SOURCES

The types of sources employed by a historian can also offer important clues about point of view. For example, a study of France's role in Vietnam that included only primary sources from French officials involved in the war's decision making clearly shows a possible bias on the part of the author. The **historiographic footnote** offers the best introduction to the most important sources in a monograph or journal article. This type of footnote is essential reading, and it generally appears in the same paragraph where the author offers the thesis statement. It offers the author's view of the major sources that have shaped his or her approach to the subject and is an abbreviated version of the bibliography. The note provides brief descriptions of major sources and comments on their respective usefulness, but it also should demonstrate that the evidence is multi-faceted and represents a variety of perspectives.

Paul McDowell included his historiographic footnote at the end of the paragraph where he made his thesis statement. The footnote appears in McDowell's paper, which appears in Appendix B. His historiographic footnote is a model; he organizes sources around major themes in his paper, offering comments on the usefulness of each source. He also includes significant primary sources.

The historiographic footnote provides helpful information concerning the significance of different sources used by an author, but a perusal of all the footnotes in a monograph or scholarly article can provide an even better idea of how sources are used. Finally, reading scholarly reviews of monographs can also provide the reader with a clearer sense of a work's value.

Having read the preface and introduction, conclusion, bibliography (if one exists), historiographic footnote, and footnotes and having consulted scholarly reviews, the historian should be able to discern the author's argument, conclusions, approach to the subject, methodology, major sources, and to some extent biases and assumptions. Thus equipped, the historian is ready to begin reading the rest of the work with the foreknowledge of what the author is trying to say and why, rather than trying to make sense of a profusion of evidence presented in a sometimes confusing narrative. Such preliminary efforts will actually result in a better understanding of the material read and should also enable the beginning researcher to complete the reading in a more expeditious manner.

No scholar working with deadlines has time to read every secondary source on a topic. The research trail, discussed in Chapter 2, provides a guide on how to select and choose the most useful sources. After narrowing the list of suitable secondary sources, the historian reads several of the important monographs and essays on a topic. Researchers may not be able to read them all but should read until they have a strong sense of both the historical and historiographical contexts. Short cuts are available to those with some degree of mastery of these contexts. To reiterate, experienced scholars often rely on book reviews and abstracts to get a sense of the argument in a particular book or article. Relying on others' expert opinions about a work helps narrow choices. Researchers should avoid an overreliance on others' critiques, but their usefulness should not be underestimated either. As such, book reviews are one of the most important tools available to historians seeking to judge the value of a monograph. Knowing how to read and write such reviews is central to the craft of a historian.

THE ANNOTATED BIBLIOGRAPHY

As researchers initiate the process of locating and selecting secondary sources through the research trail, it is essential to start an **annotated bibliography**. Most students are familiar with the format of the standard bibliography, which lists the sources consulted for completing a research paper. But serious researchers generally avoid such a bibliography in favor of one that is annotated. An annotated bibliography not only lists sources consulted but provides brief descriptions of each source as it relates to the topic. The typical annotation is two or three sentences in length. It generally offers a brief summary of the book's thesis, with perhaps some mention of who the author is and his or her interpretation. An example of a student annotated bibliography may be found by consulting Paul McDowell's paper in Appendix B.

Bibliographic Note Card

The researcher cannot wait until having completed the research to begin the annotated bibliography. Whenever a researcher encounters a new source, he or she should record the necessary bibliographic information on either a separate note card or, preferably, on a preliminary bibliography that is maintained electronically. For a monograph, this would include the following:

- Author's full name (for example, Daniel Walker Howe)
- Complete title of the secondary source (*What Hath God Wrought: The Transformation of America, 1815–1848*)
- Place of publication, publisher, and year of publication (New York: Oxford University Press, 2007)

For other sources, consult an appropriate style manual such as Kate Turabian's *A Manual for Writers of Term Papers, Theses, and Dissertations* or *The Chicago Manual of Style*.

Howe, Daniel Walker. *What Hath God Wrought: The Transformation of America, 1815-1848*

Excellent!!

New York: Oxford University Press, 2007

E338.H69 2007

(Part of Oxford History of the United States Series- David M. Kennedy, gen'l editor)

Manning, William Ray. *Diplomatic Correspondence of the United States: Canadian Relations, 1784-1860*. 4 vols. Washington, DC: Carnegie Endowment for International Peace, 1940-45.

Vol 2 - 1821-1835 , pubd 1942

E183.8.C2   Library of VA
                        Richmond
Excellent Primary!

© Cengage Learning 2013

Beginning researchers might also include other necessary information in the preliminary entry such as Library of Congress call number, library or archive where the book or article was located, and a brief annotation about the secondary source and its contents. (It would be prudent to use information located in guides and other bibliographies to supplement your own annotation.) This may seem like considerable work at the outset, but it will actually save time in the long run. Maintaining this information systematically makes it easier to retrieve materials during the research and writing process. While the preliminary annotated bibliography may look different from the finished copy, like all research and writing, it is part of a process. As you learn more about your topic, some sources will be deleted, others will be added, and your original annotations are sure to change as you become more deeply immersed in your topic.

A working annotated bibliography enables the researcher to ascertain which sources will be most useful to the various sections of the paper. Such a bibliography enables the reader to better understand the ways in which sources were useful and also to grasp the limitations of some sources. The final annotated bibliography should be arranged alphabetically with primary sources listed first, followed by secondary sources. Appendix B contains an outstanding example of an annotated bibliography. Note how Paul McDowell limits his comments to two to three sentences and not only provides a clue as to what information appears in the book but also notes its usefulness.

Many scholars, operating in the spirit of an annotated bibliography, will produce a **bibliographic essay**. A bibliographic essay is simply an annotated bibliography written in a narrative format and organized by topic or subject rather than alphabetically. Bibliographic essays often provide more insight into a source than an annotated bibliography, but writing a bibliographic essay is much more difficult than simply compiling a bibliography with annotation. An example of such a bibliography can be found in Chapter 7.

TAKING NOTES

After a preliminary reading of the key secondary sources, a researcher must begin to take notes. Most scholars who have not shifted to electronic formats use note cards. After creating a bibliographic note card, the beginning researcher should develop a system for subsequent informational note cards. All notes—whether written the old-fashioned way with pen or pencil on a note card or typed into a digital note card format—should be systematically recorded to show where information is from and to indicate the topic of the note card. Each note card should contain the author's last name and a shortened version of the title on the first line of the card. When recording notes on a card, leave a blank line between the author and title information, then indicate the page number of the book or article from which notes are taken. After taking notes from one page, skip to the next line on the card, write down the next page number, and continue taking notes. Once one side of the card is full, quickly read it and provide a few keywords on the top line. This will enable easy retrieval of information once the writing process begins. Be sure to write notes on one side only! Remember, while most writing comes from primary sources, secondary sources provide information that is essential to understanding time and place and can be very useful in filling in any holes in one's primary evidence.

These are the two examples of note cards. The first indicates notes taken from diplomatic correspondence. Notice how the note taker used << ... >> to highlight the direct quote of Enoch Lincoln's letter to Henry Clay.

Manning , Diplo. Corr, Can-Am vol 2 ①
    Gov Lincoln's on Maine Bndy

    E Lincoln (Gov of Maine) to Henry Clay
(Sec of State), Portland, Me, 3 Sep 27'
    136- Maine will ≪ . . . never
assent to the results of an
    137- arbitration unfavorable to
her interests . . ≫ Maine must
have boundary settled.

© Cengage Learning 2013

The note card below is paraphrased from a secondary source.

Howe, What Hath God Wrought ①
        Aroostook War; Treaty

    674 General discussion of
Aroostook War between Maine &
New Brunswick forces
    675- General discussion of
terms of Webster-Ashburton
Treaty

© Cengage Learning 2013

The notes taken from secondary sources reflect the different types of reading described earlier in this chapter. Initial notes may simply provide narrative description of the event or process being analyzed. The first notes of this type tend to be lengthy, but as the researcher sees different secondary sources repeating similar points, the researcher will take briefer notes. In examining more secondary sources, the beginning researcher will become aware of historical context as well as some historiographical nuances. This process of taking notes should be active; it is a written conversation between the young scholars and the scholarship.

Basics of Note Taking Software

In recent years, note-taking software intended for scholarly use has largely replaced the traditional note card method. One of the better programs is Scribe, http://chnm.gmu.edu/tools/scribe/, available through the Center for History and New Media at George Mason University. This program permits extensive notes, allows for document storage, and is easily searchable. Scholars may search their notes by keywords and may connect directly to online resources. Scribe is both flexible and easy to use. A host of programs may also be found at the Digital Research Tools Wiki (DIRT): https://digitalresearchtools.pbworks.com/w/page/17801642/Annotation%20and%20Notetaking%20Tools.

Experienced historians can offer advice on taking notes for beginning researchers. Never take notes on notebook-sized paper; too much information appears in one place, and it is difficult to organize and retrieve. Even when conducting the most preliminary research, recording notes straight from the book should be avoided since it is likely to lead to hundreds of note cards on any given source and, furthermore, increases the chances of inadvertent **plagiarism**. Plagiarism, the appropriation of another's material—intended or unintended— for one's own use, is one of the cardinal sins in academia. Those found guilty of such an offense are generally drummed out of the profession. In order to avoid plagiarism, read the source material and paraphrase what is written. If historians quote directly in their notes, they must make absolutely certain the quote is enclosed in quotation marks and appropriately labeled.

CONCLUSION

Secondary sources do more than enhance our knowledge of a specific event and provide a sense of the time and place. Scholarly interpretations also offer the reader an introduction to the historiographical context. A careful reading of the important scholarship should provide the reader with a sense of the state of the scholarship, such as the perspective of those scholars working the field, what questions they consider important, the differing interpretations of an event, and the methodologies employed to make sense of the evidence. Since any history paper is also a secondary source, good papers will engage the lines of argument in a field or test some of the theses offered on a topic.

EXERCISES

1. Based on your research trail, what is the best monograph on your research topic? How did you select this monograph instead of others?
2. What is the author's background?
3. Who published the monograph?
4. What is the author's point of view?
5. What is the historical argument?
6. What primary sources are used in the monograph?
7. How does this monograph fit into the larger historiography of the topic?
8. What aspects of historical context can be useful to your research topic?
9. Does the bibliography or footnotes contain sources (primary and secondary) that might be useful to your research topic?

4

✳

Tools for Analysis—Primary Evidence

O nce relevant secondary literature has been examined to provide background, historical context, and historiographical context, beginning historians start interpreting the primary sources identified in the research trail. They should also identify additional primary sources from their reading of the secondary sources—in particular, examining footnotes and bibliographies. The analytical process associated with primary sources is the most satisfying aspect of research because the researcher ultimately reaches independent conclusions about the evidence that goes beyond a simple summary of the documents.

The opportunities for beginning researchers to access primary sources used to be more limited. College libraries or local archives might contain scattered manuscript holdings, sources on microform, government documents, or newspapers; however, except at major research libraries such collections tended to be limited and, perhaps, reserved only for scholars. Beginning researchers usually gleaned what primary evidence they could from edited collections in print, materials on microform, or from selected document readers; thus, access to primary sources remained restricted. Such constraints often determined the kinds of topics explored, the depth of the research project, and the questions that could be reasonably posed.

But this situation has changed dramatically in recent years. The availability of materials on the Internet has transformed access to historical evidence and brought entire collections of primary sources within reach of historians almost anywhere on the planet. The possibilities for researching topics have increased exponentially as a result. In addition, many Internet websites include effective search engines that permit researchers to sift through larger quantities of evidence more efficiently than historians in past generations. While digitized technology has made an infinite variety of rich source material potentially accessible to all historians, the very volume of evidence creates the necessity for a more systematic understanding of how to evaluate and use it.

This chapter will first define primary evidence, then examine ways to read, analyze, and interpret it, with particular emphasis on digitized sources. The focus will be on the kinds of questions to ask as part of the ongoing conversation with the sources. Once students are familiar with the techniques of analysis, they are better prepared to interpret the various primary sources they have identified for their own projects. Finally, the chapter concludes with a discussion of how student historian Paul McDowell interpreted primary evidence to construct his argument.

WHAT IS A PRIMARY SOURCE?

A **primary source** is any record contemporary to an event or time period. Primary sources may be written, oral, visual, or physical. Some of these sources were produced with the intent of being preserved for the future. Such **intentional sources** include government documents, church records, autobiographies, or memoirs. On the other hand, many primary sources were produced without any intent of future use. Such **unintentional sources** may include private correspondences not originally meant for posterity but which later are deposited in archives and libraries. Physical evidence such as buildings, clothing, tools, and landscapes may also be labeled as unintentional sources.

Identifying a primary source is far simpler than analyzing such sources effectively. The most common sources used in historical research are written; any discussion of primary evidence must start with them. Before the analytical process can begin, however, researchers must read the source closely to make absolutely certain they understand its content, language, meaning, and argument—if it has one. Only then is it possible to begin to analyze. Beginning historians must learn to adopt a critical or skeptical approach to thinking about evidence and go beyond basic issues of factual content (who, what, when, where). Such an approach helps begin an active dialogue with the evidence. All researchers initiate their analyses of primary written evidence with questions to help them understand particular documents and how groups of these fit together within the context of other primary sources.

When analyzing primary evidence, certain questions are standard. Historians begin by determining the validity of the evidence. Is it what it purports to be? Where does it come from? Is it corroborated by other sources? Traditionally records found in libraries, archives, or other repositories have already been evaluated to establish their authenticity as sources—however, websites in the digital age raise new questions about reliability, accuracy, and authorship. Where trained archivists, historians, and special collections librarians could vouch for the validity of a source, the profusion of information on the web requires the practice of external criticism skills. First, one must pay careful attention to the author or creator of a website. Is the site maintained by an individual or organization with authority on the subject matter? Does the site have an ideological axe to grind? Can information contained on the site be corroborated by other evidence?

Once the historian has determined the validity of the source by applying the tools of **external criticism**, he or she moves on to consider questions about interpreting the evidence, or **internal criticism**. These include: Who authored the source? How long after the event is it being described? Is the author an eyewitness? Who was the intended audience? What is the audience's relationship to the author? What is the purpose of the source? What is the tone of the language used? Does an obvious point of view color the evidence? How reliable is the evidence? Is there anything critical missing from the account that might diminish its value? How does the source fit into the historical context established by other primary sources and secondary accounts? What new information does it provide? Does the source help explain causal or other relationships? Is the source significant? How can the source be used to advance the research project?

EVALUATING WRITTEN EVIDENCE

Author

In examining any written source, it is helpful to have some information about the author. A biographical dictionary or other resource may provide the necessary information, but in some cases information about the author must be gleaned from the source itself. This is the case when the author is either not identified or is unknown. The historian should attempt to ascertain the author's relationship to the event described.

Was the author an eyewitness to what is described or only a contemporary to the event? A scientist who observed Yuri Gagarin's successful orbit in 1961 aboard *Vostok I* provides different information from someone who happened to be alive at the time but only read about it in the newspaper or was unaware it had taken place. Some other questions to consider:

- How long after the event was the document produced? Fresh memories tend to be clearer and capture the moment more accurately.

- What authority does the author have to describe the event? How much does he or she know about what is occurring? How able is the author to understand what he or she is witnessing? For example, the frame of vision of an ANZAC infantry soldier on the beach at Gallipoli in April 1915 was necessarily limited. While that individual may well provide excellent primary documentation for the part of the battlefield he witnessed, he would be less valuable as a source for understanding the broader mission that day. A fisherman who observed the same event from a neighboring village might describe the battle very differently.

Point of View

All authors have biases, prejudices, and assumptions that influence their perspective or **point of view**. Some of the most important factors that influence point of view are family background, religious views, value system, personal experiences, age, time period, place, ethnicity, gender, education, and social class.

- What background factors might influence the author's point of view? Was there any reason for the author to misrepresent or exaggerate the account? For example, a worker's newspaper editorial would likely depict a strike differently than a speech delivered by a company manager. Despite these varying accounts, both may be credible.

- Is the author trustworthy? How do we know? Are there other primary sources that can help to corroborate the account?

Audience

Any source is written with an audience or audiences in mind. The audience may significantly influence what or how the author writes. The audience needs to be differentiated between an **intended audience**—the audience for whom the author primarily crafts his or her message—and the **unintended audience(s)**, which may also be of lesser importance. Knowledge of the audience is nearly as important as knowledge of the author.

- Who was the intended audience for this document? For example, most diaries are composed with the author alone as the intended audience. The famous English diarist Samuel Pepys even composed his diary in shorthand to guard against others reading it. While he wrote out all names, he developed a particular way of recording everything else. Thus, his diary was clearly intended to be private and personal. However, Pepys's diary has been decoded and became widely available to historians, demonstrating that many primary sources have unintended audiences; in this example, Pepys's diary provides a unique window into his life and times. Correspondence, like some diaries, is also intended for a limited, private audience. The intended audience may well influence the degree of candor expressed, the familiarity or formality of language used, and the assumptions made by the author. Knowing something about the intended audience is thus a significant part of understanding the source and using it to support a historical argument.

- If a document is produced for private or individual consumption, can the reader assume greater candor by the author? Are there reasons to stretch the truth in a personal diary or private letter? By contrast, if the document has been produced for the public, can the reader conclude its language is more guarded and its content less revealing or honest? The answers to these and similar questions require a careful reading of the document, meticulous thinking about what it says, and close corroboration with other primary and secondary sources before reaching a conclusion.

- What cultural assumptions must the reader of a private document guard against? In some cultures, formal language is more standard. In Early

Modern Europe, children and parents addressed one another differently. John Paston III's salutation to his father in March 1464 illustrates the point: "Right reverend and worshipful father, I recommend me unto you, beseeching you lowly of your blessing, desiring to hear of your welfare and prosperity, the which I pray God preserve unto his pleasure...."[1] How would many modern fathers respond to a similar greeting today? When studying evidence from other cultures, it is especially crucial to be aware of such distinctions and to evaluate all evidence thoughtfully and critically.

Once researchers have a clearer understanding of the intended audience or have concluded that such information cannot be known with any certainty, they turn next to the author's purpose in examining the source.

Purpose

When analyzing any written document it is vital to comprehend the author's purpose. Why was the document produced, and why has it survived? Some records, such as those produced by government agencies or other organizations or institutions, are intended to survive. Statutes, tax records, annual reports, and the like are recorded with the understanding that they will endure indefinitely. These documents may be more formulaic in their language, neutral in their tone, and precise in the kinds of information they provide. By contrast, private letters, diaries, memoirs, notes, and other such sources are less likely to be written with any intention they will survive to become historical documents. Writers of such documents may be more inclined to be spontaneous and open and, therefore, may be more revealing. They may also employ certain terms or references they know their reader will understand but may not be clear to those reading the letter in subsequent years or centuries. The historian must try to classify whether a document is categorized as public or private and whether it was intended to last or survived by accident.

The next step is to determine what the author was trying to achieve with this document. Often, the author's point of view influences the purpose:

- Is the author simply providing information or trying to lead the audience to a particular conclusion? Is the information accurate? That is, can it be corroborated by other primary evidence? If the source includes errors, are they intentional? Are they significant?

- What other kinds of evidence does the author introduce to support an argument or claim in the source? Why was it chosen?

- Is the coverage balanced? These questions relate to what is called the author's bias.

---

1. John Paston III to John Paston I, 1 March 1464, *The Paston Letters: A Selection in Modern Spelling*, ed. Norman Davis (Oxford and New York: Oxford University Press, 1983), 103-104.

Tone and Language

The scholar should now consider issues of tone and language within the evidence. For many beginning researchers, these considerations are complex and require attentive reading:

- What is the tone of the source? That is, what is the author's attitude toward the subject matter? It is sometimes helpful to read the document aloud to get a clearer sense of its tone. Does the author appear to be angry? Argumentative? Sarcastic? Authoritative? Judgmental? Even-tempered? Omniscient? Conversational? Consider, for example, Mohandas K. Gandhi's bitter condemnation of Western "civilization" in his 1908 pamphlet *Hind Swaraj* (*Indian Home Rule*) or the eloquence of Abraham Lincoln in the 1863 *Gettysburg Address*. Gandhi wrote:

> Formerly, when people wanted to fight with one another, they measured between them their bodily strength; now it is possible to take away thousands of lives by one man working behind a gun from a hill. This is civilization. Formerly, men worked in the open air only as much as they liked. Now thousands of workmen meet together and for the sake of maintenance work in factories or mines. Their condition is worse than that of beasts. They are obliged to work, at the risk of their lives, at most dangerous occupations, for the sake of millionaires. Formerly, men were made slaves under physical compulsion. Now they are enslaved by temptation of money and of the luxuries that money can buy. There are now diseases of which people never dreamt before, and an army of doctors is engaged in finding out their cures, and so hospitals have increased. This is a test of civilization.[2]

Gandhi's tone and examples in the passage indicate his anger at the claims of Western civilization and Westerner's attitudes toward his fellow countrymen. According to Gandhi, Westerners equate civilization with advanced technology used to kill thousands, factory work to enrich the few, and more numerous and dangerous diseases. To understand his meaning, the reader must study his tone.

In the *Gettysburg Address,* Lincoln said:

> The world will little note nor long remember what we say here, but it can never forget what they did here. It is for us the living rather to be dedicated here to the unfinished work which they who fought here have thus far so nobly advanced. It is rather for us to be here dedicated to the great task remaining before us— that from these honored dead we take increased devotion to that cause for which they gave the last full measure of devotion—that we here highly resolve that these dead shall not have died in vain,

---

2. Mahatma Gandhi, *Hind Swaraj or Indian Home Rule*, http://www.mkgandhi.org/swarajya/coverpage.htm (accessed 12 September 2011).

that this nation under God shall have a new birth of freedom, and that government of the people, by the people, for the people shall not perish from the earth.[3]

The president's tone in this speech during a particularly bloody period of the war was conciliatory and inspirational. He sought to reunite a divided nation as it remembered its fallen from this bloody battle. He does not single out Union soldiers; he mourns for all Americans who died there. His eloquent language reminded all Americans of their responsibility to the fallen at Gettysburg and to their responsibility to reunite the nation.

■ Is there a single tone employed throughout the document, or does it vary from part to part? How does the tone in one document by a particular author contrast with the tone in another, especially one written at a different time? How does a particular source's tone differ from other sources describing the same event or issue, especially when they share the same or similar positions? Obviously, an understanding of historical context obtained through a careful reading of primary sources will help the researcher to understand the tone of a particular document.

The language of a document takes many forms and reveals much about the author, the source, and the purpose. If the language is informal or conversational, the source may have been written in haste, written to a friend or someone close, or not intended to be permanent. In Early Modern England, for instance, approximately two-thirds of all wills were written within two weeks of an individual's death.[4] Such documents, including oral wills, were often dictated quickly and contain repetitions and language that suggest the individual was struggling to record his or her last wishes. Other documents may be more rigid in structure, form, and language. As noted above, salutations and closings in past correspondence were far more formal than in modern times, and researchers must understand these conventions if they are to draw appropriate conclusions from the information.

Finally, language is often period specific, and researchers must be extremely cautious not to read modern definitions into past times and thereby corrupt meaning. Words may have had a specific meaning or use in the past that is far different from current usage. Further, just as modern English has its own jargon and idioms, they were also present in the past. For example, the past use of the word *icon* would have religious connotations, while in the twenty-first century the word would often be associated with a clickable image on a computer's desktop. Having the *Oxford English Dictionary* or another etymological dictionary close at hand for reference will help

3. Abraham Lincoln, "Gettysburg Address, November 19, 1863," *The Avalon Project: Documents in Law, History and Diplomacy*, Yale Law School, Lillian Goldman Library, http://avalon.law.yale.edu/19th_century/gettyb.asp (accessed 12 September 2011).

4. Colin D. Rogers and John H. Smith, *Local Family History in England, 1538–1914* (Manchester and New York: Manchester University Press, 1991), 153.

researchers avoid this form of potential misinterpretation. This is especially important because of the instability and sometimes open-ended meaning which words may convey. In order for historians to extract precise meaning from language effectively, it is essential that they have a clear idea of how these words functioned in the context of their time.

Significance

One of the most difficult elements for beginning historians and seasoned scholars is determining the significance of a written source. Not every primary source is equal in importance. In examining written sources, a scholar should consider the following:

- What are the elements that make a particular document important? A useful convention in answering this question is to think about how the document relates to an understanding of the topic.

- First, how does the source help explain the event or topic being explored? Could the event or issue be explained as fully without the document?

- Second, does the source offer unique insights or alternative information about the topic?

- Finally, is the explanation or interpretation in this document different from others?

To this point, the discussion has focused on some of the key questions necessary to analyze primary, written evidence. While such sources are certainly the most commonly used by historical researchers, they are by no means the only kinds of evidence available. Depending upon the nature of the research project, oral, visual, or physical evidence may offer insights and information, and attention must turn to these forms.

EVALUATING ORAL EVIDENCE

Oral evidence takes several forms in today's digital environment. Recorded interviews with individuals, following guidelines and standards of the Oral History Association or other professional groups in the United States and their counterparts abroad, emerged by the mid–twentieth century as an important new source for historical research. These interviews have traditionally been either biographical or focused on specific issues. Many personal interviews have been transcribed and survive as written documents while others are available only on tape or in digitized form. Transcribed interviews generally must be evaluated as all other written primary sources. Television and video recordings added another dimension, and digitization has extended the availability of such oral evidence. Students of contemporary history now have access through their computer terminals to speeches, films, and other examples of oral evidence.

Although the format may be different, the same evaluation criteria are applied to all forms of oral evidence. Thus, the researcher asks essentially the same series of questions about **author**, **point of view**, **audience**, **purpose**, **language**, and **significance** as for any other primary source. If the source under study is transcribed, the process is relatively simple because the format of the evidence is written. When working with oral histories that have been transcribed, researchers must seek to discern whether the transcription is complete or edited. Fuller, unedited transcriptions tend to be more valuable as sources since they give the researcher complete access to the testimony as it was first recorded. If it is not transcribed, however, the process of analysis is more complex as the material is heard, not read, and may have to be replayed several times in order to understand its content fully.

The historian asks some critical questions of any oral source:

- Why was the oral source produced, and why has it survived? Is it part of a larger collection? Some collections may focus on coal miners, steel workers, or infantrymen, for example, and the historian needs to be aware of this situation. Why was the collection gathered? Speeches and television files may be preserved as part of a station or university archive.

- What is the role of the interviewer? Oral interviewers play a powerful role in the production of oral histories. The questions they pose in conducting an interview frame the discussion and may direct the person being interviewed to specific topics or themes. Thus, in evaluating oral interviews, it is important to determine the degree to which the interviewer is in control. In better oral interviews, the interviewer is less intrusive, tends to ask broader, more open-ended questions, and does not try to direct the individual to particular conclusions. When reviewing speeches or media outtakes, researchers should also be conscious of the underlying assumptions of a source. Certain idioms and allusions to places or persons may not have required explanation in the original; however, as part of the analysis of a historical source, they become more important.

Oral evidence has become more widely used in recent decades and may add significant sources to any project when evaluated critically.

EVALUATING VISUAL EVIDENCE

Paintings, photographs, cartoons, and films comprise the principal categories of visual evidence most widely used by historians. Each variety yields unique insights, and each poses specific analytical questions for researchers. When evaluating a portrait, for instance, it is useful to know whether the artist painted a flattering or accurate rendition of the individual. Charles I of England preferred portraits of himself either standing or riding to emphasize strength and manliness. Soviet realist art of the 1930s portrayed Joseph Stalin as a benevolent and caring leader. A Diego Rivera mural would likely champion the common people and the working class. When evaluating such evidence, historians must ask questions such as these:

- Who was the artist? Why was the portrait painted? Who commissioned the painting?

- What is the context of the painting? For example, a painting of Napoleon as a young man would be different from one completed after he was crowned emperor of France.

- What does the painting depict, in terms of both its primary subject as well as subjects in the background?

In assessing works of art, it is essential to know something about the artist as well as the motivation and purpose for the work. It is equally important to think about how portraits and paintings are to be used in the research being conducted. A comparison of contemporary paintings could add a useful dimension to the work.

Photographs may offer a more accurate visual image than paintings. They may also be staged, with the photographer ultimately controlling the picture that is taken. Once again, the beginning historian must ask questions about the primary source:

- What did the photographer choose to record? What was the purpose of the photograph? What assumptions does the photographer make about the subject and the audience? Has the photograph been altered? Personal photographs taken by German soldiers in the Eastern Theater of World War II can reveal much about the average German soldier's view of the Polish and Russian people. A picture may indeed be "worth a thousand words," but it is the interpretation and analysis provided by the researcher that brings meaning to the photograph.

Analysis of cartoons raises other issues because they reflect the times in which they were produced in such different ways. In the original meaning, a cartoon was a drawing on more or less permanent paper intended as a prelude to a painting of the same subject. Leonardo da Vinci's sketchbooks provide insight into the evolution of the artist's thought about a subject and may illustrate significant changes over time. In a sense, they are comparable to early drafts of correspondence or other written materials. A second meaning of the term is more familiar: a drawing, usually in a newspaper, that may be satirical or humorous. In this sense, cartoons provide rich insights into both the artist's perceptions and how individuals or events were understood by contemporaries. These sources assume certain knowledge by the viewer and must be used carefully. Gilded Age cartoonist Thomas Nast's encapsulation of the infamous Tweed Ring, portrayed here as vultures, revealed corruption in New York City to his many readers.[5]

---

5. Thomas Nast, "A Group of Vultures Waiting for the Storm to 'Blow Over'—'Let Us Prey,'" *Harper's Weekly*, 23 September 1871, 889, http://app.harpweek.com/ (accessed 16 September 2011).

Film is a final example of a visual source type used for historical analysis. This source is potentially the most enticing, especially for beginning researchers. Videotape would appear to capture the reality of the moment, but it must be scrutinized much like a photograph. On the other hand, motion pictures must be approached with extreme caution. Docudramas, feature films, and the like are produced with many different purposes, and while they may illuminate aspects of the past, they are the creation of the film artist and should not be used in the same way as written, oral, or other visual sources. They may be valuable to help achieve an understanding of the culture and times in which the film was produced or to provide insights into what it valued or found humorous, but films differ profoundly from other visual resources. For example, the movie *The Patriot* reputedly depicts events that took place in South Carolina during the American Revolution. Although there is some factual basis for the story, the film is one-sided; it distorts British behavior and misrepresents race relations in eighteenth-century South Carolina.

EVALUATING PHYSICAL EVIDENCE

Historians only occasionally use physical evidence. Weapons, tools, and other artifacts may provide valuable insights to a period and should not be ignored. Physical evidence from archaeological excavations or other sites can reveal much that is not readily found in other sources. Artifacts help scholars understand individuals and their communities. They enable historians to gain deeper and richer insights into a period and its people. Examining whalebone corsets, crinolines, and other nineteenth-century women's clothing, for example, clearly demonstrated the restrictive nature of women's wear at the time, which underscored their subservience and reinforced societal perceptions. Of course, the historian must determine whether or not these artifacts are typical or representative. Such physical evidence provides a better sense of the situation than simply reading accounts of clothing in wills or viewing pictures of it in advertisements. Students of agricultural history who examine field implements and understand their use will empathize more with written accounts of farming realities. Historians may also consider physical evidence such as landscapes, buildings, gardens, and transportation grids. All are simply other forms of text and should be critiqued in similar ways.

FINAL THOUGHTS ON ELEMENTS OF ANALYSIS

The careful researcher approaches all evidence in any format armed with a framework for analyzing it. Each document or primary source must be scrutinized critically in order to understand it and evaluate its worth as potential evidence. The questions posed in the earlier sections focus on understanding the nature and value of a source and knowing with some certainty whether or not the account or interpretation it offers can be verified and corroborated, preferably by other primary evidence. Beginning historians should scrutinize individual sources of evidence, constantly comparing a particular document or artifact with others they have already studied to determine how they are similar and how they differ. This analytical approach underlines the ongoing conversations necessary with each piece of evidence.

The first sections of this chapter have focused on matters of definition and the standard elements of historical analysis. Equipped with the techniques and terms of analysis, it is now possible to examine different types of primary sources.

SOURCE TYPES AND THEIR APPLICATIONS

Primary sources are often categorized in several ways. The first group comprises those sources that are **unpublished**. Such sources can only be found in one particular location, such as an archive, the special collections section of a research library, or a particular local library or historical society. These materials do not circulate; thus the historian must visit the facilities to view these documents. Many previously unpublished manuscripts are being digitized and posted to websites.

The second group is **published**. These primary sources include presidential papers, government documents, memoirs, autobiographies, and newspapers, which are widely available at archives, research libraries, public libraries, and websites.

A third group is **edited** or **selected**. These sources are similar to those previously mentioned; however, edited or selected collections of the writings of Mao Zedong would include very different documents from the complete works of the same individual. In these instances, an editor has culled most of the writings and organized them in a special way. (For example, this might include organizing around a theme or chronologically.) It is valuable to know why the choices for inclusion (or exclusion) were made. The active researcher should also know the nature of the collection being examined and the role played by an editor, compiler, or the group digitizing the collection.

Correspondence

Personal correspondence has traditionally been one of the most widely used primary sources. Because such correspondence was between individuals and not intended for public examination, it frequently provides a clearer understanding of the mind of the author and sometimes the recipient of the letter. Correspondence often includes the date when letters were written; the letters are often specifically focused and sometimes address issues raised in earlier letters. They may offer insights into what a person was thinking or experiencing, what he or she had observed, and what he or she chose to convey to the reader. They may either inform or persuade, and they often offer insights into an individual's point of view. Correspondence may also be official, as letters may be used to convey the wishes of an agency or a government authority. Official letters are more formal in their language and tone and may provide less insight into the individual writer than informal correspondence. While most collections of correspondence remain in archives or special collections, digitized letter collections abound on many topics and are easily accessible in manuscript or typescript formats.

One especially rich collection for U.S. history is the American Memory (Library of Congress): http://memory.loc.gov/ammem/index.html. The roughly 27,000 documents found in the Thomas Jefferson Papers include an extensive number of his letters as both a private citizen and public official: http://memory.loc.gov/ammem/collections/jefferson_papers/. A nice feature of this collection is that it provides an image of the original handwritten letter as well as a typewritten transcription. Many digitized letters have been transcribed and, while researchers must be conscious of the potential that mistakes may have occurred in the process, the probability of error is less likely for standard collections in reputable digital archives. One of Thomas Jefferson's letters to John Adams, written on 28 October 1813, declared:

> For I agree with you that there is a natural aristocracy among men. The grounds of this are virtue and talents. Formerly, bodily powers gave place among the *aristoi*. But since the invention of gunpowder has armed the weak as well as the strong with missile death, bodily strength, like beauty, good humor, politeness and other accomplishments, has become but an auxiliary ground for distinction. There is also an artificial aristocracy, founded on wealth and birth, without either virtue or talents; for with these it would belong to

the first class. The natural aristocracy I consider as the most precious gift of nature, for the instruction, the trusts, and government of society. And indeed, it would have been inconsistent in creation to have formed man for the social state, and not to have provided virtue and wisdom enough to manage the concerns of the society. May we not even say, that that form of government is the best, which provides the most effectually for a pure selection of these natural *aristoi* into the offices of government? The artificial aristocracy is a mischievous ingredient in government, and provision should be made to prevent its ascendency.[6]

This particular letter provides a good example for analysis. First, the author and audience are identified, and the letter is part of an ongoing correspondence between the two former presidents. For a deeper appreciation of the letter's purpose, it would be fruitful to review the full exchange on the topic and take the perspectives of both Adams and Jefferson into account. This is often a problem when historians rely upon personal correspondence, as one-half of an exchange may be missing, although the author may address earlier issues or suggest what was stated in earlier correspondence. One of the critical elements in reviewing this passage and the views of John Adams relates to tone and language. The two men were long retired from politics, though each remained vigorous and active. Jefferson's discussion of gunpowder as an equalizer among men reflects his tone, and the playful way in which he describes its role suggests he is gently goading Adams. The distinction he makes between natural and artificial aristocracies reinforces this point. Reading a letter aloud sometimes is helpful in evaluating tone or language.

To assess a letter's significance, the beginning historian should use other letters of the time as well as other contemporary sources to corroborate the interpretation found in the letter. In this example, was their discussion of aristocracy central to political discourse in the decade? Were their contemporaries concerned with the matter? When using correspondence as a source, the researcher should avoid whenever possible employing only a single letter. Ideas often evolve over time, and one letter, deprived of its context as part of a larger whole, may lead to erroneous assumptions. It is always important to try to read all the correspondence on a particular topic, especially if the letters extend over a long period of time. Correspondence is a vital resource for historical research and can offer many insights; however, like any other primary source, letters must be read critically and carefully.

Diaries, Memoirs, and Autobiographies

Diaries are among the most useful primary sources for examining the inner thoughts of past individuals. Although some may be eventually published, all diaries offer the historian the advantage of an internal view into the mind of

---

6. Thomas Jefferson to John Adams, 28 October 1813, *The Thomas Jefferson Papers, Series 1, General Correspondence, 1651–1827,* http://memory.loc.gov/ammem/collections/jefferson_papers/ (accessed 16 September 2011).

the author. Diaries are especially useful since they are rarely intended for the public and as a result are more likely to contain the private thoughts and views of an individual. Diarists often recount the day's events and their activities with candid thoughts. Clearly, a historian must analyze a diary in much the same way as any other primary source, but since the audience for any diary is the individual who wrote it, the author is much less likely to guard his or her comments. Although some diaries may be published, it is useful to locate and use the original diary since published diaries often are edited and sanitized for public consumption. For example, an unexpurgated version of *The Diary of Anne Frank* offers deeper insights into the life of a young Jewish girl hiding from Nazi occupiers in the Netherlands during World War II than a more selective edition.

The private nature of a diary offers clear advantages over memoirs and autobiographies as a primary source. Although all such sources are useful, the memoir or autobiography is generally written for a public audience; as a result, it is more likely to cast the author in a favorable light. For example, Richard M. Nixon's memoirs[7] say little about his involvement in Watergate.

Government Documents

Government documents offer perhaps the widest array of source types. The records kept by international, national, state, and local authorities over the centuries are voluminous and varied. These materials include, but are not limited to, legislation, resolutions, debates and speeches by government officials, records of government agencies, meeting minutes, cables, intelligence, court records, and census and statistical materials. Increasingly, government documents are being made available digitally. For example, records of the U.S. Congress from 1774 to 1875 can be found in the American Memory website: http://memory.loc. gov/ammem/amlaw/lawhome.html. The United Nations' website also provides excellent documentation of its activities: http://www.un.org/en/documents/ index.shtml.

Laws and resolutions help show an official position on a particular issue that often reflects underlying tensions within a society. An examination of laws may indicate emerging issues in a society or may help to reveal power relationships during a time or place. For example, Dutch law requires the maintenance of their extensive system of dikes, largely as a result of the massive floods that inundated the Netherlands in 1953.

Speeches by government officials not only reveal how one individual viewed an important issue of the day, but they may also say much about the audience he or she is addressing. When used in conjunction with other documents, a speech may offer insights into the strength or weakness of a particular government or political figure. The partially opened Soviet archives offer a very different perspective of government operations from those records released at the time events were taking place. Because of their very nature, however, all government records must be used with great care.

---

7. Richard M. Nixon, *RN: The Memoirs of Richard Nixon* (New York: Grosset and Dunlap, 1978).

Court records are especially valuable for providing a window into the lives of people who may not have left written records. Some court records detail the activities of individuals who have run afoul of the law. They tend therefore to be hostile accounts or to present their subjects in a less than favorable light. Despite their potential difficulties, the types of cases prosecuted offer a useful window into the issues of concern in a particular age. The court proceedings of the Old Bailey in London offer an example of trial records available digitally. The cases in the collection, numbering more than 100,000, embrace the period from 1674 to 1834 (http://www.oldbaileyonline.org/). When used in conjunction with other sources, court proceedings add an important dimension to understanding the lives of everyday people.

Wills and Inventories

Wills and inventories provide a unique glimpse into the world of those who did not usually write. Since wills were often written shortly before death, they offer insights into what occupied a person's mind at that moment. Wills can provide information about family, religious attitudes, and what an individual valued and, if accompanied by an inventory, reveal useful information about possessions and debts. Inventories were official lists of possessions on hand at the time of death with an estimate of their value. Some inventories are particularly helpful because they provide a room-by-room listing of possessions. Such evidence is extremely useful for determining an individual's wealth, social status, and lifestyle. Comparing a number of inventories in the same place over time can reveal rising or declining standards of living in a certain community. Like so many other primary sources, wills and inventories only give a snapshot into an individual's life. They are imperfect; however, they are a vital primary source, especially for the study of average people.

The typescript will of Margaret Brownson, dated 1 March 1665, found in the Church Documents section of the *Earls Colne, Essex: Records of an English Village, 1375–1854* (http://linux02.lib.cam.ac.uk/earlscolne/) illuminates the value and limits of such evidence. Because the Earls Colne online data archive cross-references all digitized records, Margaret Brownson's marriage record survives, as do tax records and other documents that assist in reconstructing portions of her life and her place in the village. Shortly before her death, she dictated her last will:

> I Martha Brownson of Earls Colne do on the 1.3.1665 make and ordain this my last will and testament imprimis I give to Wm Harlakenden of the same parish esq the bed in the parlour and all things belonging thereto with the great chest also in the parlour and whatsoever he pleaseth of any small things I leave to his dispose item I give to mrs Owens one pair of sheets a wicker chair a wainscot glass case a brazen pestle and mortar my best stuff coat a box smoothing iron a say apron item to her maid all her small wearing linen great cupboard in the hall one little table all her earthenware an old skillet a brass kettle and all appurtenances to the dairy viz

bellows firepan tongs etc one pewter dish over above and a bed with all belonging to it two feather pillows chair reel and wheel one long chest and with other things mr Harlakenden thinks fit item I give to mrs Josceling the screen as it stands by the chimney item I give to my cousin Jn Gulston 40s and to my cousin his brother 40s to my cousin Chrismas my best cloth waistcoat and 20s to her two daughters 10s each of them to my cousin Gulston her sister 20s and to her maid Ann Hutton 40s to my sister Everitt 20s to her two daughters 10s either of them to goodman Peak 5s all my debts I will to be truly paid and I appoint my loving friend Wm Harlakenden executor of this my will and if there remain any overplus of goods or money I give it to my cousin Jn Gulston to whom I give my long table in the hall and forms declared to be her last will and testament in presence of us Ralph Josselin Ann Hutton.[8]

Her inventory, valued at £24 1s, was not broken down by items.

An analysis of Martha Brownson's will reveals its usefulness as a primary source. In the first part of her will Brownson allows Harlakenden to select any small, unnamed items in the parlor and asks that he see that any surplus wealth and possessions are given to her cousin. The terminology employed to describe certain items—for example, her reference to "best stuff coat"—may suggest how she valued certain things. Specifying some individuals by name and omitting the names of others may reveal much about family structure. Many of the specific items noted in the will may be unfamiliar to modern readers and require the use of an etymological dictionary. Taken collectively, wills from a given time or place offer windows into the material world of a community and its social stratification. They tell about families, feuds, and friendships and about what was valued in communities. Furthermore, wills sometimes speak to debts owed and forgiven and indicate significant relationships. They are but one type of social history document, and historians would use them in conjunction with those exploring marriage negotiations and other varieties of evidence.

Statistical Records

Another important, and underutilized, primary source is statistical data, such as census and tax records. Such sources offer a measure of precision unavailable in other forms of written evidence. Knowing how many people were infected by a disease or migrated to a region, or how much they owned, is far more valuable than falling back on looser terms such as "some" or "many." Examining changing literacy levels or levels of employment in the same region over an extended period of time adds a dimension to understanding the past that is difficult to discern from other primary sources. Moreover, comparing statistical evidence of factors such as demography, gender balance, ethnic makeup, and per capita

---

8. Martha Brownson of Earls Colne, widow, Wills (ERO D/ACW17/80 Martha Brownson 1664/5), http://linux02. lib.cam.ac.uk/earlscolne/ (accessed 16 September 2011).

income can reveal trends over time not readily observable in other forms of evidence. Like other primary sources, statistical information must be carefully scrutinized. Researchers must know who generated the data and for what purpose. Who was the intended audience? Was there a point of view? What other evidence permits full conclusions from statistical data? How complete is the evidence? That is, were specific groups ignored? Underrepresented? What does the data reveal about the officials who gathered it or the society that generated it?

Some of the most readily accessible statistical evidence for any nation is census information. In the United States, census data has been compiled since 1790, and much of it is now available in online formats. The University of Virginia Historical Census Browser at http://mapserver.lib.virginia.edu/ provides easy access to this rich collection of data. Individual censuses may be examined and national or regional data isolated. The collection also permits sorting of variables and the creation of individual tables.

An examination of census materials for Suffolk County, Massachusetts, in the time period 1890–1920 can be helpful in explaining the strong nativist response to the Sacco and Vanzetti trial in 1921. The murder that took place just outside of Boston in 1920 reflected growing fears about immigrants in American cities. The accusation, trial, conviction, and execution of these two Italian immigrants was a leading event in the "Red Scare" in the United States and had significant anticommunist and antisocialist overtones. Local conditions influenced this response. There was a significant demographic shift in Suffolk County from 1890 to 1920. The number of native white males age 21 and over declined from 78,444 in 1890 to 59,998 in 1920, while the number of foreign-born white males of the same age increased from 66,728 in 1890 to 122,176 in 1920. One of the fastest growing groups comprised those born in Italy, whose number increased from 4,799 in 1890 to 42,052 in 1920. The statistics alone do not indicate why suburban white Bostonians reacted so strongly, but they provide clear evidence of a seismic shift in population in the generation preceding the trial. When combined with other primary evidence surrounding the case, statistical evidence provides a clearer understanding of the social tensions behind nativism.

Newspapers and Periodicals

Newspapers are among the most commonly used primary sources. Part of their appeal is their availability in print, microform, and digital formats. Most local libraries have actual copies or microfilm copies of area newspapers; major research libraries have substantial collections of historical newspapers. Many historical newspapers are online with the capability of searching for a specific article or showing an entire newspaper page. One example of these online historical newspapers is *Harper's Weekly*, a mid–nineteenth century serial: http://app.harpweek.com/. Another excellent collection covering an earlier period is the *17th and 18th Century Burney Collection Newspapers*: http://galegroup.com.[9] Despite

---

9. See also *America's Historical Newspapers, 1690–1922*: http://newsbank.com (which includes more than 1,000 newspapers) and *The Times Digital Archive, 1785–1985*: http://galegroup.com (includes nearly 8 million articles).

their usefulness and widespread availability, newspapers should be used by beginning historians with caution. Although these sources provide a popular view into
a time period, the fact that newspapers often report on events based on the evidence a reporter has collected gives newspapers and magazines some of the characteristics of a secondary source.

Many newspapers also have a point of view, which in some cases may be
muted, but in other times and places this point of view is quite pronounced.
Nineteenth-century U.S newspapers were often mouthpieces for political parties,
religious organizations, or social movements. The historian must rigorously apply
the same critical evaluation about the author, the audience, and the historical
context employed for other sources. When using newspapers to understand an
event, it is best to corroborate with other primary sources on the same event.
Newspapers are especially useful in examining a particular point of view. For
example, any examination of the politics surrounding Jacksonian fiscal policy
should include a review of leading Democratic newspapers from the period.
Newspapers can also be of great use to historians interested in examining language as a means to recover meaning. A historian might carefully scrutinize an
editorial from a particular time period and, armed with a thorough knowledge of
historical context, recover important and otherwise difficult-to-discern aspects of
an event or time.

Oral Interviews

Oral interviews open another avenue to help historians understand and explain
the past. They represent an exciting addition to existing primary source collections. Oral testimony, created with the assistance of a trained scholar, preserves
individual recollections of past events. Because this source falls into the category
of a created source—one intentionally generated through a planned and orches-
trated oral interview—knowledge of the interviewer, intended audience, purpose, and point of view are critically important in weighing the value of the
testimony. These oral sources must withstand the rigor of a critical evaluation
like any other primary source.

One of the richest oral history collections began in the 1930s and sought to
gather the accounts of former slaves, whose stories had largely been ignored as a
source for the history of slavery in the United States. Housed in American
Memory, *Voices from the Days of Slavery: Former Slaves Tell Their Stories* (http://
memory.loc.gov/ammem/collections/voices/) gives a unique glimpse into the
world of the former slaves. The interviewers are identified in the collection,
and there is information about each of them as well as about each interview subject. Studied individually, the slave narratives offer significant insights into life
experiences. One example is the testimony of Alice Gaston of Gee's Bend,
Alabama, recorded in 1941 by Robert Sonkin. Her interview opens:

> Alice Gaston: We was talking about in the old war time, the old
> slavery time. I can remember when, uh, I can remember when the
> Yankees come through and, uh, they carried my father away and
> carried away, my si, two sisters and one brother. And, uh, they left

me. And I can remember when my missus used to run in the garden, from the Yankees and tell us if they come, don't tell them
where they at. Told, don't tell nobody where they at when they
come and they all come and they told me, don't get scared now
and tell them, where they is, where they is. I told them no, we
told them no. And uh, when they come and ask for them I told
them I didn't know there they was, and they was in the woods.
And this was at the house. And my father, when my father left, he
carried with the, he went away with the Yankees, and carried two,
carried two, two girls and one son, the oldest one. Carried them
with him. And he with the Yankees. And I can remember that.
And uh, my old missus was named Mrs. M., and the master was
name Mr. F. I. [*pause*] Mr. F. I.[10]

Alice Gaston was a young child when the event she described took place,
more than three-quarters of a century earlier. Despite her inability to recall her
owner's names and the general nature of her account, it does depict the presence
of Union forces and the separation of families, both of which deeply affected the
lives of slaves. By studying this account and those of other African Americans
from this region of Alabama and the South, greater knowledge and understanding of the world known only to slaves can be reconstructed. These narratives also
illustrate the importance of studying many documents to gain an understanding
of the larger group rather than focusing on an individual interview. There may
well be factual errors that trace to the memory loss between the event and the
interview; however, the source remains critical because it is one of the few
extant collections of African Americans describing their experiences in their
own words. Had the interviews been gathered sooner, when memories were
clearer, the collection would likely be even more valuable.

Photographs and Maps

Visual evidence, like oral testimony, is an intentionally created primary source
that requires careful scrutiny. When working with this form of evidence,
researchers ask similar questions about **authorship, intended audience, purpose, perspective,** and **point of view** that they would of any other primary
source. Paintings and photographs are the creations of the artist, yet the pictures
they produce offer another type of evidence of great use to researchers. These
sources not only reveal important images; they also provide insights into the
mind and world of the artist and the times. The composition of crowds at events
may offer unique glimpses of different cultures and present information not
intended by the artist or photographer.

---

10. Interview with Alice Gaston, Gee's Bend, Alabama, 1941, *Voices from the Days of Slavery*, http://memory.loc.gov/
ammem/collections/voices/ (accessed 28 September 2011). Another excellent oral history collection is *Born in Slavery:
Slave Narratives from the Federal Writers' Project, 1936–1938*, http://memory.loc.gov/ammem/snhtml/snhome.html.

A useful example of photographic evidence is found in a digital archive in American Memory. Ansel Adams, the preeminent American photographer, photographed the Japanese American Manzanar Relocation Center in California, and his works have been gathered and preserved digitally. They record aspects of daily life and experiences of the families interned during World War II. The following photograph captures Japanese Americans in line for lunch in 1943.[11]

The black-and-white photograph illustrates the starkness of the camp and the regimented lives of its residents. It suggests the camp's isolation and documents a daily occurrence. The people seem comfortable in their surroundings and do not appear to be closely guarded. The visual evidence corroborates written accounts from those who lived in the camps, government accounts, contemporary newspapers, and other forms of evidence. The photographs also reveal what appealed to Adams. Photographs, moving pictures, and paintings provide researchers with an additional perspective on a topic under analysis.

Similar observations may be made about maps. So often maps are simply used to illustrate a point, but they should be analyzed for the subtle clues they offer about the time and place in which they were produced. All maps describing the world in 1600 are not necessarily the same. If the mapmaker was European, his perspective and focal points may have differed profoundly from those of a Chinese or Arab cartographer. The axis of the world differs from place to place, and the knowledge of places may not be identical. Maps, like other

---

11. "Mess line, noon, Manzanar Relocation Center, California," photograph by Ansel Adams, "'Suffering under a Great Injustice': Ansel Adams's Photographs of Japanese Americans at Manzanar," Library of Congress, American Memory, http://memory.loc.gov/pnp/ppprs/00100/00173v.jpg (accessed 21 September 2011).

forms of visual evidence, are sources that must be scrutinized according to the same standards of evaluation.

The two global maps published by Cornelius Wytfliet[12] and Edward Wright[13] in the late sixteenth century show the status of cartography at the time.

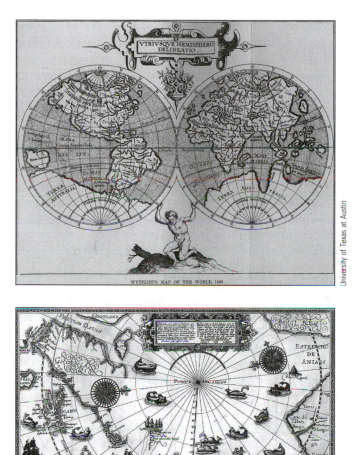

WYTFLIET'S MAP OF THE WORLD, 1598

University of Texas at Austin

National Archives of Canada

---

12. Wytfliet's Map of the World 1598, Perry-Castañeda Library Map Collection, The University of Texas at Austin, http://www.lib.utexas.edu/maps/historical/ (accessed 21 September 2011).

13. Wright's World Map of 1598, reproduced from an 1880 facsimile, National Archives of Canada/NMC 0210063, http://www.collectionscanada.ca/explorers/ (accessed 21 September 2011).

Wytfliet's map is more detailed and speculates on the sizes and locations of landmasses, while Wright's tends to focus more clearly on what has been explored and previously mapped. A comparison of these maps offers insight into the mapmaker's knowledge of the world. When evaluating these maps, the historian should consider **audience** and **perspective**. Furthermore, the historian should try to discern similarities between the maps as well as the differences to better understand the mapmaker's world. How do these maps compare with maps of today; what did the late sixteenth century cartographers know and not know about the world? What did they expect their audiences to know? A close study of maps can enhance any research project.

Artifacts

Physical, or nonlinguistic, evidence in the form of the built landscape or objects remaining from a given society constitutes another seldom studied resource. This kind of evidence survives in many forms and can enrich the historian's understanding of individuals and societies. In a sense, all other forms of historical evidence are artifacts from the past; however, buildings, furnishings, clothing, tools, coins, and the like are normally classified as artifacts. Physical remains help historians understand texture, weight, size, scale, and a host of other elements that may not be knowable from written or other types of sources. Also, it is possible to gain insights into the individuals who produced the artifacts. For societies who left no written records, their artifacts are critical in helping historians understand their place in the human past. For those societies richer in extant written sources, artifacts may be every bit as significant. As historian Leora Auslander argues, "expanding the range of our canonical sources will provide better answers to familiar historical questions as well as change the very nature of the questions we are able to pose and the kind of knowledge we are able to acquire about the past."[14] Examples from two societies, one which left no written records and the other rich in them, may illuminate some aspects of the utility of the built landscape and artifacts.

Mesa Verde in Southern Colorado contains extensive physical evidence of an otherwise unknown civilization. Its cliff dwellings are among the most extensive in the world. The Anasazi people lived here for nearly a millennium, constructing their dwellings safely beneath the massive cliff rims above. The extensive pueblos here and elsewhere across the region indicate a complex society. The following image provides a partial view of Cliff Palace. The substantial group of structures provided living, dining, social, and religious quarters. The houses also include a rich trove of images, wall paintings, and artifacts. This built environment beneath high cliffs was protected from the elements and other tribes and was accessible only by ladders. The structures

---

14. Leora Auslander, "Beyond Words," *American Historical Review* 110, no. 4 (October 2005): 1015.

and artifacts raise a number of questions. Who constructed these dwellings? When did they arrive? When and why did they disappear? Why did they build their village in this location? What does the physical evidence tell later generations about their lives, their culture, their concerns, their fears, and their worldview? Can later historians discern anything specific about the people who lived there from their remains? What can be inferred from the physical remains is limited, but it may be supplemented by examining the oral traditions of subsequent peoples throughout the region.

Michael J. Galgano

At Hall i' th' Wood, Bolton, England, the leased residence of Samuel Crompton and his family in the eighteenth century, one of the bedrooms includes the bed shown in the following illustration. It is comparable to many found throughout the region. The mattress rested on a stretched rope frame (partially visible at the base). Each evening, burning embers were put in a copper pan, which was then set on the platform in the middle of the quilt heater at the base of the bed. The bed coverings were placed over it to warm them before the couple retired for the night. The bed and heater raise a number of questions for historians with access only to written records about family life in the period. How typical was this kind of bed in the period? How comfortable was a bed whose feather or stuffed mattress rested on rope? How firm was it? How warm were the bedrooms? How long did coverlets remain warm? How common were bedroom fires? Written accounts, more often than not, rarely address these questions, and analysis of the relevant artifacts can enrich any topic.

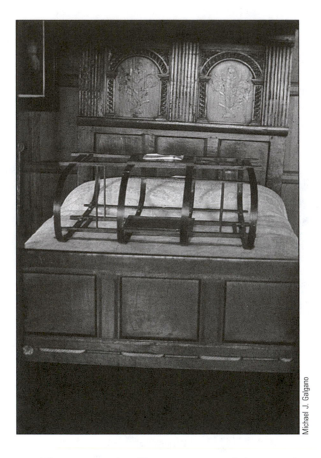

Michael J. Galgano

These examples illustrate some of the questions that may be explored by using physical remains in historical research. They offer unique insights into the past and facilitate a deeper understanding of cultures and societies.

PRIMARY SOURCES IN A STUDENT PAPER

In constructing his analysis of the murder of eleven Sicilian immigrants in a New Orleans jail in 1891, Paul McDowell used accounts from more than twenty different newspapers and contemporary magazines, census records, and correspondence exchanged between officials in Italy and the United States. The newspapers and magazines illuminated his central argument about American "nativism and xenophobia" in the period. The reports describing and explaining the event in New Orleans led him to conclude that most U.S. communities across the continent responded in similar fashion and with like anti-Italian sentiments. Paul's case is strengthened throughout by using a range of newspapers and magazines from diverse geographical regions in the United States as well as from abroad. Despite their distance from New Orleans, all shared a similar tone and perspective in expressing anti–Italian sentiments. The pages of most endorsed mob action: head-lines claimed justice had been satisfied, and one article from the *Dallas Morning News* labeled the mob's action as a vindication that "wreaked vengeance upon the Sicilian assassins who relentlessly slew David C. Hennessy." They also suggest similarities in audiences despite geographical differences. Paul did identify some variation in the conclusions drawn and views expressed by writers for the *Charlotte News* and *Houston Post*. He also relied upon a contemporary political cartoon and census returns to provide context for his discussion of popular reactions to the Ital-ian immigrant population across the nation following this incident.

The framework for analysis introduced earlier in this chapter—**author, audience, purpose, point of view, language,** and **significance**—helped focus Paul's questions as he read and evaluated the evidence. In using the evidence, especially from the popular press of the time, he is careful to consider these basic elements of analysis. He uses the newspapers to describe the incident and to exam-ine reactions to the event. The authors from the various papers are different; how-ever, they share similar audiences, points of view, and language. Each presents the event in a similar fashion, and each uses language and tone to present a largely anti-immigrant perspective. Most do not seek to offer a balanced view, and many are sensationalized.

Paul McDowell's paragraphs demonstrate an understanding of what he has read in the newspaper sources and his ability to use them imaginatively to con-struct a sound narrative. Rather than quoting extensively, he uses his primary sources to illuminate the points he is making. He avoids the common pitfall of many beginning researchers who cherry-pick from primary sources, embedding direct quotations periodically throughout their papers. Paul's paper illustrates the benefits in avoiding this practice.

The varieties of primary evidence add to the authority of McDowell's argu-ment. While his analysis properly concentrates on newspapers, he also examined a visual from *The Mascot: An Independent Journal of the Day*, printed in New Orleans. The cartoon illustrated the principal perceived stereotypes about Italian immigrants and offered methods of dealing with them. Depicted as indolent, prone to vio-lence, and living in overcrowded quarters, the suggested solutions were to dispose of them in the Gulf or beat them into submission before arresting them. Effective research must be rooted in as wide an array of primary sources as possible and the sources used as fully and critically as possible. Paul's research was conducted as part of a class assignment and was governed by time constraints. While he considered a number of primary sources, his work was by no means exhaustive.

CONCLUSION

This chapter defines primary sources and explains ways to analyze the diverse forms of evidence contained within them. It offers a framework for beginning scholars to use in analyzing that evidence. The primary sources now available to historians are virtually without limit, and the opportunity to examine firsthand evidence is unparalleled. Beginning historians can access a veritable treasure chest of evidence types and use them to construct their arguments. With the finding aids and support documentation available online and in print, researchers can more readily use their critical faculties and imagination to study aspects of the past, which was impossible for most a short generation ago. The volume is daunting, and scholars must be conscious of what may reasonably be examined and studied closely to strengthen a particular project. They must weigh the number of examples required to make a compelling case without tipping the scale to make an argument that overwhelms a reader. The process of assembling and blending information to support a well-reasoned and well-written historical argument is found in the next chapter.

EXERCISES

Select four different varieties of primary sources identified for your research project with at least one being an oral, a visual, or a physical piece of evidence. Apply each of the suggested tools for analysis to each source. What are your conclusions?

1. Author or producer
2. Point of view or perspective
3. Intended audience
4. Purpose
5. Significance

5

✳

Writing—The Research Paper

Writing is an ongoing process that starts when research begins. Although it seems that research and writing are independent tasks, they are not. Writing is to historical inquiry what oxygen is to life; it surrounds all that the historian does, and one cannot practice history without writing. The writing process begins when a researcher enters an archive or library; it continues as he or she critically analyzes what has been gleaned from research; it informs further research on a topic; it enables students of history to develop a clear and organized understanding of the subject; and it provides a medium by which these students may clearly present their interpretation of the process or event they have examined. Writing history is a constant conversation—with the sources, with ideas, with other historians, and with oneself. No clear understanding of the past is possible without following a painstaking yet rewarding process of writing. Writing is the best way to learn about history.

BEGINNING THE WRITING PROCESS

Inexperienced historians still believe that writing is a process that begins after the research has been completed. For the uninitiated, this means that after spending hours and hours reviewing the pertinent primary and secondary sources, the beginning historian sits in front of a computer, notes and books nearby, and bangs out an essay that is "complete" with few revisions. Such an approach might be common, but it is seldom good writing. Nor is it good history. As the central component to the critical thinking process, writing should consume considerably more time than the hours spent researching. The final product is, after all, what is read and judged by others.

All historians must ask themselves several questions as they begin to write. The first is, "What is the purpose of the writing assignment?" Writing a book review or a reaction paper is different from writing a research paper or analyzing a document or preparing an annotated bibliography. Some writing assignments have limitations.

Book reviews, for example, tend to be about 400 to 1,000 words in length and offer critical evaluation of a single book. For larger writing assignments, some instructors impose page limits or word counts or restrict the assignment to specific books or sources. Formal research papers usually take the form of a scholarly journal article, about twenty to twenty-five pages in length, with appropriate footnoting and bibliography. Beginning scholars should be aware of the writing assignment's purpose as they begin their work. Some basic questions are:

- Who is the audience? Those individuals who read book reviews have different expectations than those who read a journal article, historiographic essay, or research paper. Historical writing may include several audiences. Some historians write for the general public. Most professional historians write for their peers and students and thus have certain assumptions about topic knowledge and understanding. The historical knowledge and sophistication of one's intended audience often shapes a historian's approach to a subject.

- What voice should the paper take? Historical writing should always assume a scholarly tone that presents a thoughtful analysis and interpretation of the past.

- What interpretation does the paper take? Many forms of historical writing offer interpretations. Historians analyze the sources (both secondary and primary), construct an argument supported by this evidence, acknowledge alternative interpretations, and demonstrate why their perspective is most suitable through a preponderance of evidence.

Early Writing

Historical writing is initiated in the "early writing" stage. This occurs when a historian first begins to think about a topic. This might involve little more than jotting down ideas on a subject, listing terminology, or beginning a timeline of events. But such freeform thinking is irrelevant if uninformed. This preliminary investigation may begin with reading a general source such as an encyclopedia entry or book chapter, but it will quickly lead to the important secondary sources described in Chapter 3. As the beginning historian reads these general and secondary sources on a subject, the ideas about a topic begin to take shape and should evolve into a group of written questions. For many historians, this is a useful time to formulate a prospectus.

Prospectus

The prospectus illustrates an initial conversation between research and writing. The drafting of a prospectus is outlined in Chapter 2 as one of the first steps of the research process, but it also is an early step in writing a research paper. Without fully reiterating what was written earlier, the prospectus is an informal writing assignment in which the beginning historian jots down initial ideas and begins to formulate a series of questions about a topic based upon preliminary research.

Ideally, such informal thinking committed to the written word will allow the researcher to begin to develop a central question or hypothesis about the topic.

THE JURY OF OUR PEERS

Nearly all historians recognize that their work will eventually be submitted to their peers for scrutiny. It is essential, especially for beginning historians, to make use of a peer reviewer while writing. In the best sense, a peer reviewer is someone who either knows something about the subject or someone who can discern a well-constructed, thoughtful essay supported by evidence. An effective peer is not one who reads the early drafts of a paper, stating, "That's great." Rather, it is someone who critically evaluates numerous aspects of the essay, offering constructive criticism on how it might be improved, often raising questions for the historian to consider. It is helpful to seek constructive criticism from the peer reviewer at all stages of the written work.

In evaluating another's writing, a peer reviewer should consider some of the following questions:

- How well organized is the essay? Is there an effective ordering of main points and information? How might it be improved?

- How well written is the essay? Are the main points clearly presented? In what ways might the draft be improved?

- What is the historical argument of this paper? Is it clearly presented? In what ways might it be improved?

- Does the author provide adequate background information and historical context for the topic? How could this section be improved? What are the strengths and weaknesses of the essay?

- In what ways might the topic be better developed?

- How well are primary sources and secondary works used? Are they adequate to support the historical argument and the interpretation?

- How analytical is the paper? How interpretative? In what ways could the analysis and the interpretation be improved?

Few activities are more valuable to a writer than a good peer review. Effective peer reviewing is, however, a two-way street. Constructive criticism from a peer, if heeded, can greatly improve a paper. Conversely, careful analysis of a peer's paper can help improve one's own analytical and writing skills.

THE FIRST PARAGRAPH

In many ways drafting the first paragraph of the paper is the culmination of the research, reading, and thought on the research topic. It is often one of the hardest paragraphs to write. Although not especially informal in its grammar or organization, the first paragraph is a rough draft that sets a paper's direction. The first paragraph serves as a rudimentary roadmap, but it also requires initial thoughts about the organization of the project.

Several elements are essential to a quality first paragraph. Like a good first impression, the opening paragraph must interest readers and draw them into reading further. Failure to do so may mean that the rest of the paper is ignored. Developing an interesting opening to an essay is a difficult task even for the most experienced writers. Many historians attract readers' interest by beginning with dramatic tension. For example, an essay explaining who fired the first shot at Lexington in 1775 might not begin with background causes but might start with a brief description of the exchange of fire or the immediate aftermath of the event. In presenting this tension, the writer should offer a cursory sketch (no more than a few sentences) of historical context, often placing the event in the time period, noting the place of the events, as well as introducing the main characters. Having briefly established a central tension that draws readers' interest and offers some background, it is important to next develop a central question that the paper will answer. Only after considerably more research, analysis, and writing of subsequent drafts will the beginning historian be able to develop a historical argument from this preliminary hypothesis. This statement of hypothesis (and eventually historical argument) should appear at the end of the first paragraph. A thesis statement that appears early in the paper is an effective cue to the historical argument; it also serves as the central spine around which an essay is organized. The historical argument must be stated clearly, and it must be developed and supported with evidence throughout the paper. The paper, then, should be organized and flow from one point to another while periodically returning to the historical argument.

At the end of the first paragraph, historians often include a **historiographic footnote.** Some historians use two or three footnotes in the first few pages to address historiography. This footnote (or footnotes) offer(s) a brief commentary on the most important secondary sources, and sometimes on primary sources, on the topic. Historiography is the history of the study of history. It can include anything ever written on a topic, but frequently it depicts how historians examined and interpreted past events. This can range from the use of new primary source materials to asking new questions about the sources or the development of a new interpretation. The historiographic footnote tends to be organized with the most important general scholarly works on the time period or subject listed first, then it narrows to more specific secondary sources on the topic. After listing the scholarly works, most historians include a brief list of the most important primary sources on the topic. This feature offers readers a shorthand guide to the sources that shaped the approach to the topic.

Student Paul McDowell follows these conventions in his first paragraph. He creates a tension, a curiosity about the lynching of Italians in New Orleans in 1891. His historical argument comes at the end of the first paragraph and is clear: he examined the reaction of a number of newspapers to this incident. McDowell's first paragraph and historiographic footnote are below:

> **They had been found innocent. After six months of uncertainty, the jury had finally awarded the defendants their freedom. Tomorrow, they would go back to their families and celebrate the birthday of**

King Umberto I[1] with singing, dancing, and feasting. Life would return to normal. They would go back to working on the docks, along the streets, or in the stores. The nine Sicilians accused of murdering New Orleans Police Chief David Hennessy went to sleep on March 13, 1891, with freedom in their minds and hope in their hearts. Unfortunately, seven of those nine would never experience their freedom. The next morning, thousands of New Orleans residents stormed the Parish Prison and brutally executed eleven Italians locked inside, claiming to bring justice when the American courts failed to do so. Newspapers around the United States quickly seized the opportunity, using the event to display anti-immigrant sentiments. Many newspapers favored the extreme measure to which the upper-class New Orleans residents had carried out justice upon the devious Sicilians, and only a few factions of the American press condemned such rash action. Despite different political and social reasoning, most newspapers from all around the United States shared the same underlying anti-Italian sentiment in their reports of the 1891 lynching of eleven Sicilians in New Orleans.[2]

A first paragraph is an ideal short essay to submit to a peer for constructive criticism. Since the first paragraph provides some historical context and sets the

---

1. Italian monarch during the late nineteenth century.

2. Any in-depth research on the results of immigration into the United States begins with John D. Buekner and Lorman A. Ratner, *Multiculturalism in the United States: A Comparative Guide to Acculturation and Ethnicity* (New York: Greenwood Press, 2005). John Higham, *Strangers in the Land: Patterns of American Nativism, 1860–1925* (New Brunswick: Rutgers University Press, 1955), and Desmond Humphrey Joseph, *The APA Movement* (New York: Arno Press, 1969), provide excellent overviews and analyses of general American nativism around the turn of the nineteenth century. Alexander DeConde, *Half Bitter, Half Sweet: An Excursion into Italian-American History* (New York: Scribner, 1971), provides a good introduction to the overall Italian American experience during the height of Italian immigration. Edwin Fenton, *Immigrants and Unions, a Case Study: Italians and American Labor, 1870–1920* (New York: Arno Press, 1957), and Donna Gabaccia, *Militants and Migrants: Rural Sicilians Become American Workers* (New Brunswick: Rutgers University Press, 1988), adequately describe Italian Americans and their roles in the American labor system throughout different parts of the United States around the turn of the twentieth century. For information on the city of New Orleans itself during the 1890s, Joy J. Jackson, *New Orleans in the Gilded Age: Politics and Urban Progress, 1880–1896* (Baton Rouge: Louisiana State University Press, 1969), and Joy J. Jackson, "Crime and the Conscience of a City," *Louisiana History* 24, no. 4 (Summer 1968): 229–244, analyze the general background of New Orleans around the time of the 1891 lynching. To discover detailed reports of other lynchings of Sicilians in the South, see Clive Webb, "The Lynching of Sicilian Immigrants in the American South, 1886–1910," *American Nineteenth Century History* 3, no. 1 (Spring 2002): 45–77. For a combination of extended narrative and in-depth analysis on the events surrounding the actual lynching on 14 March 1891, see Richard Gambino, *Vendetta: A True Story of the Worst Lynching in America, the Mass Murder of Italian-Americans in New Orleans in 1891, the Vicious Motivations Behind It, and the Tragic Repercussions that Linger to this Day* (Garden City, NY: Doubleday and Co., 1977); Joseph Gentile, *The Innocent Lynched: The Story of Eleven Italians Lynched in New Orleans* (New York: Writer's Showcase Press, 2000); Tom Smith, *The Crescent City Lynchings: The Murder of Chief Hennessy, the New Orleans 'Mafia' Trials, and the Parish Prison Mob* (Guilford, CT: The Lyons Press, 2007); Humbert S. Nelli, "The Hennessy Murder and the Mafia in New Orleans," *Italian Quarterly* 19, no. 75 (1975): 77–95. Other works focus on different aspects of the event: J. Alexander Karlin, "New Orleans Lynchings of 1891 and the American Press," *Louisiana Historical Quarterly* 24, no. 1 (January 1941): 187–204, examines the nationwide media's reaction to the event. Barbara Botein, "The Hennessy Case: An Episode of Anti-Italian Nativism," *Louisiana History* 20, no. 3 (1979): 261–279, discusses how the trial and lynching were cases of extreme nativism during a time of heightened xenophobia. For contemporary reports on the lynching, the most trustworthy works include "Correspondence in Relation to the Killing of Prisoners in New Orleans on March 14, 1891," Harvard University Library Virtual Collections, http://pds.lib.harvard .edu/pds/view/4987805; *New York Times*; *Washington Post*; *Harper's Weekly*; and the *New Orleans Daily Picayune*.

direction for the future development of the paper, a critical eye is essential to ensure that the paper is not on the wrong track. A good peer will review the first paragraph with some of the following points in mind:

- Did the opening sentences of the paragraph attract the reader's attention?
- Did the paragraph set the historical context?
- Can you identify the central question or hypothesis or historical argument?
- Was the paragraph well written and well organized?
- Does the historiographic footnote present the major scholarly works on this topic?
- Was the correct footnote style used?
- What are your suggestions to improve the first paragraph and historiographic footnote?

ELEMENTS OF EFFECTIVE WRITING

Writing well is not a trait one is born with, although some individuals may have more innate ability in this area than others. Effective writing is the result of drafting, editing, rewriting, and polishing. While effective writing is difficult to describe, most individuals know it when they read a few paragraphs. Most good writers developed an eye for good writing through a love of reading. The more that an individual reads, the more attuned they become to clear writing. A beginning historian might improve his or her writing skills by emulating the writing style and tone of a favorite historian.

TIPS FOR EFFECTIVE WRITING

Effective writing requires hard work. While there is no simple set of suggestions that can easily turn a weak writer into a good one (except practice through repetition), all types of effective writing share certain elements in common.

Know the Audience

It is essential for a writer to have a clear sense of the audience. Writing that might be appropriate in some venues might not be acceptable in others. Most historians assume that their audience consists of academic peers with an interest in scholarly deliberation. This requires writing in a serious tone and in a style that conforms to accepted scholarly practice. Scholarly journals or monographs provide clues to this standard.

Be Clear and Concise

Although many inexperienced writers attempt to impress their readers with flowery or obscure language, such writing belabors and clouds the point being made. Successful writers use clear, simple language, making even difficult concepts easy to understand. The **active voice** is the best means for making writing clear and more concise. Sentences that begin with a subject followed by a verb that acts upon an object are examples of the active voice; conversely, the passive voice places the object first in the sentence, followed by the verb, with the subject coming toward the sentence's end. While many novice writers may believe that the active sentence "Gandhi viewed the British *raj*[3] as an enemy" is too simple and brief, the passive version of this sentence "The British *raj* was viewed as the enemy by Gandhi" indicates how wordy and occasionally confusing the passive voice becomes. The increase in the number of words adds nothing to the concept expressed and, indeed, in more complicated sentences can be confusing. One of the easiest ways to identify passive voice is to look for tenses of "to be" or "to have" as modifiers for other verbs. While these verb tenses are perfectly fine alone and are among the most used in the English language, when they stand in front of or near another verb, trouble lurks. For example, the above passive sentence includes the phrase "was viewed." All writers should use sentences that clearly indicate the subject.

Be Organized

One of the most difficult tasks for any historian is to write in an organized, logical manner. It is important that an essay proceeds logically from sentence to sentence, from paragraph to paragraph, and from section to section. Whether a sentence, a paragraph, or a section of the paper, each is simultaneously discrete and connected with what came previously and what follows. One of the important aspects of creating a well-organized paper is to offer transitions from one point to another. This may require a clause at the end of one sentence or the beginning of the next to ease the transition, or sentences at the beginning and end of paragraphs that make the transition to the next paragraph. In some instances, subheadings can be useful to assist the transition from one section to another (especially in earlier drafts).

Write in Sentences and Paragraphs

This point may seem almost too obvious to state, but many writers fail to follow this essential adage. All sentences should contain a subject and verb. Many sentences also include an object. Sentences that lack these essentials are known as **sentence fragments**. Perhaps more problematic are those sentences that have too many subjects, verbs, and objects. The **run-on sentence** is one that does not know when it is time to stop. A good rule of thumb to avoid run-on sentences is to place a period after a sentence that contains two clauses connected by the words *and, but,* or *however*. The additional points may be closely connected, but they deserve a sentence of their own. Indeed, two sentences may reinforce an important point. It is also essential to have proper transitions between sentences. In some cases, including a clause at the end of one sentence or the

---

3. *Raj* derives from the Hindu word for "reign" that Indians used to describe British rule in India.

beginning of the next makes for easier reading. Sometimes an entire sentence may be necessary to achieve this end.

Paragraphs are somewhat more problematic. Paragraphs are like sentences in that they have a central point to make, but beginning historians often do not know when to stop. Each major point deserves its own paragraph. One of the best means for making a paragraph a self-contained entity is through the use of topic and concluding sentences. A **topic sentence** in a paragraph serves as an introduction to the topic of the paragraph and is followed by sentences that illustrate this point. A **concluding sentence** briefly summarizes the paragraph. Not only are these useful for setting limits for a paragraph, but topic and concluding sentences are helpful to make the transition from one point to another.

Vary Words, Sentences, and Paragraphs

Even technically correct prose may not be especially good writing if it lacks variety. Most historians recognize when writing their first essay that some words are essential, but writing can become repetitious and boring if the same words are used over, and over, and over again. A **thesaurus** is a valuable tool that enables a writer to find words with the same meaning, thus adding variation to one's language. Similarly, the length of sentences should vary. A string of grammatically correct, short, declarative sentences is exhausting to read. Good writing varies between short sentences, long sentences, and compound sentences to maintain a reader's interest. Paragraphs should also vary in length for similar reasons. When writing, think of the audience; it should not be a chore or difficult to read history.

Words Matter

Effective writers take great care to select the right word for the occasion. Writers who try to impress by using longer, flowery, or obscure language often confuse their readers. They use inappropriate words or even words that, if used correctly, may offend their readers with an approach that seems patronizing. Even the most experienced historians must regularly consult a dictionary or thesaurus to find just the right word that conveys precisely the point. Be sure to avoid words that suggest uncertainty or doubt. Historians often are tentative in what they can assert, but they should never write, "It appears that maybe it is time to possibly change strategies." Effective use of the language also means that even the most inexperienced scholars must avoid clichés (such as "a stitch in time saves nine"), colloquial or conversational language, or slang. One would never write, "When James Madison first met his future wife Dolley, he thought she was a hottie."

Word choice should also be precise. One of the most misused words in the English language is *feel* or *felt*; for example, "The beginning scholar felt she had written an excellent paper." But to feel is a sensory perception, such as a bee sting or a cold breeze; it is not thought. A more appropriate sentence might read, "The beginning scholar believed she had written an excellent paper" or perhaps, "The beginning scholar knew she had written an excellent paper." Effective writers are also economical in the use of language; never use ten words if fewer convey the point clearly. Finally, avoid contractions and abbreviations in all formal writing.[4]

Avoid First and Second Person in Academic Writing

Writing in the third person provides two important benefits to an essay:

- It provides a sense of scholarly detachment from the subject that sets a tone of academic seriousness and evenhandedness.

- More importantly, it avoids the first person. Authors, especially inexperienced authors who use the first person, often slip from clear prose to conversational language that is inappropriate for the task at hand.

Check for Agreement

Effective writing exhibits agreement and parallel construction. A singular noun must be accompanied by a singular verb, and a plural noun must be accompanied by a plural verb. For example, "The beginning historian was busy with her research" is grammatically correct, but "The beginning historian were busy with her research" is not. Authors should also attempt to be as consistent with tenses as possible. Most historians write about the past, so they make almost exclusive use of some form of the past tense in their writing. For example, "Mr. Lincoln determined to supply Fort Sumter after assuming the presidency. South Carolina officials responded by firing upon the fort" is grammatically correct, but "Mr. Lincoln determined to supply Fort Sumter after assuming the presidency. South Carolina officials respond by firing upon the fort" is not.

Quote Appropriately

Experienced historians use quotations to provide their readers with a sense of how a historical figure thought about or reacted to a specific situation. Many beginning historians are much less effective in their use of quotations. Quotations should be used to illustrate or provide specific evidence, not to make a point. The following hypothetical example highlights this issue. In discussing Robert E. Lee's reaction to the death of Stonewall Jackson, it would be better to write "Jackson's death stunned the general. Lee remarked, 'I have lost my right arm,'" instead of "Jackson's death led Lee to remark, 'I have lost my right arm.'"

Direct quotations should come from primary sources, and the writing should clearly identify the author or speaker of these words. Extensive, excessive, and

---

4. One exception to this rule is the use of abbreviations as acronyms. Historians generally use the full name with the first mention followed by the acronym—Central Intelligence Agency (CIA) or Federal Bureau of Investigation (FBI)—and use the acronym in all following instances—CIA or FBI.

awkward quotations should be avoided. Remember, quotations exist to enhance the narrative, not to take up space or make it more cumbersome. They are to illustrate a point you have made, not be the point.

Use Proper Punctuation

Poor punctuation can mar otherwise fine writing. Overuse of commas or semi-colons often indicates poor punctuation, generally the result of an inexperienced writer. All writers regularly consult a grammar manual for appropriate use. Over-punctuation can often contribute to choppy writing that is painful to read.

Proofread and Edit

The most important piece of advice for beginning historians is to proofread and edit. And proofread and edit. And proofread and edit. Proofreading and editing requires looking at different aspects of the paper. A beginning historian might initially proofread for organization, then proofread for content, then proofread for writing and grammar. The final proofread should be done aloud as the ear picks up errors often missed by the eye. A more detailed examination of proof-reading and editing can be found in Chapter 7.

TYPES OF WRITING

All historians make use of four basic approaches to writing. While they go by a variety of names, for our purposes they are **narration, description, interpretation,** and **persuasion**. The first two, narration and description, are often closely related and provide a visceral sense of an event or period. The second two, interpretation and persuasion, are similarly interdependent but function on a more intellectual level. Historical writing requires all four methods to be effective. Although each method is different, they often overlap and intertwine. For that reason, a brief explanation of the four methods and their usefulness is necessary.

Narration

Narration is a critical element of historical writing that tells what happened in the past—the series of events that when combined narrates the story. Thus, the historian must resurrect past events and organize these events in a manner that the reader can follow. The key to narration is to tell a good story about what happened.

The beginning historian should consider several ideas when narrating events.

- Narration has a purpose beyond simply telling what happened. Like the historical argument, narration must create curiosity in the reader to want to continue reading. It introduces information that will be explained later.

- The beginning historian should tell the story in a manner that enables the reader to understand what happened. Be efficient in this presentation: what to include or not include are critical decisions. Too much detail will burden the reader with unnecessary information, while too little will leave the reader wondering what actually transpired. Provide sufficient information so that the reader can make connections later in the paper or so he or she can understand the analysis of events. Always keep the audience in mind while writing.

- Tell the story from multiple perspectives, if possible. This is particularly important if various viewpoints are to be addressed or if historians provide differing interpretations of the events. Where possible, the beginning historian should reveal the contradictions and tensions in the sources while trying to remain faithful to retelling what happened.

In the following selection, Paul McDowell provides a lively narrative of Police Chief David Hennessy's murder and the subsequent trial of the nine Italians accused of his murder.

> David Hennessy would not live to see that trial. On the foggy, rainy night of October 15, exactly one week before he was to testify, David Hennessy walked into an ambush. As he headed back to his house from the police headquarters late at night, several dark figures came out of nowhere and riddled him with bullets. The assassins scattered, dropping their weapons in the process. David Hennessy lived on for nearly nine more hours, during which he repeatedly denied knowing who had attacked him. Despite his consistent denial, however, fellow police officer William O'Connor,[5] who was the first to find Hennessy following the attack, declared that Hennessy had indeed told him who had committed the assassination. According to O'Connor, "the Dagos did it."[6] The police force quickly rounded up scores of Italian males, while the Provenzanos quickly accused the Matranga faction with the murder. The New Orleans police chose to believe the Provenzanos' declaration and released any Italian affiliated to the Provenzanos. After deliberation, the police indicted nine suspects for the murder of David Hennessy, and a trial was set for February 28, 1891.[7]

---

5. O'Connor, Hennessy's police partner and close friend, claimed that Hennessy had told him that "the Dagos did it" when he first found Hennessy following the assault. Hennessy, however, repeatedly denied ever knowing the identity of attackers during the nine hours between the attack and his final death. Once Hennessy was dead, it was merely assumed that O'Connor was telling the truth, and the New Orleans newspapers instantly began constructing explanations for why the Italians would have committed the murder. "Assassinated, Superintendent of Police David C. Hennessy Victim of the Vendetta," *New Orleans Daily Picayune*, 16 October 1890; "Shot Down at His Door," *New York Times*, 17 October 1890; Gentile, 14–21.

6. *Dago* is an offensive term for an Italian. The root of the term traces to the name "Diego," and it was once used as a demeaning term for Italians, Spaniards, or Portuguese. Gentile, 15; "Assassination of the Chief of Police," *New Orleans Daily Picayune*, 16 October 1890; "The Slain Chieftain," *New Orleans Daily Picayune*, 17 October 1890.

7. Gentile, 14–21.

The prosecution had absolutely no evidence that the suspects had committed the murder. All of the accused Italians were able to provide alibis, and the prosecution's reliance on witness testimonies collapsed when cross-examination of the witnesses revealed that the night of the murder was too clouded with fog and rain for anyone to clearly distinguish any individual more than five feet away. On March 13, 1891, the jury announced their verdict: the defendants were found not guilty.[8]

Description

Description is a vivid presentation that appeals to the senses. It describes the way things smell, look, feel, taste, or sound. Description provides a sensory perception of the situation in the past so that readers can relate to these past events through their own experiences. For example, those who have spent time outside on a cold winter day might better understand the situation facing Napoleon's army as it retreated from the failed invasion of Russia in 1812. Or those who have canoed on a river or hiked in the wilderness might have a better appreciation of the Lewis and Clark expedition. Description can also help the reader visualize different circumstances. Words can describe the confusion, the jumble of a battlefield, the acrid smell of gunpowder. They can also present the loneliness of life on the frontier or the mixed emotions of European immigrants as they were processed though Ellis Island.

Description can also be used to explain geography. Any discussion of European colonialism in East Asia must address the geographical importance of cities such as Shanghai and Hong Kong. Similarly, it would be hard for any reader to understand the Battle of Iwo Jima in the Pacific in 1945 without a description of the surrounding terrain.

It is important that beginning historians use narration and description carefully. For example:

- Narration and description should not dominate a paper. They are devices, methods to draw the reader into the topic and to provide the reader with enough information to understand the situation.

- The beginning historian should provide sufficient information but not overwhelm the reader with a blizzard of excessive detail. The basic question at this juncture is, "What does the reader need to know at this point in the paper in order to understand later sections?"

- Description should be based directly on the sources or what can be inferred from them. **Never** make up information. Be as historically accurate as possible.

---

8. "NONE GUILTY!, the Jury in the Hennessy Case Deliver their Verdict," *New Orleans Daily Picayune*, 14 March 1891; "The Hennessy Case," *New Orleans Daily Picayune*, 14 March 1891; Gentile, 32–40.

Interpretation

This method of writing, which is intertwined with persuasion, explains or analyzes the meaning of events or ideas. **Interpretation** most often involves a close analysis of primary sources to determine, as best as possible, **why** something happened. The beginning historian defines terms or ideas in a historical context and seeks to explain past writings and actions for the present-day reader to understand. Such analysis often produces different interpretations of past events based on the weight of the primary source evidence. The goal is to advance a convincing interpretation supported by such evidence.

The beginning historian should consider the following elements in interpretative writing.

- **Interpretation is central to historical writing.** The analysis of human actions is often complex and must be fully explained. There are often contradictions or exceptions that must be considered and evaluated. Such critical thinking requires marshalling evidence to support an interpretation while also acknowledging—and sometime refuting—other existing viewpoints.

- Historians are critical readers of the scholarship on their topic. They must be alert to the interpretations that are presented. Sometimes it is best to write down a brief description of the scholar's interpretation, as it will be helpful in developing a historiographic footnote or an annotated bibliography. Remember, be skeptical of the sources. Understanding the various scholarly interpretations will enable the beginning historian to confidently develop an interpretation based on the weight of the primary source evidence.

- Beginning historians should present their interpretations carefully and in an organized and logical manner. Make sure that the interpretation is consistent throughout the paper. Make use of evidence to support the interpretation while also acknowledging that other interpretations and contradictions in the primary sources exist.

Persuasion

Modern academic writing must contain a thesis or argument. While persuasion may actually form a small part of the paper, it is likely to be the most important part. **Persuasion** is the argument and the evidence that supports it. Persuasive writing is easiest to locate in the introduction, where the historical argument is first stated, and in the conclusion, where the argument is restated and subsidiary conclusions are presented. But persuasion will also appear throughout the paper. Historians interpret evidence throughout the course of their written arguments to clarify how they use evidence. The argument functions as the framework of a historical essay; the reader must be frequently reminded about the argument and be shown how the evidence supports such an assertion.

Student Paul McDowell effectively uses all four forms of historical writing in his conclusion: narration, description, interpretation, and persuasion:

> While not all newspapers openly celebrated the 1891 lynching of eleven Sicilians in New Orleans, every single one exhibited anti-Italian prejudice in one way or another. From San Francisco to New York, the entire country believed that the victims were guilty. Even the newspapers that eased up on the eleven lynched Sicilians demonstrated clear prejudice against the Italian people. The same anti-Italian fervor that plagued the Hennessy case lasted well into the twentieth century, and the belief in the Mafia's existence in the United States never disappeared. The trial of those accused of David Hennessy's murder and the subsequent lynching of eleven Sicilians soon became lost in history,[9] but the event nevertheless altered the American outlook towards Italians for many years afterward.[10]

ORGANIZATION

The first paragraph, discussed earlier in this chapter, implies a form of organization by providing a central core for a paper. Historians generally follow the writing of their first paragraph by creating a roadmap of what should follow. All essays, whether a scholarly journal article, a critical biography, or a scholarly monograph, contain the same basic elements as the classic five-paragraph essay: an introduction, the body of the paper, and the conclusion. This might be presented as the argument (introduction), support for the argument with evidence (body), and restating the argument and summarizing subsidiary arguments (conclusion). Often, a historian begins with a brief outline which can be gradually fleshed out as he or she conducts more research. But most essays eventually contain the following sections.

Introduction

Although the first paragraph attempts to elicit the reader's attention while also introducing the historical argument and the main focus of the essay, a good introduction should seamlessly continue by offering the reader historical background and context. Some scholars devote a paragraph or more to what select previous historians have written on the topic by briefly acknowledging the schools of thought or interpretations. This section often explains how their

---

9. Edward Holmes, a native New Orleanian born in 1922, never recalled having heard of the Hennessy trial or the lynching of eleven Sicilians just a few decades prior. "I've never heard of anything like that," he commented, "but people didn't like Italians, that was for sure." Almost forty years after the incident, the event had been discarded, even in New Orleans; yet the legacy of anti-Italianism clearly kept on chugging.

10. Gentile, 107–115.

particular argument complements or challenges the earlier interpretations. One of the great difficulties for many beginning historians is knowing how much material to include. Since the historical past is a foreign country, it is important to help the reader make sense of that different place. The best place to begin is to provide historical background. The development of this historical background may be organized in a variety of ways, but often it begins with more general comments about the historical time and place, which are followed by information that is more focused on the event or process described. In a monograph, establishing context may take a chapter or more; in a twenty-page essay it usually consumes several pages. The best rule of thumb is to provide enough historical background so that the reader can make sense of the event. Student Paul McDowell's twenty-two-page narrative on newspaper reactions to the lynching of Italians in New Orleans in 1891 provides an excellent example of how to provide historical background. He presents information about Italian immigration to the United States, the presence of Italians in New Orleans, and the two antagonistic factions within this immigrant community. He also depicts the nativist responses. By devoting several pages to these subjects, McDowell gives the reader a sense of the situation in New Orleans on the eve of Police Chief David Hennessy's murder. The stage has been set appropriately for McDowell to delve into the body of his paper. One of the hallmarks of an effective introduction is that it is difficult to tell when the introduction ends and where the body of the paper begins.

Body

The most important part of any historical essay is the body. Here, the historian narrates the story of what happened, describes the sights and sounds that can make the past come to life, elaborates on points that would otherwise remain obscure, explains and interprets the significance of various points, and presents the core of evidence that supports the argument or rebuts evidence that might point to other possible conclusions.

The organization of this part of the paper is critical to presenting a clear and coherent argument. Historians generally have two choices for organizing a paper—**chronological** or **thematic**. If the beginning historian organizes his or her paper chronologically, events taking place contemporary to one another might need to be presented thematically. Conversely, if the thematic approach is chosen, material under each theme will likely be organized chronologically. Effective organization makes for a more coherent essay; it helps to show cause and effect more clearly.

Conclusion

The conclusion is the researcher's last opportunity to make his or her point. It is the lasting impression of the research paper. Most conclusions offer a summary of the major points made in the paper. They often contain a restatement of the historical argument. Some historians like to include this restatement in either the first or last paragraph of their conclusion. A conclusion should also tie up any loose ends, elaborate on the points that support the historical argument, and may offer suggestions for further research on the topic.

THE FIRST DRAFT

Because writing is a way to analyze critically, historians—novice and experienced—should begin to write a first draft long before they complete their research. A beginning historian said it best:

> Write! Get something down. It forces you to grapple with the sources and scholarship. Besides, a working draft, no matter how poor, is better than nothing. It is easier to edit and rewrite than to stare at a blank piece of paper or computer screen and hope something happens.

Since historians write from primary sources, a good rule of thumb is to write after completing most of the secondary source reading and at least some of the primary source research. The first draft is precisely that—a draft. As such, it need not be particularly formal, nor does it need to cover all aspects of a topic, nor does it need to be especially well organized. The draft is simply an effort to get ideas into a written format. For most historians, producing a draft essay is a messy affair. It is full of gaps in logic and information. The important point is to get thoughts and ideas into writing. A historian should attempt to follow many of the conventions discussed earlier in this chapter, but an effective draft attempts to present ideas as clearly as possible, although it may not be perfectly written and organized. The first draft is a conversation between the beginning historian, his or her sources, and the draft itself. Thus, the draft may also include questions, comments about points that need additional evidence, or more thorough analysis. These might be stated parenthetically, in boldface or italics in the text, or placed in a footnote. A draft should be clear enough that a fellow historian can read it and provide commentary on strengths and weaknesses. It should also include footnotes to indicate where information, ideas, and direct quotes have been obtained. No draft is perfect; hence its name.

It is absolutely essential to review one's own first draft and have a peer read it as well. A review of a draft essay is often something of a draft itself. It may offer less commentary on writing for the simple fact that the essay is a draft. But a good peer will offer considerable constructive criticism about the essay's strengths and how the essay might be improved. Authors should review their own work with the same critical eye. Some of the questions to keep in mind in reviewing a draft include the following:

- Is the historical background or context sufficient?
- What are the strengths of the essay?
- What points would you like more information about?

- Is the thesis clearly presented? Does the subsequent evidence support the thesis?

- How might the paper be better organized? How might it be better developed? Were there any sections that were not clear? What were they?

- What suggestions would improve the writing and organization?

- How well are primary sources and secondary sources used?

- Is the historiography addressed?

- How analytical is the paper?

- What are the initial conclusions? Does the evidence support them?

REVISING AND EDITING

The first draft should **never** be a final draft. Following the author's own review of the essay coupled with peer comments, a beginning historian will discover that the first draft needs considerable work before it can be submitted as a final paper. Early reviews of one's work often reveal that important pieces of essential evidence are missing, that the thesis might need modification because of some initially fuzzy thinking, that the research has excluded some types of potentially useful sources, or that the organization and writing need improvement. Because historical writing is a conversation between the author and the sources, most beginning historians' first step after receiving peer comments is to conduct further research.

The additional research must be integrated into the paper, but editing and rewriting involves more than simply plugging more information into the same narrative. As the beginning historian finds more evidence, it is essential to consider the extent to which the new material supports the historical argument. Often, a draft or the research conducted subsequent to the draft review will turn up information that refutes or at least casts doubt on some initial assertions.

Revising and editing also requires attention to writing and organization. Historians revise for content; then consider their analysis, argument, and conclusions; and then review their essay for clarity of expression, effective organization, appropriate grammar, and proper word choice. Often reading a draft sentence or paragraph aloud can make the writer aware of problem. Since it is virtually impossible for anyone to catch every problem in just one reading, good historians continually revise and edit based on their own reviews and those of their peers. Many historians find it useful to have a peer consider specific requests for constructive criticism. Such a request might ask about the quality of the argument or the essay's organization or use of sources. The important point is that beginning historians should seek additional constructive criticism of their work and should continue to revise and edit until the essay reaches a final stage.

The editing and revising of drafts is made easier with word processing programs. It is relatively easy to write and rewrite sentences, and many programs have automatic spell-checks or grammar checks to alert a writer. While such programs are convenient, careful proofreading is still necessary because some words may be spelled correctly but are used incorrectly, such as *there* and *their* or *then* and *than*. In addition, most word processing programs include a simple process to move blocks of written material or a sentence to another part of the paper, thus allowing the reorganization of the paper. But the electronic file also allows for the peer reviewer(s) to examine the draft in meaningful ways. Most word processing programs have an editor function that permits the inclusion of comment "bubbles" where questions or concerns can be raised. They also contain features where peer reviewers can suggest changes in the narrative text in a different color font so that the beginning historian can readily see the suggested changes in the draft. All these features are designed to improve the writing so that the final draft is a more polished and accomplished piece of writing.

The paper has now evolved from a vague idea scribbled on paper, to a first draft, to a nearly final paper—at all stages aided by the constructive criticism of peers as well as one's own proofreading and editing. The final paper is the next and concluding step in the process. The research paper is not the only type of writing one needs to master. The following chapter discusses the writing of short essays and the preparation of vitae and resumés.

EXERCISES

1. Write a paragraph that makes use of the four forms of writing: narration, description, interpretation, and persuasion.

2. Write an introductory paragraph for your paper that includes some historical context and time and place, the historical argument, as well as a historiographic footnote.

6

$\ast$

Writing—The Short Essay

One of the best ways to improve critical thinking and writing skills is by writing short essays. Such essays force the writer to commit ideas to paper but also to grapple with essential points in an efficient way. As a follow-up to a prospectus or as a reflection upon reading material, the short essay offers the historian an opportunity to sharpen his or her thoughts on a particular subject. Toward that end, this chapter will discuss different types of short essays common to historical writing. Many of the forms are regularly used in undergraduate history classes. The first group relates to subjects that teach student historians basic skills in abbreviated forms. They are common to academic or classroom settings. The second relates to writing forms essential to all students of history as they prepare themselves for careers or professions.

SUMMARY AND ANALYSIS

The simplest short essay assignment is the **summary**. Although even the most inexperienced historians believe that they can easily summarize a reading, many discover that when put to the task they struggle. An effective summary is succinct, and being succinct requires the writer to make difficult decisions about the material. Virtually anyone can offer a lengthy commentary of a document they have read, a lecture they have heard, or a movie they have seen, but how many can do it in 300 words or fewer? Writing a summary involves the ability to express points clearly and concisely as well as requiring the author to understand the material well enough to make choices about what is most important. Beginning historians can quickly hone both their writing and critical thinking skills by performing such exercises regularly. For example, writing short 100- to150-word summaries of daily reading assignments or course lectures forces the writer to grasp the most essential details. In completing summaries, consider only what is genuinely essential. What are the key points?

CourseReader Assignment 1: Summary

You can practice summarizing articles on your own, but Appendix C contains instructions for a specific assignment within CourseReader that will help you create an effective summary about an article concerning Europe during World War I.

ANALYSIS

Any summary should offer some **analysis**. Effective analysis requires describing the historical argument and main points, the historical context, and historiographical issues as well as indicating important conclusions. A more sophisticated analysis might go so far as to offer some interpretation of cause and effect or meaning. Many of the critical skills outlined in Chapter 4 will be particularly useful in performing analysis and should be consulted. But effective analysis often requires an ability to deduce meaning from the written account. Here, knowledge of the historical context and the event in particular can help to corroborate interpretations of cause and effect or meaning. Analysis is an essential skill when reading, and one can improve the ability to take notes in class or for research by mastering this skill.

The ability to summarize in an analytical way is essential to effective writing. As the beginning historian works through sources, he or she must be an active reader who thinks constantly about the material before committing preliminary ideas to the written word. (The passive reader, by contrast, does little more than thoughtlessly transcribe material from one medium to another. It is comparable to highlighting a page in a text. All that is really accomplished is changing the color of the page.) When reading any source, consider its tone, how it uses language, and its argument, purpose, and audience. By developing the skills involved in effective summarizing of individual readings, beginning historians are better able to learn to integrate multiple readings into more complex essays.

The processes of external and internal criticism discussed in Chapter 4 are central to the evidence analysis process. But how does one examine different pieces and types of evidence and generate conclusions, particularly when the varying accounts and other forms of evidence may be conflicting? There is no easy answer to this question. Historical questions such as "What roles did women play in the French Revolution?" or "Who discovered America?" and "Did Germany Cause World War I?" have invited hosts of interpretations from historians over the years. To answer such questions, one is bound by the evidence. But as Chapters 3 and 4 make clear, not all sources are equal. Begin by first practicing external criticism on each document—"How do I know this source is authentic?" Generally, however, the more fundamental preoccupation will center on internal criticism. Carefully review the author—if there is one; his or her authority and relationship to the audience, perspective, biases, and reliability. Such an examination will suggest which evidence is likely most useful, but to answer historical questions such as those noted above, first check to see where other sources corroborate this evidence.

But corroboration can only take one so far. Perhaps answering the big questions should be thought of as a Venn diagram.[1] On what points do the sources agree? Determining how much evidence is necessary to corroborate an event is something of an art. When all of the evidence reveals that an event took place, then it may be accepted as established fact. But what about when the sources conflict, or where sources may be mute on a point? There are no clear guidelines in such cases, but if a few accounts describe an event while others do not, one might assume that the other accounts either did not notice or chose not to comment on a specific event. In instances where the evidence differs the result is more problematic. In such cases, disagreements may actually be minor, where an account may be correct in most respects but contain minor errors such as names or dates. But in some instances, historians are confronted by wildly differing testimony. In such instances, it is important to carefully employ the analytical skills outlined earlier and discern which source is likely most accurate. Where sources differ slightly, what is the agreement necessary among them that most indicates reliability? Ultimately, one is left to one's own analytical skills and historical intuition in developing an interpretation of the past.

CourseReader Assignment 2: Analysis

Go to Appendix C for instructions on the CourseReader assignment that will help you practice analytical skills.

SYNTHESIS

Writing a synthesis illuminates the progression from summary through analysis to integration. Historians construct their arguments by synthesizing primary sources, which form the foundation for their conclusions, and secondary scholarship, which establishes historical and historiographical context. In blending the evidence and using it thoughtfully to offer interpretations of the past, historians move from analysis to synthesis. In composing the synthesis, consider also the tone of the documents and the language used.

THE FIVE-PARAGRAPH ESSAY

The five-paragraph essay is a time-honored approach employed for short writing assignments, including responses to essay questions such as "Did Germany Cause World War I?" Such essays require one to go beyond a simple narration of events and instead consider the sources in order to develop a historical argument based on the weight of the evidence. The five-paragraph essay includes an opening paragraph that briefly introduces the topic, provides a general overview of the evidence, and offers a clear statement of the historical argument. The next

---

1. A Venn diagram represents corroborating evidence through the use of overlapping circles.

three paragraphs contain the body of the essay. Here, one must provide a narrative of events that describes what happened, but this evidence must be used to explain motive, consider counterarguments, and in particular support the historical argument. The concluding paragraph provides a summary of the essay's main points with an eye toward underscoring the historical argument. Even though some essay assignments may require writing considerably more than five paragraphs, the same approach may be employed, with the additional paragraphs enabling one to offer more evidence to better support the historical argument and consider some of the basic elements of analysis.

CourseReader Assignment 3: Essay

Go to Appendix C for instructions on a CourseReader assignment that will help you practice writing the five-paragraph essay.

THE ANNOTATION

Another useful short writing exercise is the annotation. Annotations are usually associated with bibliographies, but knowing how to write an annotation fuses the skills of summary and analysis. The length of annotations can vary, so be certain of the requirement before undertaking this task. Most annotations tend to be a few sentences long, or in some cases no more than three lines of text, though others can be nearly one page long. Annotations include a summary of the work as well as provide the historian's interpretation. In some instances, some commentary on the sources is appropriate.

For examples of annotations, see Appendices A and B. Other excellent examples can be found in *The American Historical Association's Guide to Historical Literature*, third edition.[2]

SHORT ESSAYS: BOOK REVIEW

One of the best ways that young scholars can master the short essay and learn to evaluate a secondary source is by writing a book review. Regardless of the sophistication of the audience or the length of a review, all reviews should accomplish the following:

- Give the reader a sense of the book
- Comment on the quality of the work
- Compare the work with other, similar works
- Assess the work's contribution to the scholarship
- Discuss the appropriate audience for the monograph

---

2. Mary Beth Norton, ed., *The American Historical Association's Guide to Historical Literature*, 3rd ed. (New York: Oxford University Press, 1995).

It is crucial in every instance to be fair to the book as written. Although reviews vary in length, most are between 500 and 1,000 words.

The prospective reviewer begins the review by including a heading that indicates the book's author, title, and publication information. The following heading appeared in a review completed by student Sean Crowley:

Flight and Rebellion: Slave Resistance in Eighteenth-Century Virginia. By Gerald W. Mullin. (New York: Oxford University Press, 1972. pp. xii, 219.)

The text of the review starts with a statement that simultaneously draws the reader's interest while hinting at the central idea or tension discussed in the book. After this opening, the reviewer provides the reader with a brief description of the author and a statement of the author's thesis. Knowing who the author is enables the reviewer to discern something about the quality of the work and the point of view as well as to provide insights into the author's level of expertise on the subject matter. Many monographs contain brief descriptions of the author at either the beginning or end of the book. At any rate, a reviewer should seek more information about the author. One of the most convenient ways to find this information is by searching reference works such as the *Encyclopedia of Historians and Historical Writing*, *A Global Encyclopedia of Historical Writing*, *Biography and Genealogy Master Index*, and the *Directory of American Scholars*. In some cases, simply conducting a Google search of the author's name will yield results.

The reviewer must provide a sense of the thesis of the monograph. While it is important to practice the techniques of critical reading discussed earlier in this chapter, authors often clearly state the thesis or central argument in their prefatory or introductory comments. If not, a careful reading of the book should make clear the author's central point.

The first two paragraphs of Sean Crowley's review follow. Note how he draws the reader's attention and then identifies the author and his thesis:

Late one evening on July 10, 1800, a few miles outside the city of Richmond, Virginia, a black slave named Ben Woolfolk is cutting wood. A man steps out from the surrounding "scrubby, pine woods." "Would you join a free Mason society?" asks the man. Ben replies, "All free Masons would go to hell." Undaunted the man replies, "It [is] not a free Mason society I have in mind [but] a society to fight the white people for [our] freedom." George Smith, himself a slave, stepped out of the woods that night in search of recruits—recruits for what would become the "most sophisticated and ambitious slave conspiracy" in United States history, recruits … for Gabriel's Rebellion.

Although Gabriel's Rebellion (named after its leader, Gabriel Prosser) failed before it began, it nonetheless represented a significant shift in slave behavior toward the institution of slavery. Using this event as the culminating and defining moment in his book *Flight and Rebellion*, California State University professor of history

Source: L. Sean Crowley

Gerald W. Mullin looks to explain how slave resistance escalated from individual acts, like running away, to group action in the form of outright rebellion. Examining the patterns of slave resistance in eighteenth-century Virginia and the degree to which slaves differed in their reactions to slavery, he offers this central thesis: that the level of slave acculturation (or assimilation) and the type of work performed were the determining factors in the type of resistance that was engaged in and "that as slaves acculturated they became outwardly rebellious and more difficult for whites to control."

At some point in the review, the reviewer must also comment on the author's conclusions and sources. Often, the last chapter of a book or last paragraph of an essay will summarize the main points and offer the author's conclusions. It is more difficult to discern the sources used by an author. While many historians provide a bibliographical essay or an annotated bibliography that provides commentary on sources, it is often best to examine the footnotes to see which sources are consulted most frequently.

The heart of a review is the summary. Summarizing a monograph is challenging work. An effective summary should not only reflect how the author supported and elaborated on his or her thesis but should provide an abstract of the main points and give the reader a sense of the book's organization. This requires reviewers to be selective in their comments. Inexperienced writers who attempt to write a paragraph about every chapter will produce incoherent summaries of little use. An effective summary elaborates on how the thesis is supported, citing selected sections that will be explored in greater depth because they more clearly illustrate the author's main point or because they are simply more interesting.

In the following paragraph, Sean Crowley summarizes the main points of the book while including some commentary on sources:

Mullin analyzed and interpreted the primary sources often known to historians as "witnesses in spite of themselves"; for example, court, county, and plantation records, ledgers, and census returns were used. His primary focus, however, rested upon examination of notices for runaway slaves published in Virginia newspapers. He analyzed approximately 1,500 such ads from 1736 to 1801 and from these exhumed a wealth of insightful information, such as the origin of the slaves who ran away and the type of work they performed; he even gained an understanding of their use of English. He was thus able to develop a good idea of various types of slaves and their behavior toward slavery. The newly arrived African (or "outlandish") slaves often attempted escape, either seeking to return to Africa or establish settlements to "re-create their old life." Those Africans who remained within the plantation system and became what Mullin calls "new Negroes" often engaged in relatively minor forms of "inward-directed" rebellion, such as truancy, thievery, property destruction, "feigned illness," and general laziness. This type of resistance produced only short-lived gains and temporary relief yet often resulted in more suffering on the part of the slave. Lastly, and most importantly, were the highly acculturated, American-born, skilled or artisan slaves. This group, with its variety of occupational skills, good command of the English language, and useful understanding of the ways of the whites—all elements of a high degree of acculturation—included men like Ben Woolfolk and George Smith. It was these slaves, the "artisans and waitingmen," who had the means, the understanding, and the desire to organize and fight for their freedom. As individuals, these skilled artisan-slaves initially exhibited "outward-directed" resistance by becoming fugitives and often attempted to pass themselves off as free men. By 1800, however, partially influenced by the ideals of the American Revolution, many of these individuals had begun to view resistance as a collective effort. It was they who would become the motivators and leaders of America's first large-scale slave insurrection.

If the heart of a review is the summary, the brain of the review is the analysis. Indeed, it is analysis that makes a review different from, and much more useful than, a book report. Analysis may be of many different types. For example, a review in a professional journal includes commentary on where the work fits into the existing scholarship as well as what, if any, scholarly contribution has been made to a field. Professional reviews might also discuss the use of sources, whether their use was appropriate, and if other extant sources were ignored. Beginning researchers often lack the experience and knowledge of the field to make such judgments. But a careful review of the book should enable them to comment on many aspects of a scholarly work. For example, they can determine if the thesis is clear and supported by the evidence. Are the author's main conclusions consistent with the thesis? Might other conclusions be drawn from the evidence presented?

A review needs to comment on the sources. Historians ask: What types of primary sources are used? Who wrote them? Do these primary sources seem appropriate to the topic? Have sources that might have been used been neglected? What secondary sources does the author use? What do these works focus on? Who wrote them? When? Is there some significance to the works selected by the author?

Reviews should also comment on additional features within the book. These frequently include maps, illustrations, charts, and graphs. All reviewers should answer questions about a book's readability, clarity, and organization. Although many inexperienced reviewers may find some words outside of their existing vocabularies, writing about history does not involve the same type of vocabulary and technical knowledge as writing about nuclear physics. Historians write about people and the cultures and institutions they create. Beginning researchers do not need a special vocabulary to decipher an author's meaning.

Reviews also include a brief commentary on the appropriate audience for such a work. Remember, a review should provide scholars with a sense of the book's value. Identifying the appropriate audience for a monograph is not easy, and a few guidelines might be helpful. A heavily footnoted volume written on a relatively narrow topic is likely meant for specialists; a book that contains no or few citations written about an event that has been covered in detail by other historians might be intended for a popular audience. But a reviewer should not automatically jump to such a conclusion if footnotes are not present; some scholars' reputations are so great that their expertise is taken for granted. The publisher might also suggest the intended audience. Books produced by university presses are intended for a scholarly audience. Books produced by trade presses are meant for a broader readership. The tone of a work might also indicate its potential audience. Is the writing scholarly? Are the author's findings and interpretations dispassionately presented? The depth of a book might also be a clue to audience. For example, does it provide an overview or introduction to a topic, or does it examine a more esoteric point in careful detail?

Reviewers conclude by commenting on the quality of the work. Suggesting that a piece of historical scholarship is too long or repetitive is more often a sign of a short attention span than an informed commentary on the work. Instead, the reviewer should consider whether the argument is supported by the evidence, whether the work is clearly written and easy to understand, and in particular where the monograph fits into the existing scholarship and what specific contribution it makes to this scholarship. In passing this final judgment, it is essential that the reviewer always remember to review the work as it was written, not as he or she wishes it had been written.

The final paragraphs of Sean Crowley's review analyze the book and offer comments on the appropriate audience. The author's name and institutional affiliation appear on separate lines at the end of the review.

> *Flight and Rebellion* is full of quotes and outtakes from the runaway slave notices and other primary source material. Mullin weaves these excerpts into his prose almost flawlessly; however, they do, at times, slow the pace of the book. That professor Mullin was able to glean so much information from these ads is remarkable, but this reviewer is left wondering if it is enough to make the case beyond contestation. Nonetheless his argument is very persuasive and despite the book's short length (it weighs in at only 163 pages of actual text), it still serves well to bolster his argument. Mullin efficiently packs a lot into a tiny space, presenting his ideas in five chapters, each showing a progressive step in the slaves' development towards rebellion. Mullin also provides for his readers a few maps of Virginia counties and towns as well as some tables showing, among other things, the differing value of slaves, their jobs, and their destinations when they ran away. The maps did not seem to be entirely necessary, but the tables were helpful and easy to use. The most interesting was "Table Two: The Assimilated Slaves' Jobs." This table outlines the type of jobs performed by the slaves whom Mullin studied in the notices and shows both the number of slaves who held the various jobs and the percentage they

represented of the whole. The index is adequate yet could be more detailed with its entries. Finally, there are also 39 pages of extensive endnotes as well as a bibliography listing the primary materials but only "selected" secondary sources.

Mullin has produced a book that is inclined toward the academic audience more than toward the general reader, but as its thesis is so intriguing and the evidence presented appears to solidly back it, anyone interested in slave resistance should read this book. It must be said, though, that it will be helpful if one has a serious interest in the subject of slave resistance and also does not mind stopping to think and reflect every few paragraphs. Despite its sometimes dry tone, Mullin does manage to draw the reader into his vision of slavery from the "bottom up" and is ultimately successful in his attempt not only to prove his thesis but also to provide the reader with a "new perspective on slave behavior."

L. Sean Crowley
James Madison University

THE ARTICLE REVIEW

Reviewing a journal article is nearly identical to reviewing a book. That said, journal articles are nearly always more difficult to review. Where most modern historical monographs offer some information about the author, journal articles rarely provide more than an institutional affiliation. Journal articles also lack the prefatory materials found in most modern monographs and biographies. Such prefaces often discuss the author's point of view, historical arguments, methodology, historiography, important sources, approach, and sometimes even important conclusions; journal articles generally offer little more than a statement of historical argument accompanied by a historiographical footnote. Because of these limitations, reviewers of journal articles generally have to conduct more research into both the author and the scholarship to write an effective review. Although reviewing a journal article may seem easy because articles are considerably shorter than books, looks are deceiving—writing article reviews requires a greater level of expertise than what is usually required for reviewing a book.

Read student Paul McDowell's essay in Appendix B and prepare a 500-word review of it using the elements discussed in this section. Assume the study is an article in a scholarly journal. What are some of the difficulties you encountered in preparing the review?

WEBSITE OR EXHIBITION REVIEWS

Reviews of websites are in many ways similar to the conventions followed for book and article reviews. While website reviews share most of the same characteristics as book and article reviews, there are some important differences. Any website review must comment on the look, accessibility, and navigability of a site as well as describing the types (recordings, images, videos) and quality of the media that are available at the site. The sheer diversity in the types of websites led the *Journal of American History* (*JAH*) to list the different types.

- "**Archive**: a site that provides a body of primary documents.
- **Electronic Essay/Exhibit**: something created/written specifically for the Web—that is, a secondary source that interprets the past in some fashion. This would include "hypertexts" that offer a historical narrative or argument.
- **Teaching Resource**: a site that provides online assignments, syllabi, and other resources specifically geared toward using the Web for teaching.
- **Gateway**: a site that provides access to other Web-based materials.
- **Journal/Webzine**: an online publication.
- **Organization**: a site devoted to providing information on a particular organization.
- **Virtual Community**: a site on which a historical community—popular or academic—interacts"[3]

The type of website plays an important role in the reviewing process. For example, reviewing an online archive requires commentary on the materials contained, who the editor is and his or her qualifications, how the materials are organized, whether they appear as originals or have been edited, whether they possess introductions, and the site's navigability. Someone reviewing an online essay would have to answer some of the same questions, but essentially his or her task is very similar to that of a book or article reviewer. Discerning the audience of a website, much like a book or journal, can be extremely helpful in determining the purpose and usefulness of a site. Examine a website related to your area of interest and prepare a 500-word review of it. In what ways is this review similar to book or article reviews you have completed?

WRITING FOR THE WEB

The growing popularity of websites presents a set of new challenges for historians. The qualities of good analytical writing must be reevaluated because of the nature of the medium. The first difference is the audience. Readers are less likely to read each word on a website than they are the printed page. If the writing and visuals do not attract attention immediately, a click of the mouse moves the reader to another site, and the opportunity to convey ideas is lost. Writing in this environment, therefore, requires the author to consider which words in a

3. "Web Site Reviews," http://www.journalofamericanhistory.org/submit/websitereviews.html (accessed 4 November 2011).

scanned text to draw attention to by using such devices as different colors or hypertext links. Thus, the page layout becomes a critical concern. Text sections must be briefer and should be divided by thoughtful subtopics to set off bodies of information. Tone and language must hold the reader's attention. The question of what the reader needs or even wishes to know about the topic must be considered in different ways than for the printed page since it is possible to introduce hypertext links at any time. Where and when will they be most effective? How many links are useful? When does their use overwhelm and turn the reader to his or her mouse? Paragraphs must also assume a more journalistic style emphasizing only a single idea, and each paragraph should be as sparse as possible. Each page should include visuals that enhance the layout and encourage the reader to continue. How to select appropriate visuals, images, graphs, and charts to improve a page is much more vital than on a page of printed text.

Since the environment is relatively new, there are fewer good models to employ as guides. By contrast, many websites created by merely uploading text files without paying adequate attention to potential audiences fill cyberspace. Student historians have a genuine opportunity to shape this new writing and communication environment. Because they rely more fully on the web in their daily lives, they are likely better judges of what is effective and what is not. Taking existing writing assignments or developing new ones and shaping them for online use will sharpen traditional research and writing skills and may better prepare undergraduates for the world of writing in the future. Take a relatively brief writing assignment similar to one already described in the chapter and convert it for a website. What questions should be considered about purpose, audience, argument, and evidence? How can the paper best illuminate these elements in the new environment? What kinds of visuals will highlight the message? How should the paper be revised for the web? What is sacrificed? What is gained?

SHORT ESSAY WRITING FORMS BEYOND THE IVIED WALLS

To this point, the focus has been on enhancing writing skills as they directly relate to academics and potential forms of classroom writing assignments. Students need also to consider aspects of short essay writing that relate to more practical considerations once formal education ends. While the skills associated with effective writing transfer in many ways, this discussion will address two to illustrate. Both connect directly to skills in persuasion: grant writing and the search for employment beyond the university.

Grants and Job Applications

One of the most practical writing skills for all historians is learning the basics of grant writing. Grants from public or philanthropic agencies have traditionally been regarded as essential for completing many successful personal research

projects or for supporting museums, sites, and organizations as they inform, edu-
cate, and entertain a variety of publics. The support provides the time to devote
to planning and completing the project. One place to begin developing the skills
involved in successful grant writing is as part of studying undergraduate history.
Learning about grant writing constitutes another way students can actually learn
the processes involved in doing history. Begin with a recent good term paper
and consider the ways it might be expanded and made more comprehensive.
What is the paper's argument? What does the research add that is unique?
What sources were available to conduct the research? What sources are extant
but were not available when you were completing it? With more time and
other resources, what aspects of the topic would be open to examination? With
these and similar questions in mind, consider what would be necessary to prepare
a successful grant application. Examine the guidelines for personal grants and fel-
lowships found at the website for the National Endowment for the Humanities
(NEH), http://www.neh.gov/grants/guidelines/fellowships.html, or similar sites
for national or regional awards. What are the kinds of grants the NEH funds?
What is required in an application? Who is eligible to apply? What restrictions,
if any, are placed on the kinds of projects eligible for funding? What specific
guidelines exist?

Begin drafting a narrative that addresses clearly and succinctly each element
requested in the application guidelines. The NEH, for instance, limits the application narrative to three single-spaced pages. In the narrative, applicants must
explain the significance of the proposed study, detailing four particular items:

1. The research and the contribution it will make
2. The methods and work plan (what specifically will be accomplished during
   the period of the grant)
3. The researcher's competencies and special skills to conduct the research
4. The final product, its audience, and how the results will be made available to
   its intended audience.

The brief narrative will be reviewed by experts and must convince them of
the project's merits and benefits. It must, therefore, be meticulously constructed
and persuasive. Every word counts. Consider why you are using each word and
whether or not you can be more precise without sacrificing clarity. The review
of sentences and words is especially important since many grant submissions are
now completed online and require applicants to fill in allotted spaces in a tem-
plate that will only accept a given word count. You will need to be equally persuasive and pointed in recounting your special abilities and how you will use the
time and support efficiently to complete the project on schedule. It is insuffi-
cient, for example, to indicate a need to examine records in Buenos Aires or
Beijing. You must justify why such travel is essential to the successful completion
of the work. Next, construct a budget that thoughtfully explains the costs and
the rationales for each expenditure. Many agencies require evidence of cost sharing, either by the individual or institution. During the process, discuss your idea
with faculty who have applied for, or held, research grants to solicit their

thoughts. While it is obvious that few, if any, student papers meet the criteria necessary for funding by the NEH, it is important that student historians begin to develop some skills in grant writing as another way to reflect critically about their own scholarship and improve short-essay writing skills that will be important after graduation.

Preparing grant proposals for historic sites, museums, or agencies follows a pattern similar to personal grants. Students might identify a local group that depends upon outside grants for its ongoing operations or to plan special projects or exhibits. Many have websites that can be readily checked for ideas regarding the kinds of projects such groups might wish to seek funding to support. Once some background study is completed, try to schedule an appointment with an official in the organization to listen to their ideas about needs, potential funding agencies, and the like. As the assignment, prepare a draft grant proposal for the organization that includes an explanation of the project, its purpose, audience, budget, and so forth. Share the completed draft with the agency officers and seek their response and guidance. If the draft is something useful to the organization, offer your services to actually complete a final proposal for submission. It is a useful experience and another dimension of the ability to conduct historical research. The skills enhanced in preparing grant proposals are similar to those used in reviewing, as described earlier in the chapter, and in preparing conference paper submissions and abstracts, outlined in Chapter 8.

JOB APPLICATION LETTERS, VITAE, AND RESUMÉS—NOT SHORT ESSAYS BUT ESSENTIAL TO ALL HISTORIANS

Another writing skill that nearly everyone must develop is the ability to prepare a resumé and write a job application letter. After all, everyone needs a job (and your parents or guardians will insist upon it)! Below are some basic considerations when preparing a job application letter and resumé.

The typical job application letter (sometimes referred to as a "cover letter") contains about three to five paragraphs.

- The introductory paragraph includes information about who you are, why you are writing, and where you learned of the opening. If you learned of the position through an individual or through earlier correspondence, it is useful to mention the person by name or reference the earlier communication.

- The next paragraph, or if necessary paragraphs, contain information about you and your skills that pertain specifically to the position. Highlight important features of your resumé that make you an attractive candidate for the job. In addition, incorporate your knowledge about the position and the organization to which you are writing. In many ways, this section of the letter is your sales pitch.

■ Make the concluding paragraph brief, indicating the steps that should happen next, culminating in an interview. There are two basic approaches to take. The passive approach puts the responsibility on the employer to make contact with you (you will wait for the employer to contact you for more information or an interview). With the active approach you offer to initiate further contact with the employer, perhaps indicating that you will call or arrange an appointment.

All historians, from beginners to the most seasoned professionals, must be able to describe who they are on paper. For most students, this is a resumé. For academics, this is a curriculum vitae (vitae[4] or CV). A vitae is generally needed when applying to present at a conference and is required when applying for an academic job. It is never too early to begin to develop a resumé or vitae.

Vitae

Student Jillian Viar provides an example of what a vitae should look like. At the top of her vitae she has listed her contact information. Like many students, she has two addresses—one at the university she attends and another for her home address. One might list two phone numbers, especially since most people have cell phones, but in Jillian's case one is sufficient. Finally, it is essential to include an email address. Remember that many first impressions are important. Be sure your phone message sounds professional, and if your email refers to an old nickname or some aspect of a long-lost weekend, change your email address to something more formal and professional.

Each section of this vitae is clearly delineated from the preceding section. In listing her degrees, Viar indicates where she received or expects to receive her degree, as well her major field. Furthermore, she includes important information such as the title of her master's thesis and name of her thesis advisor. This information can be helpful for a conference program committee or potential employer to determine Viar's qualifications and interests.

Since Viar is interested in a position as a historical interpreter, she includes her teaching experience followed by her conference presentations. The section of the vitae "Teaching Experience" presents her role as a teaching assistant, but this may not provide enough information. She might improve this section of her vitae by briefly listing her teaching assistant responsibilities. Her guest lecture might also list the exact date rather than simply the year. The following section focuses on her research experience. Although the order in which she lists her experiences may appear arbitrary, it is connected to the specific position she seeks. Finally, Viar lists work and travel experiences. This section is excellent, clearly describing positions held and responsibilities required for each position. But her section on international travel seems almost an afterthought. She might consider presenting more about this experience as well as any foreign language skills. Here is Jillian Viar's vitae.

---

4. The Latin word for "life."

Jillian Viar

800 South Main Street
Harrisonburg VA 22801
viarjl@dukes.jmu.edu

100 Long Drive
Lynchburg VA 24503
Cell 555-555-5555

Education

M.A., James Madison University, Harrisonburg, VA, in process for May 2012.
    Major: United States History, focus on Colonial America
    Thesis Title: "Friendship and the Awakening of Political Consciousness: The Letters of Mercy Otis Warren and Abigail Adams"
    Advisor: John Christopher Arndt
B.A., Christopher Newport University, Newport News VA, 2010.
    Major: History. Phi Alpha Theta member.
    Minor: Art History
    Advisor: William Connell

Teaching Experience

Teaching Assistant, James Madison University, Harrisonburg, VA, 2010-2012.
    History 225: United States History
Guest Lecturer on the United States and Early 1900s Immigration, James Madison University, Harrisonburg, VA, 2011.
    History 225: United States History

Conference Experience

Moderator, "History Through Art," James Madison University MadRush Research Conference, Harrisonburg, VA, 2011.
Presenter, "The Spanish American War for Independence: A Struggle Against the Control of the United States," Christopher Newport University Paideia, Newport News, VA, 2010.
Presenter, "1607-1614: Jamestown's Interaction with the Powhatan Tribe," Christopher Newport University Paideia, Newport News, VA, 2009.

Work Experience

Intern, Poplar Forest, Bedford, VA, summer 2011. Under the supervision of the Director of Interpretation and Education, Octavia Starbuck.

- Worked on establishing a hands-on history activity for children that will be used for future programs.
- Coordinated and ran multiple history summer day camps and one five day archaeology camp for children from ages 6 to 12.

Editor, *Madison Historical Review* for James Madison University, Harrisonburg, VA, 2011.
Intern, Colonial Williamsburg, Williamsburg, VA, fall semester 2010. Under the Department of Education Outreach.

- Initiated the process of archiving and digitizing their files on all of the Electronic Field Trips.

Library Assistant, Paul and Rosemary Trible Library at Christopher Newport University, Newport News, VA, 2007-2010.

- Assisted undergraduate students in researching.

International Experience

Study Abroad to China, May to June 2008

- Completed under the direction of Dr. Xu, Christopher Newport University.
- Visited Shanghai, Suzhou, Hongzhou, Beijing.

Resumé

If Viar were applying for jobs outside of academia, her resumé would look somewhat different. The resumé might contain much of the same information, but since employers would need a clearer explanation of her skills Viar's resumé might look as follows:

Jillian Viar

800 South Main Street	100 Long Drive
Harrisonburg VA 22801	Lynchburg VA 24503
viarjl@dukes.jmu.edu	Cell 555-555-5555

Education

M.A., James Madison University, Harrisonburg, VA, in process for May 2012.
    Major: United States History, focus on Colonial America

B.A., Christopher Newport University, Newport News VA, 2010.
    Major: History, Phi Alpha Theta member, Minor: Art History

Skills

    Advanced research, analytical, writing and editorial skills
    Fluent in French (Reading and conversational)
    Mastery of Microsoft Office
    Oral presentation experience
    Experience facilitating group meetings and discussion
    International Experience

Work Experience

Intern, Poplar Forest, Bedford, VA, summer 2011. Under the supervision of the Director of Interpretation and Education, Octavia Starbuck.

- Worked on establishing a hands-on history activity for children that will be used for future programs.
- Coordinated and ran multiple history summer day camps and one five day archaeology camp for children from ages 6 to 12.

Editor, *Madison Historical Review* for James Madison University, 2011.
Intern, Colonial Williamsburg, Williamsburg, VA, fall semester 2010.

- Initiated the process of archiving and digitizing their files on all of the Electronic Field Trips.

Library Assistant, Trible Library at Christopher Newport University, 2007-2010.

- Assisted undergraduate students in researching.

Teaching Experience

Teaching Assistant, James Madison University, 2010-2012.
    History 225: United States History

Research Experience

Moderator, "History Through Art," James Madison University MadRush Research Conference, Harrisonburg, VA, 2011.
Presenter, "The Spanish American War for Independence: A Struggle Against the Control of the United States." Christopher Newport University Paideia, Newport News, VA, 2010.
Presenter, "1607-1614: Jamestown's Interaction with the Powhatan Tribe." Christopher Newport University Paideia, Newport News, VA, 2009.

Source: Jillian Viar.

The inclusion of "Skills" as a discrete category immediately following "Education" is the major distinction between Viar's resumé and her vitae. Inclusion of this section is essential since it alerts employers to abilities you possess that may not seem apparent or that they may not have considered. Like many students, Viar may be reluctant to refer to some of her skills as excellent, but her experiences as a history student certainly support her claim. If Viar were applying for a position as an exhibit developer for a museum and the job advertisement indicated primary-source research skills and the need to coordinate with various groups within the museum to develop and maintain exhibits as well as design the actual exhibit, then the resumé and cover letter would indicate her ability to meet these specific job requirements. She might wish to emphasize her research as a history major as well as some skills developed in her work as a museum intern and library assistant.

This chapter has offered guidance on preparing short writing assignments in the classroom as well as writing that has professional or career application. The forms suggested in the first part are some of the more common types all students experience in classes or seminars. It is important to consider the form and structure of each type and to see these forms in the same light as more formal or more intricate writing exercises. Grant writing and job applications illustrate the transfer of some of the same skills practiced in the academy to the professional world. If anything, these skills are more critical to individual students than anything else discussed in the chapter.

EXERCISES

1. Find as many secondary sources as possible pertaining to your research topic. Briefly note the various interpretations of the scholars.

2. Find primary sources that pertain to your research topic. First, perform external and internal criticism on the documents. Second, using the secondary sources as context, write an essay in which you use the primary sources to answer the question posed in number.

3. Go to the career, planning, and placement office at your university. Take a draft of your resumé and job letter and work with one of the professionals to critique it.

7

✳

Finishing the Paper

Polishing a successful research project into finished form demands a different set of skills than those involved in research and writing, yet they are every bit as critical to the work's ultimate success. It is, after all, the final version of a research paper that will be read and subsequently evaluated. The last review of a paper is a tedious and time-consuming process that requires careful attention to detail. It also requires an understanding of—and precise adherence to—the discipline's conventions. Beginning researchers must follow this fundamental aspect of research and writing, especially in the rush to meet deadlines.

This chapter will emphasize the principal aspects of finishing a project successfully: accurately completing the necessary scholarly apparatus (footnotes and bibliography according to *The Chicago Manual of Style* or its abbreviated form, *A Manual for Writers of Term Papers, Theses, and Dissertations* by Kate L. Turabian) and reviewing a suggested checklist of the paper's mechanical and stylistic elements necessary for the final written presentation. Beginning researchers should be thinking of these matters throughout the research and writing process; however, they assume a more central place as the project nears completion.

FOOTNOTES

When historians read scholarly monographs and journal articles, they quickly understand that footnotes are an essential part of the work. Footnotes assist the audience in following the thought processes and questions posed by fellow scholars to shape their arguments. The reader also learns how other historians use information. Reading footnotes carefully and thinking about the ways historians use evidence transfers readily when beginning researchers frame their own studies and give form to their own arguments. Footnotes, then, are fundamental to historical analysis. Whenever writing takes place, footnoting should be done simultaneously to document the sources used. Three basic questions are central to footnoting: Why do historians footnote? What do they footnote? How do they footnote?

Why Do Historians Footnote?

Footnotes serve several purposes in the research paper and appear in several varieties.

- The most common type of footnote may be called a **citation footnote**. These footnotes inform the audience where the author found the evidence that supports a particular argument or case. Since historical scholarship is a collaborative effort, identifying the sources and crediting the works of others is a fundamental responsibility for all students of history. In footnoting, historians acknowledge publicly how previous scholarship has strengthened and influenced their interpretation.

- Footnoting primary sources indicates that the historian has examined the original materials and used them fully to substantiate an argument.

- Footnotes provide audiences with the ability to locate, analyze, and corroborate the evidence used in the paper, and enable them to determine the validity of the conclusions reached. Footnotes, therefore, credit primary and secondary sources to establish reliability for the historian's argument.

In sum, the historian uses footnotes to credit his or her sources. Footnotes are part of an ongoing series of conversations the historian has undertaken with the sources and the audiences. They help the historian better understand the quality of an argument and inform readers about the level of care that has gone into the selection of evidence to support conclusions.

Another type of footnote is the **explanatory footnote**. Historians use explanatory footnotes in several ways. As the name suggests, this footnote form helps to further explain material, terms, individuals, places, or ideas that are mentioned in the paper. The explanatory footnote usually contains a few simple sentences that enhance or clarify a point presented in the text. A general rule for using an explanatory footnote is as follows: in the author's judgment, this information would disrupt the narrative flow of the paper or it is an interesting aside that may not be appropriate for presentation within the body of the paper. For example, if someone is named in the paper and that individual is not well known, the historian may want to provide some brief biographical information. Less familiar places may also be identified, or terms may be defined. The explanatory footnote can also be used to clarify sources, to comment on historical and historiographical discrepancies, or to explain foreign-language material. In all instances, the explanatory note is included to enhance understanding. Explanatory footnotes also help to sustain conversations between the historian and the evidence to the improvement of the historical argument. For an example, see footnote 4 in student Paul McDowell's paper (Appendix B).

The **historiographic footnote** is the third footnote form. It is usually one of the first footnotes in a research paper or scholarly article, often appearing at the conclusion of the first paragraph. In some instances, scholars opt to use two or three footnotes to address historiographic issues rather than one footnote. There is a detailed explanation of the purpose and composition of the historiographical footnote in Chapter 5; an example appears in Paul McDowell's paper in Appendix B. The historiographic footnote illustrates the historian's familiarity with what has been written on the topic.

What Do Researchers Footnote?

One of the most difficult concepts for less experienced historians to grasp is when to footnote. There are two possible approaches to footnoting. The first is to footnote each sentence or sentences containing information taken from a specific secondary or primary source. Whenever a direct quotation is used, it must be footnoted. This approach works best during the draft writing stage of the paper. It allows the author to see the sources, and it facilitates editing since the footnote is clearly linked to a sentence or sentences that may be edited or perhaps moved to another part of the paper. It also gives beginning researchers confidence that any ideas or words not their own have been attributed to the appropriate sources. Because historians use many sources in crafting a paper, this approach also means that many paragraphs will contain a number of footnotes.

A second approach, and one increasingly used by scholars, is the multiple-citation footnote. This footnote usually appears at the end of each paragraph and lists the various sources employed to write the paragraph, with the sources generally arranged in the order of their appearance in the paragraph. This ordering allows the reader to determine with some degree of certainty the source used to write a particular part of the paragraph. The multiple-citation footnote is preferable to having a discrete footnote for each sentence or groups of sentences within a paragraph. Although it reduces the number of footnotes in the paper, it still provides the necessary documentation. A semicolon (;) is used to separate one citation from another in the multiple-citation footnote. An exception to the use of the multiple-citation footnote is when the historian employs a direct quotation from a primary source; that sentence should be footnoted and attributed to the specific source.

The following are examples of the two approaches to footnoting as demonstrated with a paragraph from Paul McDowell's paper. The first paragraph shows the approach of footnoting each sentence or sentences:

> Even the newspapers throughout the West held underlying prejudices against the Italians. Although most of the western reports gave a fairly objective account of the event for that time period, they still erroneously accused the Italians as members of the Mafia and labeled them as merciless killers. The *San Francisco Bulletin* clearly reported that the jury found the accused not guilty, yet

hastily called them "Sicilian assassins" who had murdered David Hennessy.[1] The *Idaho Statesman* emphasized the role of the Mafia in its report, despite the fact that there was no valid proof of the Mafia's existence at this time.[2] The initial wire from the *San Jose Mercury News* reported that the Italian victims were "alleged murderers," providing much more defense for the lynched victims than most other newspapers. Yet the very next sentence of the report stated that the jury had "failed" to convict the eleven "members of Lamafia," clearly demonstrating the writer's underlying belief that the victims were truly guilty.[3] The *Tacoma Daily News* of Washington provided an almost southern-like prospective, blindly citing the Italians as "members of the Mafia society, a lawless organization of Italians." The Tacoma paper even resorted to manufacturing its own truths, declaring that the Mafia "had decreed the assassination of several [other] prominent citizens," a statement that had not been reported anywhere else, even in New Orleans.[4]

The following shows the same paragraph using the multiple-citation footnote:

Even the newspapers throughout the West held underlying prejudices against the Italians. Although most of the western reports gave a fairly objective account of the event for that time period, they still erroneously accused the Italians as members of the Mafia and labeled them as merciless killers. The *San Francisco Bulletin* clearly reported that the jury found the accused not guilty, yet hastily called them "Sicilian assassins" who had murdered David Hennessy. The *Idaho Statesman* emphasized the role of the Mafia in its report, despite the fact that there was no valid proof of the Mafia's existence at this time. The initial wire from the *San Jose Mercury News* reported that the Italian victims were "alleged murderers," providing much more defense for the lynched victims than most other newspapers. Yet the very next sentence of the report stated that the jury had "failed" to convict the eleven "members of Lamafia," clearly demonstrating the writer's underlying belief that the victims were truly guilty. The *Tacoma Daily News* of Washington provided an almost southern-like prospective, blindly citing the Italians as "members of the Mafia society, a lawless organization of Italians." The Tacoma paper even resorted to manufacturing its own truths, declaring that the Mafia "had decreed the assassination of

---

1. "Latest Telegraph, A Violent Uprising in New Orleans," *San Francisco Bulletin*, 14 March 1891.

2. "The Mafia Case," *Idaho Statesman* (Boise), 14 March 1891; "A Crime Revenged, Eleven Mafia Assassins Are Killed in New Orleans," *Idaho Statesman* (Boise), 15 March 1891.

3. "Lynched, A Mob in New Orleans This Morning," *San Jose Mercury News*, 14 March 1891.

4. "Eleven Lynched, Citizens Break into New Orleans Jail," *Tacoma Daily News*, 14 March 1891; "Mafia Murderers, The Crimes for Which They Were Executed," *Tacoma Daily News*, 16 March 1891; "The New Orleans Mob," *Tacoma Daily News*, 16 March 1891.

several [other] prominent citizens," a statement that had not been reported anywhere else, even in New Orleans.[5]

An exception that some historians make with the multiple-citation footnote is the block-indented quotation. It is often footnoted immediately after the quoted material with the citation referring to the single, specific source. Scholarly writing convention suggests that when a direct quotation exceeds five typed lines, it should be indented "one tab stop from the left margin" and the quotation marks removed. A good rule to follow is to introduce the block-indented quotation and reference the author. Block-indented quotations must be single spaced. The footnote number should appear outside the punctuation following the block quotation. Block-indented and other quotations should be used judiciously to illustrate arguments made by the researcher; they do not replace the arguments themselves. When using any direct quotation, be extremely careful to check each word carefully to make certain it appears in the text exactly, including punctuation and spelling,[6] as found in the source.

Plagiarism   Students of history, whether budding historians or long-term faculty, are part of a community of scholars who acknowledge or recognize historical knowledge is cumulative. One of the hallmarks of this community is the honest and explicit attribution of words, thoughts, ideas, or interpretations of others and not claiming the work of others as your own. For these reasons, historians document and footnote sources to give credit to others.

Failure to footnote appropriately may result in charges of **plagiarism**, which is academic dishonesty of the highest order. Plagiarism occurs when an author claims words, thoughts, ideas, or interpretations that are not his or her own. This act may be committed consciously or inadvertently; either way, it is plagiarism. In most instances, plagiarism involves carelessness in paraphrasing, quoting, or citing evidence. Students of history would be well served to establish and maintain good habits of footnoting to attribute the contributions of others in the profession.[7]

5. "Latest Telegraph, A Violent Uprising in New Orleans," *San Francisco Bulletin*, 14 March 1891; "The Mafia Case," *Idaho Statesman* (Boise), 14 March 1891; "A Crime Revenged, Eleven Mafia Assassins Are Killed in New Orleans," *Idaho Statesman* (Boise), 15 March 1891; "Lynched, A Mob in New Orleans This Morning," *San Jose Mercury News*, 14 March 1891; "Eleven Lynched, Citizens Break into New Orleans Jail," *Tacoma Daily News*, 14 March 1891; "Mafia Murderers, The Crimes for Which They Were Executed," *Tacoma Daily News*, 16 March 1891; "The New Orleans Mob," *Tacoma Daily News*, 16 March 1891. Many of these newspapers are available at America's Historical Newspapers, http://infoweb.newsbank.com/ (accessed 14 December 2011).

6. Any error, such as misspelled words, factual mistakes, etc., in direct quotations should be followed by [sic]. The Turabian manual indicates that [sic] should be italicized. The use of [sic] indicates that the misspelling or error was not the author's mistake; rather, it appeared in the original document.

7. The American Historical Association website includes a full, clear explanation of the issues involved in plagiarism and how to avoid them. It also includes a fine article intended for beginning researchers: The American Historical Association, "Statement on Professional Standards," Chapter IV, Plagiarism, http://www.historians.org/pubs/Free/Professional Standards.cfm (accessed 14 October 2011); Michael Rawson, "Plagiarism: Curricular Materials for History Instructors," http://www.historians.org/governance/pd/Curriculum/plagiarism_defining.htm (accessed 14 October 2011).

A growing number of colleges and universities have turned to software programs to help students become more aware of plagiarism and to prevent the malicious cutting and pasting of materials from websites or online sources without proper attribution. Programs like SafeAssign or Turnitin.com take the text of papers and compare it to materials in existing databases and the Internet. The programs then highlight the wording similarities and indicate the located source so that students can see the potential problems and remedy the word choice to avoid plagiarism. Should students have access to such programs, they should take advantage of the opportunity.

How Do Researchers Footnote?

Many different style manuals specify footnote form, and, it seems, nearly every scholarly discipline observes its own style format.[8] Historians prefer *The Chicago Manual of Style*, 16th ed. (Chicago: University of Chicago Press, 2010). A copy of this style manual can be found in most college libraries. The entire book is available at: http://www.chicagomanualofstyle.org/16/contents.html. It is especially useful in documenting the growing number of online books, journals, and primary sources. *The Chicago Manual of Style* has been condensed into a more manageable form by Kate L. Turabian in *A Manual for Writers of Term Papers, Theses, and Dissertations*, 7th ed. (Chicago: University of Chicago Press, 2007). Both manuals include clear explanations of types of footnotes as well as examples. Beginning researchers should be consistent in following *Chicago Manual*/Turabian style throughout the research paper, including the bibliography.

One of the strengths of *Chicago Manual*/Turabian style is its unobtrusiveness. Within the narrative of the paper, a footnote is simply indicated by a superscripted (raised one-half letter) number that appears after the punctuation mark. Most software programs perform this task automatically when the footnote function is enabled. The actual text of the footnote can appear at the bottom of the page or as an endnote at the end of the paper. The advantage of footnotes is the ease of having them at the bottom of each page while reading through the text, instead of flipping back and forth from the text to the endnotes. Historians prefer *Chicago Manual*/Turabian style because it allows for long citations of sources, explanation, or commentary on sources at the bottom of the page or the end of a paper without disrupting the narrative flow of the paper.

The first time a source is cited, a complete footnote citation is required. A typical footnote for a book should contain the following information:

- Author's name, generally first name, middle initial, last name, followed by a comma.
- Full title of the book in italics. No punctuation follows the title.

---

8. For example, most English Literature scholars follow the Modern Language Association (MLA) style, while most psychologists observe the American Psychological Association (APA) style.

- Publication information, enclosed within parentheses: city of publication, followed by state abbreviation unless it is a well-known city like Boston, followed by a colon (:); name of the publisher, followed by a comma; and year of publication. After the last parenthesis, place a comma.

- The page or pages cited, followed by a period. No *p.* or *pp.* is required.

Each footnote should be single spaced and numbered consecutively throughout the paper. Most word processing programs automatically handle these tasks and superscript the number in the text and to begin the footnote. This is different from *The Chicago Manual of Style* and Turabian, where footnote numbers are superscripted in the text, but the actual footnotes are numbered in regular font without superscript followed by a period (for example, 23.). The footnotes in this text follow *Chicago Manual*/Turabian format.

The following examples cover the major types of footnotes that appear in *Chicago Manual*/Turabian style. The footnote numbers are superscripted and flush with the author's name to show the different approaches to footnote numbering. For a complete listing, beginning researchers should consult these references directly. When working to complete footnotes for any research project, a copy of or link to either *The Chicago Manual of Style* or Turabian should be close at hand and regularly consulted to make certain that the form used is consistent with the standard.

Books

1. Single author book

[1]Elizabeth McKellar, *The Birth of Modern London: The Development and Design of the City, 1660–1720* (New York: St. Martin's Press, 1999), 221.
[2]Daniel Walker Howe, *What Hath God Wrought: The Transformation of America, 1815–1848* (New York: Oxford University Press, 2007), 363.

Both examples include the full title of each book as it appears on the title page. Beginning researchers who sometimes cite directly from sources like WorldCat or online library catalogs often overlook this point. The form used on these online reference works may differ dramatically in style from what appears on the title page. This difference is most common in matters of capitalization and punctuation and must be manually corrected by the historian.

2. Shortened form footnote reference for second or later references

In subsequent footnotes that refer to an earlier cited work, list only the author's last name and page number.

[3]McKellar, 219.
[4]Howe, 232.

However, in instances where an author has published more than one work on a subject, or where a different author with the same last name has published a source **used in the paper**, the short title should include key words from the title of the book or article as well as the author's last name.

[5]Howe, *What Hath God Wrought*, 323.

The same short title must be used consistently throughout the paper.

3. Two or more authors

If a book has two or three authors, list the full names of these individuals in the order they appear on the title page of the book.

[6]J. L. Hammond and Barbara Hammond, *The Village Labourer, 1760–1832: A Study in the Government of England Before the Reform Bill* (London: Longman, Green and Company, Ltd., 1911), 26–29.

If a book has four or more authors, use the term *et al.* after the first author's name instead of listing each author separately.

[7]James West Davidson, et al., *Nation of Nations: A Concise Narrative of the American Republic*, 4th ed. (Boston: McGraw-Hill, 2006), 471.

4. Editor(s) as author(s)

When citing an editor as an author, the format is similar to that used for author(s), except the abbreviation "ed." or "eds." is added to indicate that the work has been edited.

[8]Lloyd deMause, ed., *The History of Childhood* (New York: The Psychohistory Press, 1974), 41–57.

[9]A. L. Beier and Roger Finlay, eds., *London 1500–1700: The Making of the Metropolis* (London and New York: Longman Group Ltd., 1986), 28.

5. Author's work edited or translated

Scholars often edit writings such as diaries and memoirs for publication. In this case, the editor is selecting and editing the work of another author.

[10]*The Diary of John Quincy Adams, 1794–1845: American Political, Social, and Intellectual Life from Washington to Polk*, ed. Allan Nevins (New York: Longman, Green and Company, 1928), 244.

Works originally published in another language are often translated to facilitate wider scholarly use. When such works are cited in footnotes, it is important to credit the author but also to acknowledge the translator. In some cases, there may be more than one translator, and all should be referenced by name. Such citations inform the audience that the book was originally published in another language.

[11]Philippe Ariès, *The Hour of Our Death*, trans. Helen Weaver (New York: Alfred A. Knopf, 1981), 222.

6. Edition other than first

Second and subsequent editions of a book may include significant revisions and modifications; thus, it is important to specify the edition actually used.

[13]Walter George Bell, *The Great Fire of London*, 2nd ed. (London: The Bodley Head, 1951), 17.

7. Multivolume work

[14]Robert Hamlett Bremner, ed., *Children and Youth in America: A Documentary History*, vol. 2, *1866–1932* (Cambridge, MA: Harvard University Press, 1971), 61–74.

8. Published correspondence

Many historians make use of published correspondence that has been collected and edited by scholars. A letter from one correspondent to another appears as follows:

[15]Oliver Cromwell to Sir William Spring and Mr. Barrow, 28 September 1643, *Oliver Cromwell's Letters and Speeches with Elucidations*, ed. Thomas Carlyle, vol. 3 (New York: Peter Fenelon Collier, Publisher, 1897), 166–169.

Articles

1. Scholarly journal article

Scholarly journal articles are one of the most important secondary sources. They should be cited as follows:

[13]Gregory D. Massey, "The Limits of Antislavery Thought in the Revolutionary Lower South: John Laurens and Henry Laurens," *Journal of Southern History* 63, no. 3 (August 1997): 522–523.

Increasing numbers of scholarly journals appear in online format such as JSTOR. Some scholars opt to indicate this format in their footnote.

[13]Gregory D. Massey, "The Limits of Antislavery Thought in the Revolutionary Lower South: John Laurens and Henry Laurens," *Journal of Southern History* 63, no. 3 (August 1997): 522–523, http://www.jstor.org/stable/pdfplus/2211648.pdf?acceptTC=true (accessed 14 October 2011).

2. Article in published collections

[10]Christopher Clark, "The Consequences of the Market Revolution in the American North," in *The Market Revolution in America: Social, Political and Religious Expressions, 1800–1880*, ed. Melvyn Stokes and Stephen Conway (Charlottesville: University Press of Virginia, 1996), 24.

3. Article in popular magazine (author named)

Popular magazines are often useful primary sources for historians.

[31]William Bradford Huie, "The Shocking Story of Approved Killing in Mississippi," *Look*, 24 January 1956, 46–50.

4. Article in popular magazine (author unnamed)

[32]"Making the Black Sox White Again," *Literary Digest*, 20 August 1921, 13–14.

5. Article in newspaper (author named)

[22]Bob Woodward and B. C. Colen, "Bugging Case Suspect Is Free on Bail," *Washington Post*, 24 June 1972.

Often, in citing a newspaper article, the headline is used either as it appeared in the newspaper with most words capitalized, or a sentence-style capitalization is used. In either case, be consistent throughout the paper, as newspapers use both. Page numbers are not used because a newspaper may have several editions and the article may appear on different pages.

6. Article in newspaper (author unnamed)

[16]"Pacifists Condemn and Praise Wilson," *New York Times*, 11 February 1917.

7. Article in newspaper, place of publication not included in title

If the newspaper title does not indicate place of publication, or if the location of the city is not readily apparent from the newspaper name, the city name and state should be included within parentheses following the newspaper title.

[17]"State of Maine!," *Eastern Argus* (Portland, ME), 14 March 1820.

Government Publications

1. Presidential papers

[37]"Farewell Radio and Television Address to the American People," *Public Papers of the Presidents of the United States: Dwight D. Eisenhower, 1960–61* (Washington, D.C.: Government Printing Office, 1961), 1035–1040.

2. Testimony before a congressional committee

[25]Congress, Senate, Subcommittee on Unemployment Relief, "Statement of Miss Dorothy Kahn," *Hearings before the Senate Subcommittee on Unemployment Relief, Senate Committee on Manufacturers*, 72nd Cong., 1st sess. (28 December 1931), 73–77.

3. Congressional committee report

[22]Congress, *Report of the Joint Committee on Reconstruction*, 39th Cong., 1st sess. (Washington, D.C.: Government Printing Office, 1866), 435.

4. Congressional debates

[24]Congress, Senate, Albert J. Beveridge, "Policy Regarding the Philippines," 56th Cong., 1st sess., *Congressional Record* (9 January 1900), 704–712.

5. Supreme Court

[14]Brown v. Board of Education of Topeka, Kansas, 347 U.S. 483 (1954).

6. Other

[1]Public Record Office, "Marc Antonio Giustinian, Venetian Ambassador in France, to Doge and Senate," 12 October 1666, *Calendar of State Papers and Manuscript, Relating to English Affairs, Existing in the Archives and Collections in Venice, and in Other Libraries of Northern Italy 1202–[1675]* (London: Longman, Green, Longman, Roberts, and Green, 1864), no. 87, 86.

Electronic sources   The proliferation of web-based sources has been a boon to historical research.[9] Like traditional footnotes, the reference to an electronic source should contain the following information:

- Author's name
- Title of document or article in quotation marks

---

9. Students of history should understand that the historical profession has yet to settle on an accepted standard for documenting information taken from websites.

- Title of complete work in italics (if relevant)
- Date of publication
- URL of the website
- Date website was accessed

1. Website

[21]Hannah Spires, "Killing: Infanticide, 16 January 1751," *The Proceedings of the Old Bailey* Ref.: t17510116-52. http://www.oldbaileyonline.org/ (accessed 15 September 2011). [1]Thomas Jefferson to James Madison, 28 August 1789, *The Thomas Jefferson Papers, Series 1, General Correspondence, 1651–1827.* http://memory.loc.gov/ammem/collections/jefferson_papers/ (accessed 10 October 2011).

2. Email message

Personal email messages are treated as written correspondence and are cited similarly.

[1]Michael Roth to John Smith, 22 February 2003, "Re: A Note on Polish Immigrant Sources," personal email.

3. Listserv or newsgroup message

Many Listservs and newsgroups archive messages that can be readily accessed. These archives contain valuable insights and information on various topics. These messages should be cited in a manner similar to unpublished papers.

[1]Phil VanderMeer, "Re: WWI Era Harassment of Germans," 12 February 2003, http://www2.h-net.msu.edu/~shgape/ (accessed 5 May 2010).

Because the names and addresses of websites can change over time, it is important to cite the website and date accessed. Historians should also include the full web address since this will often link directly to the source cited.

Other Sources

1. Unpublished dissertation or thesis

[13]Michael Joseph Seth, "Education, State and Society in South Korea, 1948-1960" (PhD diss., University of Hawai'i, 1994), 28. [13]Michael Joseph Seth, "Education, State and Society in South Korea, 1948-1960" (PhD diss., University of Hawai'i, 1994), 28. http://search.proquest.com/docview/304102767/fulltextPDF/13186D196F43894E25B/27?accountid=11667 (accessed 12 September 2011). [17]David G. Bloom, "Divergent Paths: John L. Lewis, Walter Reuther and World War II" (MA thesis, James Madison University, 1996), 45.

2. Manuscript collections

[11]Samuel E. Dutton to Reuel Williams, 14 July 1807, Folder 11, Box 2, Reuel Williams Papers, Maine Historical Society, Portland, Maine. [15]Diary of Henry L. Stimson, 9 December 1941, Henry L. Stimson Diaries, George C. Marshall Library, Lexington, Virginia.

3. Video

[8]*Cold War, 23: The Wall Comes Down, 1989*, prod. Sir Jeremy Isaacs and Pat Mitchell, 47 min., Turner Original Productions, 1998, videocassette.

4. Interview

[12]James McPherson, "Fresh Air from WHYY," interview by Terry Gross (National Public Radio 22 June 2004) http://www.npr.org/ (accessed 10 June 2011).

5. Interview by author of paper

[21]John Baugh, president of SYSCO Foodservices, interview by author, 15 October 2004, Houston, Texas, tape recording in author's possession.

6. Indirect source (quoted in)

In some instances a primary source is located in a scholarly work. While it is always preferable to read the original source, sometimes this is not possible. When citing such a source it is important to attribute the secondary work that contains the primary source material.

[22]J. C. Peoples to A. W. Buchanan, 12 December 1890, J. A. Rose Papers, The University of Texas Library, Texas Archives Division, Austin, Texas, quoted in Norman Pollack, ed., *The Populist Mind* (Indianapolis: Bobbs-Merrill Company, 1967), 22–23.

Historiographic Footnote

Here is another example of a historiographic footnote. It comes from student Lelia H. T. Smith's paper on the legal and illegal confiscation of women's property in early modern England, which makes use of the rich Old Bailey collection of legal documents. Her footnote addresses the scholarship on women and the work of women as well as the legal practices affecting women, then provides an introduction to some of the important primary sources.

[1]The best secondary sources used in this essay are Alice Clark, *Working Life of Women in the Seventeenth Century* (New York: A. M. Kelley, 1968); Miranda Chaytor, "Household and Kinship: Ryton in the Late 16th and Early 17th Centuries," *History Workshop* 10 (Autumn 1980): 25–60; Amy Louise Erickson, *Women and Property in Early Modern England* (London: Routledge, 1993); A. L. Erickson, "Common Law versus Common Practice: The Use of Marriage Settlements in Early Modern England," *The Economic History Review* 43, no. 1 (1990): 21–39; Malcolm M. Feeley and Deborah L. Little, "The Vanishing Female: The Decline of Women in the Criminal Process, 1687–1912," *Law & Society Review* 25, no. 4 (1991): 719–757; Michael Galgano, "Out of the Mainstream: Catholic and Quaker Women in the Restoration Northwest," *The World of William Penn*, ed. Richard S. Dunn and Mary Maples Dunn (Philadelphia: University of Pennsylvania Press, 1986), 118–137; Geoffrey L. Hudson, "Negotiating for Blood Money: War Widows and the Courts in Seventeenth-Century England," in *Women, Crime and the Courts in Early Modern England*, ed. Jennifer Kermode and Garthine Walker (London: Routledge, 1994), 146–169; Josephine Kamm, *Hope Deferred: Girls' Education in English History* (London: Methuen, 1965); Carole Shammas, "The World Women Knew: Women Workers in the North of England During the Late Seventeenth Century," in *The World of William Penn*, ed. Richard S. Dunn and Mary Maples Dunn (Philadelphia: University of Pennsylvania Press, 1986), 99–115; Eileen Spring, *Law, Land, and Family: Aristocratic Inheritance in England, 1300 to 1800* (Chapel Hill: University of North Carolina Press, 1993); Susan Staves, *Married Women's Separate Property in England, 1660–1833* (Cambridge: Harvard University Press, 1990); Garthine Walker, "Women,

Theft, and the World of Stolen Goods," in *Women, Crime and the Courts in Early Modern England*, ed. Jennifer Kermode and Garthine Walker (Chapel Hill: University of North Carolina Press, 1994), 81–105. The best primary sources used in this essay are *Old Bailey Proceedings Online*, www.oldbaileyonline.org (accessed 18 October 2009), trial of Christian Brothers (t16951203-3); Mary Clavering Cowper Countess, "Diary of Mary Clavering Cowper, Countess, October, 1714," in *Diary of Mary, Countess Cowper, Lady of the Bedchamber to the Princess of Wales, 1714–1720*, ed. Charles Spencer Cowper (London: John Murray, 1864); Elizabeth Carter, "Letter from Elizabeth Carter to Elizabeth Robinson Montague, June 21, 1765," *Letters from Mrs. Elizabeth Carter to Mrs. Montagu between the Years 1755 and 1800* (London, England: F.C. & J. Rivington, 1817), 399, http://solomon.bwl2.alexanderstreet.com/cgi-bin/asp/philo/bwl2/getdoc. pl?S4452-D073 (accessed November 5, 2009); Mary Wollstonecraft, *By a Woman Writt: Literature from Six Centuries by and about Women*, ed. Joan Goulianos (New York: The Bobbs-Merrill Company, Inc., 1973); and Earls Colne, Essex: Records of an English Village, 1375–1854, "Wills (EROD/ACW20/79D/ACR10/144 Ralph Josselin 1683 1683)," http://linux02.lib.cam.ac.uk/earlscolne/probate/4901085.htm (accessed November 4, 2009).

Explanatory Footnote

In the sample student paper, Paul McDowell uses an explanatory footnote to define the label *Dago*. If he stopped in the text to explain this offensive label and its origins, he would clutter the narrative. Instead, he provides a brief explanatory note to inform the reader.

[1] *Dago* is an offensive term for an Italian. The root of the term traces to the name "Diego," and it was once used as a demeaning term for Italians, Spaniards, or Portuguese. Gentile, 15; "Assassination of the Chief of Police," *New Orleans Daily Picayune*, 16 October 1890; "The Slain Chieftain," *New Orleans Daily Picayune*, 17 October 1890.

Sometimes explanatory footnotes are used to provide additional information about the topic or to act as an aside to the reader. They can also be used to describe discrepancies in the sources as well as comment on scholarly interpretations.

BIBLIOGRAPHY

A bibliography is the last part of a paper, and it reveals much about the research process. It indicates the extent of the research, the kinds and types of sources that were used, and the different disciplines that helped inform the study. The proper bibliographic citation is necessary so that interested readers might find and read the sources for themselves. As emphasized earlier, bibliographies are valuable for finding sources on particular topics. Finally, the bibliography provides a window to the research for the paper while also allowing the reader to make a discerning judgment about that research. Having a complete bibliography is therefore essential to a finished piece of research.

Beginning researchers should create a **selected bibliography**. A selected bibliography only includes those sources—both primary and secondary—that were cited (footnoted) in the paper. Historians do not pad or inflate the bibliography with sources that were consulted but not actually footnoted.

There are three basic types of bibliographies.

1. **Standard bibliography**. The simplest is the standard bibliography, which is a listing of works used in the paper. It is arranged into subcategories beginning with a listing of primary sources, followed by secondary works. The primary sources category may be further subdivided into the following order: unpublished materials, published materials, and newspapers. Secondary sources are often subdivided into the categories of books, journal articles, and unpublished works. In each category and subcategory, sources are arranged alphabetically.

2. **Annotated bibliography**. The annotated bibliography is more useful to students of history. Its arrangement is the same as a standard bibliography, but each entry has an annotation or critical commentary. The annotation should be brief, usually not more than three lines of text. It generally indicates the author's coverage of the subject, the historical interpretation, and the overall value of the work.

3. **Bibliographic essay**. The bibliographic essay provides commentary about sources in a narrative format. Rather than arranging sources in alphabetical order, the bibliographic essay is arranged by topic or subject in paragraph form. The author determines how the sources are arranged in this essay, though the basic bibliography organization of first addressing primary sources, then secondary sources prevails. The bibliographic essay must be readable, informative, and, like the annotated bibliography, provide critical analysis of the sources. It is helpful to the author of the paper because he or she must have a good sense of the works in order to write about them in a clear narrative style. Constructing a bibliographic essay is a good exercise in learning history by writing. But the essay is also useful to the historian's audience because of its topical or thematic organization.

Since students of history know they must prepare a bibliography, it is important that they arrange the required information as they conduct their reading and research. Maintaining an ongoing computer file of works consulted is a good starting point. For each source consulted, add a bibliographic entry to this file according to *The Chicago Manual of Style*/Turabian format. This ongoing endeavor will make creating the final bibliography much simpler. It is useful to indicate the call number of a book in this file, as the work may need to be located again after it has been returned to the library.

A typical bibliographic entry contains the following information:

- Author's last name, followed by a comma; generally first name, middle initial, then a period.
- Full title of the book in italics. Place a period after the title.
- Publication information: city of publication, followed by a colon (:); name of the publisher, followed by a comma; and year of publication. Place a

period after the publication date. Parentheses are not used in the bibliography entry, although they are used in footnotes.

■ When consulting online sources, be sure to include the name of the site, URL, and date accessed.

Guiding Points

What follows is a basic guide for considering annotations, comments in the bibliographic essay, or remarks in the historiographic footnote, especially for secondary or interpretive works. Keep the answers to these questions in mind for reference and later use.

1. What is the author's point of view? Examine the book's preface or introduction for clues or information.

2. What is the author's historical argument? Authors of books often indicate the historical argument of the study in the preface, while authors of articles usually do so in the first few paragraphs.

3. What evidence supports the historical argument? Examine the bibliography and footnotes to determine the variety and kinds of sources that were used.

4. What is the value of this study? This is the judgment of the scholarly work.

Examples of Bibliographical Citations

Books

1. Single author book

Note that all lines after the first one are indented one tab stop. Most software programs have a "hanging indent" function that can arrange this indentation automatically.

Howe, Daniel Walker. *What Hath God Wrought: The Transformation of America, 1815–1848*. New York: Oxford University Press, 2007.

McKellar, Elizabeth. *The Birth of Modern London: The Development and Design of the City, 1660–1720*. New York: St. Martin's Press, 1999.

2. Two or more authors

If there are two or more authors, list the first author by last name, then first name, followed by a comma. List the remaining authors in standard order. All authors, regardless of number, should be included.

Davidson, James West, William E. Gienapp, Christine Leigh Heyrman, Mark H. Lytle, and Michael B. Stoff. *Nation of Nations: A Concise Narrative of the American Republic*, 4th ed. Boston: McGraw-Hill, 2006.

Hammond, J. L., and Barbara Hammond. *The Village Labourer, 1760–1832: A Study in the Government of England Before the Reform Bill*. London: Longman, Green and Company, Ltd., 1911.

3. Editor(s) as author(s)

Beier, A. L., and Roger Finlay, eds. *London 1500–1700: The Making of the Metropolis.* London and New York: Longman Group Ltd., 1986.

deMause, Lloyd, ed. *The History of Childhood.* New York: The Psychohistory Press, 1974.

4. Author's work edited or translated

Ariès, Philippe. *The Hour of Our Death.* Translated by Helen Weaver. New York: Alfred A. Knopf, 1981.

The Diary of John Quincy Adams, 1794–1845: American Political, Social, and Intellectual Life from Washington to Polk. Edited by Allan Nevins. New York: Longman, Green and Company, 1928.

5. Edition other than first

Bell, Walter George. *The Great Fire of London*, 2nd ed. London: The Bodley Head, 1951.

6. Multivolume work

Bremner, Robert Hamlett, ed. *Children and Youth in America: A Documentary History.* 3 vols. Cambridge, MA: Harvard University Press, 1970–1974.

7. Published correspondence

Cromwell, Oliver. *Oliver Cromwell's Letters and Speeches with Elucidations*, ed. Thomas Carlyle. 3 vols. New York: Peter Fenelon Collier, Publisher, 1897.

Articles

1. Scholarly journal article

Massey, Gregory D. "The Limits of Antislavery Thought in the Revolutionary Lower South: John Laurens and Henry Laurens." *Journal of Southern History* 63, no. 3 (August 1997): 495–530.

Increasing numbers of scholarly journals appear in online format such as JSTOR. Some scholars opt to indicate this format in their footnote.

Massey, Gregory D. "The Limits of Antislavery Thought in the Revolutionary Lower South: John Laurens and Henry Laurens." *Journal of Southern History* 63, no. 3 (August 1997): 495–530. www.jstor.org/.

2. Article in published collections

Clark, Christopher. "The Consequences of the Market Revolution in the American North." In *The Market Revolution in America: Social, Political and Religious Expressions, 1800–1880*, ed. Melvyn Stokes and Stephen Conway, 23–42. Charlottesville: University Press of Virginia, 1996.

3. Article in popular magazine (author named)

Huie, William Bradford. "The Shocking Story of Approved Killing in Mississippi." *Look*, 24 January 1956, 46–50.

4. Article in popular magazine (author unnamed)

"Making the Black Sox White Again." *Literary Digest*, 20 August 1921, 13–14.

5. Article in newspaper

When more than one article is used from a newspaper, indicate the name of the newspaper and the range of dates of the articles used in the paper.

> *Eastern Argus* (Portland, ME). 14 March 1820–28 March 1820.
> *New York Times*. February 1917–April 1918.
> *Washington Post*. June 1972.

Government Publications

1. Presidential papers

Public Papers of the Presidents of the United States: Dwight D. Eisenhower, 1960–61. Washington, D.C.: Government Printing Office, 1961.

2. Testimony before a congressional committee

U.S. Congress. Senate. Subcommittee on Unemployment Relief. "Statement of Miss Dorothy Kahn." *Hearings before the Senate Subcommittee on Unemployment Relief, Senate Committee on Manufacturers.* 72nd Cong., 1st sess., 28 December 1931.

3. Congressional committee report

U.S. Congress. *Report of the Joint Committee on Reconstruction.* 39th Cong., 1st sess. Washington, D.C.: Government Printing Office, 1866.

4. Congressional debates

U.S. Congress. Senate. Albert J. Beveridge, "Policy Regarding the Philippines." 56th Cong., 1st sess. *Congressional Record*, 9 January 1900.

5. Supreme Court

Brown v. Board of Education of Topeka, Kansas. 347 U.S. 483 (1954).

6. Other

United Kingdom. Public Record Office. "Marc Antonio Giustinian, Venetian Ambassador in France, to Doge and Senate," 12 October 1666. *Calendar of State Papers and Manuscript, Relating to English Affairs, Existing in the Archives and Collections in Venice, and in Other Libraries of Northern Italy 1202–[1675].* London: Longman, Green, Longman, Roberts, and Green, 1864.

Electronic Sources

1. Website

If only one citation from a website or digital archive is used, cite as follows:

Spires, Hannah. "Killing: Infanticide, 16 January 1751." *The Proceedings of the Old Bailey* Ref.: t17510116-52. http://www.oldbaileyonline.org/ (accessed 15 September 2011).

If more than one document is used from a website, then indicate the collection as follows:

The Thomas Jefferson Papers, Series 1, General Correspondence, 1651–1827. http://memory.loc.gov/ammem/collections/jefferson_papers/ (accessed 10 October 2011).

2. Email message

Roth, Michael to John Smith. "Re: A Note on Polish Immigrant Sources," 22 February 2003, personal email.

3. Listserv or newsgroup message

VanderMeer, Phil. "Re: WWI Era Harassment of Germans," 12 February 2003, http://www2.h-net.msu.edu/~shgape/ (accessed 5 May 2010).

Other Sources
1. Unpublished dissertation or thesis

Bloom, David G. "Divergent Paths: John L. Lewis, Walter Reuther and World War II." MA thesis, James Madison University, 1996.

Seth, Michael Joseph. "Education, State and Society in South Korea, 1948–1960." PhD diss., University of Hawai'i, 1994.

Seth, Michael Joseph. "Education, State and Society in South Korea, 1948–1960." PhD diss., University of Hawai'i, 1994. In Proquest Dissertations and Theses, http://search.proquest.com/docview/304102767/fulltextPDF/13186D196F43894E25B/27?accountid=11667 (accessed 12 September 2011).

2. Manuscript collection

Lexington, Virginia. George C. Marshall Library. Henry L. Stimson Diaries.

Portland, Maine. Maine Historical Society. Reuel Williams Papers.

3. Video

Cold War, 23: The Wall Comes Down, 1989. Produced by Sir Jeremy Isaacs and Pat Mitchell. 47 min. Turner Original Productions, 1998. Videocassette.

4. Interview

McPherson, James. "Fresh Air from WHYY." Interview by Terry Gross (National Public Radio, 22 June 2004). http://www.npr.org/ (accessed 10 June 2010).

5. Interview by author of paper

Baugh, John. Interview by author, 15 October 2004. Tape recording. In author's possession.

Annotated Bibliography

The annotated bibliography is far more valuable to the audience than a simple list of sources consulted because it includes a brief commentary about each source. The typical annotation is usually no more than three lines of text, though some variations in length are acceptable. Drawing upon the notes and answers to the "guiding points" questions that were placed within the ongoing computer file bibliography, annotations to the sources can be developed readily. The organization of an annotated bibliography is the same as the standard bibliography, with primary sources listed in alphabetical order first, then secondary sources listed in alphabetical order.

Student Paul McDowell's annotated bibliography illustrates the usefulness of this bibliographic form. His annotations are brief but descriptive. The audience gains a sense of the varieties of historical interpretations and the nature of the primary evidence used. Paul McDowell's annotated bibliography appears at the end of his paper located in Appendix B.

Bibliographical Essay

The bibliographical essay is presented in essay format with a narrative flow. It contains a brief review of the primary and secondary sources used to write the paper. The organization and style for entries are different from the standard and annotated bibliographies. While primary sources are still addressed first in the bibliographic essay, the traditional alphabetical organization is dropped. The author of the bibliographic essay decides how to organize the material. Some approaches include grouping sources around particular topics, themes, issues, personalities, or interpretations. A brief commentary about the sources is an essential component of the essay. Like the annotated bibliography, it is useful to draw upon the notes and answers to the "guiding point" questions that were developed during the research process. Because of the essay format, the bibliographic entry takes a form similar to a footnote. A typical bibliographic essay entry for a monograph or bibliography uses a different format from other bibliographic forms. It should contain the following information:

- Author's name, generally first name, middle initial, last name, followed by a comma.

- Full title of the book in italics. No punctuation after the title.

- Publication information enclosed within parentheses: city of publication, followed by a colon (:); name of the publisher, followed by a comma; and year of publication.

Below is student Paul McDowell's bibliographic essay, which conforms to the appropriate style of such an exercise.

Bibliographic Essay

While the 1891 lynching of eleven Sicilians in New Orleans was a controversial and sensational event for its time, it attracted nominal scholarly attention until the late twentieth century. Fortunately, the number of historical surveys and analyses of the event has risen during the past few decades, although primary sources on the topic outnumber secondary sources by a substantial margin. The most detailed primary source is the "Correspondence in Relation to the Killing of Prisoners in New Orleans on March 14, 1891," in the Harvard University Virtual Collections, http://pds.lib.harvard.edu/pds/view/4987805, which includes all written communication between local, state, national, and international officials within the United States and Italy regarding the events immediately prior to, during, and following the Hennessy trial and subsequent lynching.

Many newspapers recounted the events of the lynching, but the most thorough reports came from *Harper's Weekly* and the various New Orleans papers, especially the *New Orleans Daily Picayune*. For some reasonably unbiased reactions and somewhat critical repots, consult the *New York Times, San Jose Mercury News, Houston Post, Daily Register* (Mobile, AL), and *Charlotte News*. A few newspapers that illustrate the South's positive support of the lynching include the *Dallas Morning News, Knoxville Journal*, and *Macon Weekly Telegraph*, while newspapers that demonstrate the North's cloaked support of the lynching include the *Baltimore Sun, Chicago Inter Ocean, Frank Leslie's Illustrated Newspaper, New Haven Register, The Illustrated American, Philadelphia Enquirer*, and *Washington Post*. For a variety of Western perspectives, consult the *Idaho Statesman* (Boise), *San Francisco Bulletin*, and *Tacoma Daily News*.

U.S. Bureau of the Census, *Population of the United States in 1860: Compiled from the Original Returns of the Eighth Census under the Direction of the Secretary of the Interior* (Washington, D.C.: Government Printing Office, 1861) provides a fair guess of the numbers of Italian immigrants in 1860. Census takers of the nineteenth century, however, were certainly not immune to many mistakes and errors regarding someone's racial profile or ethnic heritage. Furthermore, many immigrants may have been skipped over or simply not reported in the census. The same can be said for the 1880 census, provided by U.S. Bureau of the Census, *Statistics of the Population of the United States at the Tenth Census* (Washington, D.C.: Government Printing Office, 1883), and the 1900 census, U.S. Bureau of the Census, *Twelfth Consensus of the United States Taken in the Year 1900* (Washington, D.C.: Government Printing Office, 1901). Unfortunately, a fire in 1921 destroyed most of the 1890 census, and virtually no data remains from that report.

Apart from primary sources, some secondary works contain a wealth of information regarding the subject. For the first and arguably most thorough monograph regarding the subject, consult Richard Gambino, *Vendetta: A True Story of the Worst Lynching in America, the Mass Murder of Italian-Americans in New Orleans in 1891, the Vicious Motivations Behind It, and the Tragic Repercussions that Linger to this Day* (Garden City, NY: Doubleday and Co., 1977). Gambino provides some of the best overview and analysis of the 1891 lynching, although the author proves slightly biased towards the Italians. Nevertheless, the work is an excellent presentation of abundant information and contains very detailed comments on the event as a whole. Another excellent monograph, and one of the more recent ones, is Joseph Gentile, *The Innocent Lynched: The Story of Eleven Italians Lynched in New Orleans* (New York: Writer's Showcase Press, 2000). Gentile provides basic descriptions of the events and attempts to present the hard facts without supplying too much analysis, purposely leaving the much of the conclusion up to the reader. A third study is Tom Smith, *The Crescent City Lynchings: The Murder of Chief Hennessy, the New Orleans 'Mafia' Trials, and the Parish Prison Mob* (Guilford, CT: The Lyons Press, 2007), who draws upon nearly all other works concerning the 1891 lynching and provides an incredibly detailed narrative, resulting in a well-written story.

There are far more journal articles on the 1891 lynching than monographs. For general overviews of the sequence of events and immediate consequences, consult Barbara Botein, "The Hennessy Case: An Episode of Anti-Italian Nativism," *Louisiana History* 20, no. 3 (1979): 261–279, and Humber S. Nelli, "The Hennessy Murder and the Mafia in New Orleans," *Italian Quarterly* 19, no. 75 (1975): 77–95. Botein focuses on how the anti-Italian sentiments in New Orleans led to the accusation of Italian suspects, the trial of the nine Italians, and their ultimate deaths, while Nelli emphasizes the actual ambush and possibility of the Mafia's involvement rather than the actual court case and subsequent lynching. Alexander J. Karlin, "New Orleans Lynchings of 1891 and the American Press," *Louisiana Historical Quarterly* 24, no. 1 (January 1941): 187–204, also gives an overview, focusing especially on the press's reaction to the lynching in 1891. Finally, Clive Webb, "The Lynching of Sicilian Immigrants in the American South, 1886–1910," *American Nineteenth Century History* 3, no. 1 (Spring 2002): 45–77 describes and explains a multitude of violent acts committed against Sicilians in the South around the turn of the twentieth century, including, but not limited to, the 1891 lynching in New Orleans.

For works on other subtopics within this paper, such as American nativism, see John Higham, *Strangers in the Land: Patterns of American Nativism, 1860–1925* (New Brunswick: Rutgers University Press, 1955). He provides a detailed analysis about the constant anti-immigrant sentiments that plagued the United States around the turn of the twentieth century and provides examples of nativism exhibited against many different ethnicities. Desmond Humphrey Joseph, *The APA Movement* (New York: Arno Press, 1969) also provides an excellent monograph regarding American nativism, specifically concerning the American Protective Association.

For works concerning New Orleans during the nineteenth century, Joy Jackson remains the best scholar on the subject. Joy J. Jackson, "Crime and Conscience of a City," *Louisiana History* 24, no. 4 (Summer 1968): 229–244, focuses on the underground world in New Orleans during the turn of the twentieth century, including the alleged existence of the Mafia, the infamous Committee of Fifty, and the 1890 Hennessy trial and following lynching. An even better work on greater New Orleans during that time period by Joy Jackson, *New Orleans in the Gilded Age: Politics and Urban*

Progress, 1880–1896 (Baton Rouge: Louisiana State University Press, 1969), analyzes New Orleans just before the twentieth century, focusing more on the political and social world than the 1891 tragedy.

Studies of Italian immigration are numerous, but some of the best works include Patrick J. Gallo, *Old Bread, New Wine: A Portrait of the Italian Americans* (Chicago: Nelson, Hall, 1981), which provides a general overview of the Italian American experience and criticizes much of the American response to Italian immigration, especially around the turn of the twentieth century. Luciano J. Iorizzo and Salvatore Mondello, *The Italian Americans* (Boston: Twayne Publishers, 1980), also offers a very broad overview of Italian Americans and their experiences and lifestyles since coming to the United States. Alexander DeConde, *Half Bitter, Half Sweet: An Excursion into Italian-American History* (New York: Scribner, 1971), gives a well-developed introduction to the overall Italian American experiences during the height of Italian immigration as well, highlighting both the positive and negative effects of the mass migration to the United States. Edwin Fenton, *Immigrants and Unions, a Case Study: Italians and American Labor, 1870–1920* (New Brunswick: Rutgers University Press, 1988), examines Italian immigrants and their larger roles in American labor around the turn of the twentieth century. And finally, for a general overview of immigration and ethnic tensions in American history, consult John D. Buekner and Lorman A. Ratner, *Multiculturalism in the United States: A Comparative Guide to Acculturation and Ethnicity* (New York: Greenwood Press, 2005). This dense work provides general background to immigration and its effects on the United States, encompassing the country's entire ethnic history into one massive study.

HISTORIOGRAPHIC ESSAY

By definition, **historiography** is the study of how historians interpreted a particular topic and the ways in which their work may be characterized. It is not the study of the actual events or personalities; rather, it examines the secondary studies of various scholars. The historiographic essay differs from the bibliographical essay in one essential way: it reviews only secondary sources.

The essay begins with an introduction that sets the context and outlines the major issues, interpretations, or other patterns that will be used to explain the works of those scholars whose works will be discussed. One method is to approach the topic chronologically, beginning with those scholars who first studied the topic, then considering in a systematic way how and why interpretations changed over time. In some cases, new primary source materials came to light, causing a reinterpretation. In others, historians began asking different questions of the same or similar evidence.

The historiographic essay groups major and lesser historians according to their approaches, methods, or types of conclusions. It seeks to explain how historians once viewed a topic and why interpretations have changed. Thus, it must describe each work and analyze its place along a continuum. What does each work contribute to the subject? What new interpretations or fresh examination of evidence is offered? How does each use evidence? What kinds of evidence does each rely upon? It may also seek to place the works of particular historians in specific categories or schools: Marxist, Annales, or postmodern, for example.

To modify Paul McDowell's essay into a historiographic one, it would be necessary to revise the introduction, eliminate the primary source references, and regroup the discussion of secondary sources either chronologically or topically. Greater emphasis would be placed upon a critical analysis of each book and article with the author explaining the various interpretations and schools as well as the uses of evidence.

FINAL CHECKLIST

Once the scholarly apparatus is complete and proofread for accuracy, beginning researchers examine the entire paper one final time to make absolutely certain they have satisfied all the criteria necessary to produce the desired best effort. A comprehensive checklist recording each component helps beginning researchers make certain they have completed each part. It is also helpful to have a peer read the final paper critically. The checklist may seem pedestrian, but it is a significant step in the successful paper writing process. It may be adapted to suit individual needs; however, it does illustrate important aspects that are often ignored.

Proofread!

While it is enticing to rely on the automatic spelling and grammar functions of most word processing programs, it is far better to reread the finished paper aloud and slowly to yourself. The ear will often pick up awkward constructions the eye may miss. It is also a good idea to have a peer read the paper. If a peer does not understand a point or a paragraph, the point or paragraph should be made clearer.

Be sure to proofread more than once. Does the introductory paragraph provide some historical context? Is there a clear statement on the historical argument? Is this argument evident throughout the paper? Does the evidence support the argument? Does the paper have a conclusion? How well organized is the paper? How well does the paper make transitions between points? In some instances, inserting a brief title for a subsection of the paper can assist in bridging challenging transitions from one portion of the paper to another.

Is the Paper Grammatically Correct?

Many software programs contain both spelling and grammar functions that can assist the beginning researcher in the proofreading process. It is also prudent to consult a grammar guide. Historians should consult these throughout the writing and proofreading process. British English spellings in sources (*labour*, for instance) will be changed in most spellcheck programs. In quoted material, if an electronic program modifies the spelling or grammar, the result will be an error.

Are the Arguments Clear and Supported by Solid Evidence?

By this point in the process, the beginning researcher has read and reviewed the historical arguments several times; there may be a temptation to read through the points in haste. It is important to read closely and check each argument against the specific evidence used to support it. Has anything that would strengthen the case been left out? Is there other evidence that might help clarify the case?

Are the Correct Elements on the Title Page?

A title page should be the first page of the paper. A page number should not appear on this page. The title page should include your name, title of the paper, and date. If the research is being prepared as part of a course assignment, include the semester of the course, course name and number, and instructor's name. See Appendix B for an example.

Number the Pages

Number the pages of your paper. Software programs can place page numbers easily in a variety of locations; just be consistent in the location.

Is an Appendix Needed?

Does the paper need an appendix for materials that add to the paper but cannot be included, such as images, maps, or lengthy documents? Especially in the digital age of cutting and pasting, such appendices may be more helpful.

Check the Footnotes or Endnotes

Footnotes should appear at the bottom of each page; endnotes should appear after the text of the paper. They should be numbered consecutively. Historians follow *Chicago Manual*/Turabian format when documenting materials in a footnote or endnote. Use a short-title footnote or endnote after a full citation.

Check the Bibliography

The bibliography should be divided into two sections—primary sources and secondary sources. If annotated or an essay, the bibliography should include the author's interpretation as well as the usefulness of the work. The bibliography should conform to *Chicago Manual*/Turabian format.

Once the historian has completed the steps outlined in the previous chapters and has reviewed his or her work numerous times, the paper can be submitted to the jury of peers for their consideration, and it will add to the continuing conversation about the historical past.

EXERCISES

Identify each of the following resources used in your paper according to *Chicago Manual*/Turabian format.

1. List the two most useful monographs in the following ways:
   a.   Bibliographic style
   b.   Footnote style and shortened-form footnote
2. List the two most useful scholarly journal articles in the following ways:
   a.   Bibliographic style
   b.   Footnote style and shortened-form footnote
3. List four primary sources in the following ways:
   a.   Bibliographic style
   b.   Footnote style and shortened-form footnote

8

✳

Sharing Scholarship

Scholarship is intended to be shared publically. Professional historians present their initial research findings at academic conferences. Once their peers have reviewed and commented on their preliminary ideas, they then revise their work and submit it to scholarly journals or book publishers, where experts in the field peer review it again and recommend it for publication, return it for revisions, or reject it outright. The process of sharing and critiquing is therefore fundamental to being a professional historian. As students develop their own research and writing skills, it is appropriate that they also gain exposure to the same kinds of scholarly sharing and reviewing for their better work. It is important to recognize that research papers have an audience beyond one's classmates and professor.

Fortunately, there are increasing possibilities for undergraduates to present their best research at conferences intended for beginning historians. Many of these conferences also encourage poster sessions. Some academic departments organize conferences to highlight student work; some colleges and universities, national honor societies, or professional associations sponsor conferences to showcase undergraduate scholarship. In addition, in the digital age, it is increasingly possible for students to share their research on websites or publish in peer-reviewed electronic publications. Students who have successfully followed the research process described in the previous chapters are encouraged to take this final step after their term has ended and their course instructor has evaluated the finished work. This chapter will suggest some of the rewards for student researchers and examine some of the steps involved in the process.

THE SEMINAR ORAL PRESENTATION

The first step in sharing undergraduate scholarship often takes place after several rounds of drafting, editing, and revising, by presenting a polished, but not yet final, version of the research project to an audience of peers. For undergraduate researchers, the presentation frequently occurs in the final weeks of the seminar and is followed by questions. The oral presentation is among the most daunting parts of the drafting and editing process, but it is essential to receive constructive criticism to improve an essay. It can be one of the most rewarding aspects of the entire writing process. It may also encourage students to consider presenting their work to audiences beyond the classroom.

Oral presentations vary little from those delivered in a small, friendly seminar to sessions at a larger professional conference. There are several ideas to keep in mind in preparing the oral presentation for any venue. These are:

- Understand the kind of presentation to be made. Prepare accordingly. Is the purpose simply to offer information about the topic? Is the presentation a persuasive argument that presents only one side of an issue? Is it designed to solicit questions or open a dialogue on the topic?

- Know the audience. How much knowledge and understanding do they have of the topic? This will dictate how much, or how little, historical background to provide. It will also determine how much explanation is needed.

- Know the time limitation for the presentation. Is the presentation to be 10 minutes, 15 minutes, 20 minutes? It takes about 2½ minutes to read one typed, double-spaced page of text or comment on one outline slide. Will the text be read or presented from an outline? Will the presentation make use of visuals or maps? Will presentation software be used? If so, is there a reason for using it? When using such software, make certain to test it before the actual presentation.

- As the topic is introduced, be certain to open with something that makes the audience want to listen. A brief description of a specific event that captures the central tension of the essay is very effective. Can the audience easily discern the thesis or major thrust of the presentation? In the introduction, do voice and demeanor convey confidence and credibility? Will the presentation convey knowledge of the topic?

- How will the presentation be organized? Can the audience follow the argument easily? Is there a clear separation between points? Does the presentation flow naturally from one idea to the next? Are the meaning and purpose of the presentation clear?

- Is there sufficient evidence to support the thesis? Were direct quotations identified and clearly presented? Statistics? Was evidence displayed or circulated in handouts? Were sources referenced, especially the primary evidence?

- Was the topic presented enthusiastically? Could the audience hear clearly? Were varieties of pitch, intonation, and pace of delivery employed to avoid a monotone?

- Were the pronunciation and articulation clear? Avoid vocal distractions such as repetitive use of *you know* or *like*. Avoid visual distractions like running hands through your hair or flipping hair. Use good posture before the audience. Do not slouch or lean upon podium.

- Maintain good visual contact with the audience.

- Reach conclusions. Make certain to return to the main points of the argument. Did the presentation come to closure?

- Presentations should allow time for questions from the audience. What questions were asked? Were there comments or suggestions? All constructive criticism should be taken seriously. Such comments can be used to improve subsequent drafts of the paper.

- When using PowerPoint or some other presentation software, keep the information on each slide brief and do not simply read your slides.

Preparation for an oral presentation is obviously central to its success. Careful attention to each element offers an opportunity to highlight what has been learned and to share personal enthusiasm for the topic with the audience. The same level of preparation and attention to detail will also produce a written paper that reflects the same high standard.

The paper has now evolved from a vague idea scribbled on paper, to a first draft, to a nearly final paper—at all stages aided by the constructive criticism of peers as well as one's own proofreading and editing.

CONSIDERING A CONFERENCE PRESENTATION

When the finished research project is returned at the end of the term, read it over carefully and consider particularly the instructor's comments. Look at those addressing the use of primary evidence, the strength of the analysis, and the overall contribution. The professor's evaluation is the second step in sharing research following the classroom oral presentation. If the comments are largely positive, consider what would be necessary to revise the work for submission to a conference. If additional primary sources are suggested, for example, are they readily accessible? If the comments on the paper relate more to matters of analysis or evidence, organization, writing, or interpretations, can the modifications be made while you are working on the next term's coursework? Finally, are you sufficiently satisfied with the quality of your work to want to share it with an audience beyond your individual course setting? If the answers to these questions are positive, consider submitting a proposal to one of the many student or mixed conferences. It is a wonderful occasion to continue the conversations begun when the topic was first considered. A first step at this point is to schedule a meeting with the faculty member to discuss revisions and seek additional feedback.

Conferences intended primarily for undergraduate students have proliferated over the past two decades as more history programs place emphasis on student research and writing. These conferences exist to encourage students to share their scholarship and to mingle with their peers from other colleges who may share common interests. They offer a nonthreatening, unintimidating environment in which to test ideas and discuss research. They also provide an introduction for beginning scholars into the world of the professional conference. There are many questions to consider when contemplating whether or not to offer a finished work for conference presentation. Student Paul McDowell's thoughts about his own experience anticipate many of them:

> Turning a 20+ page research paper into a 10-minute oral presentation requires a good deal of preparation and practice. Just like the writing process, you have to remember that everything in the oral presentation must revolve around your argument statement. The first step is always the most difficult; figuring out what you *don't* need to include in your presentation. This process becomes especially challenging after you realize that even though you've spent months researching and writing your research paper, a large amount of the information, and usually the most interesting little tidbits or anecdotes you've come across, simply won't fit into a 10-minute presentation. You have to be able to distance yourself from the paper and look at it through objective lenses in order to determine what is *absolutely vital* to the audience's comprehension of your thesis. Remember, everything should revolve around your thesis, so if it doesn't contribute directly to your thesis, it probably isn't worth cramming into a 10-minute oral presentation.

Paul's first observation is fundamental. Can you look critically at your own research paper and decide what is essential for an outside audience and put everything else aside? Can you then identify only those points that directly illuminate the argument and strip away everything else? If your answers are affirmative, Paul offers more sound suggestions about using your original outline (if you wrote from one) or constructing an outline of your paper if you did not. He observes:

> In deciding what to present, it might also help to make an outline (or if you wrote an outline earlier in the research or writing process, try to recover it and look it over again). A proper outline will provide a skeleton of your paper, and this skeleton can help you figure out the bare minimum an outsider needs to know to understand your thesis. An outline will also allow you to remember your main points. Use these main points as checkpoints in your presentation. The first part of your presentation can be about your thesis, and the rest can be organized by your main points, followed ultimately by your conclusion and bibliographic references.

The critical examination of your paper and the construction of a workable outline serve also to simplify the process of preparing a conference proposal and abstract to submit to the conference program committee. Most conferences for undergraduates insist upon a written proposal that identifies the argument of the research, indicates the evidence used to support its claims, and suggests its appropriateness for a potential audience. Some conferences also ask for a supporting letter from the faculty member who evaluated the initial work. Finally, many require an abstract or brief summary statement about the work. Some abstracts are very brief. Phi Alpha Theta, for instance, requests an abstract of twenty-five words or less for its national biennial conference.

In preparing the abstract, follow student Paul McDowell's recommendation concerning the oral presentation. Ask the question, "What does the audience really need to know?" Strip away everything else. If the paper is accepted for presentation, the abstract may be printed in the conference program. There are two online resources to assist undergraduates in drafting successful abstracts: *America: History and Life* and *Historical Abstracts*, published by EBSCO, and *Dissertation & Theses*, published by ProQuest. Both include thousands of illustrative historical abstracts that may be used as guides. Successful abstracts should be clear, brief, and conscious of the potential audience. Here is Paul McDowell's 2009 abstract submitted to MARCUS (Mid-Atlantic Regional Conference of Undergraduate Scholarship) sponsored by Sweet Briar College in Virginia:

Guilty Until Proven Innocent: A New Orleans Tragedy That Swept the Nation

Anti-Italian sentiment in New Orleans reached a new height after beloved Police Chief David Hennessy was suddenly assassinated one foggy October night in 1890. As Hennessy's maimed body was rushed to the hospital, fellow policeman William O'Connor erroneously claimed the Dagoes had slain Hennessy in cold blood. Thirteen Italians were quickly arrested for the crime as anti-Italian fever quickly consumed New Orleans' white citizenry. Matters became worse six months later when the indicted Italians were declared not guilty. Taking justice into their own hands, thousands of New Orleanians charged the Parish Prison and attacked the innocent Italians, murdering eleven in the process. This presentation examines the nationwide reaction to the lynching of the eleven Sicilian immigrants in New Orleans in 1891 through the examination of contemporary newspapers and magazines to identify the scope of anti-Italian sentiment in the United States in the late nineteenth century.

His abstract is sharply focused and relatively free of adjectives. It defines the event and notes the trial, its results, and the reactions to the murders of the eleven Sicilian immigrants. Paul provides insights into his argument and the principal sources he uses to support his claims. He also indicates his own unique contribution.

CHOOSING THE CONFERENCE

With outline and abstract in hand, the student historian tries next to choose the most suitable conference, considering such factors as location and time of year. It must ultimately suit your schedule as a student researcher. Does the conference meeting conflict with your current classes? Is it over a weekend? Will it take place during a holiday? In addition, unless your college or university will help defray the expenses, what are the costs? What is involved in submitting an application? Does the conference require a proposal? A letter of support? An abstract? A copy of the full paper? A resumé?

More substantive than these more mundane considerations, student historians should consider the intellectual reasons for participating. Do you intend to more fully develop the finished paper into an undergraduate thesis? Will you use it as a writing sample for graduate applications? In such instances, strive for those conferences intended primarily for history undergraduates since it is more likely your audience will be more interested and more knowledgeable about your topic. Will the conference participants also include professional historians? Their presence may also yield more useful questions. Discuss potential submissions with faculty mentors or with fellow students who may have presented in past years. Department bulletin boards, websites, or word of mouth from peers who may have presented earlier provide good information about upcoming conferences. Phi Alpha Theta, the national history honor society, holds annual regional conferences and a national meeting every second year. Whether local, regional, or national, these conferences communicate their calls for papers broadly, and many now have webpages. All offer benefits to beginning practitioners and provide an occasion to share your scholarship with others in the best tradition of the academic profession.

CONFERENCE PRESENTATION

When you receive official notice that your paper has been accepted for presentation at a conference, review the same points introduced at the beginning of this chapter about preparing an oral presentation for seminar. Consider your argument and audience and reflect upon the time constraints. Will you have access to a computer and projection system? Will you need to upload your presentation from a flash drive? Will you produce handouts for the audience? If so, how many are likely to be sufficient? What plan do you have if the technology fails? Paul McDowell offers some helpful thoughts as to your final preparations:

> Once you have formulated your presentation through index cards, PowerPoint slides, or the like, it is necessary to practice and time yourself. After your first run-through, your recorded time will tell you whether you have too little information in your presentation or, a more likely scenario, whether you have too much information. Conferences tend to be quite strict on time limits, so if you are more than two minutes over your designated time, you have some serious cutting to do. If you are thirty seconds over your designated time, try crossing out one or two lines from your presentation. Adjust as you see fit, and then time yourself again. Continue to edit your presentation until you are no more than thirty seconds over or no less than one minute under the designated presentation time.

The presentation experience itself can be unnerving, but there are ways to combat some of that anxiety. You will almost certainly be nervous before your presentation, but just remember—so are all of the other presenters. And besides, *you* will know more about your particular topic than anyone else in the room. *You* did all the research, analysis, and writing, so everyone will see *you* as the authority on the subject. When you are in the process of presenting, you also must remember to make a good amount of eye contact, enunciate, and avoid monotony at all costs. *Don't read your paper.* The worst presentations at conferences are the ones where the presenter simply reads his or her research paper like a book. Unless it is written like a Dr. Seuss story or a Mark Twain novel, it will not be enjoyable or useful for the audience to hear you drone on about your project word for word. Be energetic. Add a few subtle jokes or hints of sarcasm if you have to (but don't go overboard). Engage the audience. Smile when you talk. And most importantly, show them how much you care about your topic. People will pay attention to your presentation if they think it is worth paying attention to, so it is in your best interests to captivate your audience as best you can.

Ultimately, the presentation experience is highly rewarding. If your presentation has made a significant impact upon the audience, there will be no shortage of questions after you have finished speaking, and questions are good things for a presenter. They allow you the chance to address things you were not able to in your presentation, clarify certain points, or mention other facts that support your claims. And while it is not quite the same as finishing a road race, going skydiving, or addressing a crowd of thousands at a football stadium, there is a certain "presentation high" after you've finished your talk. You feel as though you have accomplished something. You've just done something that many other people either cannot or will not do at the undergraduate level. A weight has been lifted off your shoulders, and now you can simply sit back, relax, and enjoy the show.

POSTER PRESENTATIONS

A growing number of history and related conferences intended for undergraduate students use poster presentations to complement or replace formal papers or oral presentations. Initially used in the sciences, poster sessions combine texts, graphics, and visuals in a pleasing way to illustrate research conclusions to a large audience over a more extended period of time than what is normally provided during a conference presentation. Poster presentations permit the intended audience to examine work leisurely on the poster board and discuss its findings with the researcher one on one. At some poster sessions, the presenter is asked to deliver a brief presentation periodically during the time allotted to the program.

Poster presentations should always strive for clarity and visual attractiveness. They should illuminate the project's results, its argument, and the evidence in a pleasing manner, as the poster itself is what will attract the audience. Like the oral presentation using presentation software, the writer must keep in mind how best to create a visual effect through words and how to balance text with appropriate visuals for the audience. The visuals (images, charts, graphs, etc.) must complement and enhance the text and should never simply fill empty space.

Work from your finished paper rather than an outline. Consider how much text is sufficient to explain the arguments. How much is too much? What textual elements will draw attention and elicit questions? In recent years, some organizations are also turning to Internet sessions in which the author is invited to post a poster presentation electronically so that interested people can reference it on the web and ask their questions. In preparing for any poster session format, consider the venue and be certain to have handouts that focus on key elements for the audience.

Whether your presentation is in the form of a formal session, a poster session, or is offered online, successful researchers should pay close attention to the observations offered by the audience. Jot down as many questions and comments as possible for your subsequent review and consideration. Pay particular attention to those observations that raise questions about the clarity of the argument, the use of evidence, the need for more or different examples, and the overall organization or presentation. Such information is critical to sharing historical research and contemplating the next level in the research process: seeking publication.

PUBLISHING THE PAPER

The ultimate in sharing historical research is publishing your paper. Few are able to achieve publication, and the competition to succeed is stiff; however, the rewards for trying more than justify the energy expended. Publication opens your research to a potentially global audience, and it is enduring. If your work is accepted and published, it exists forever. Opportunities for undergraduates to have their work reviewed for possible publication have increased significantly. Online undergraduate research journals, either sponsored by individual history departments for their own undergraduates or those open to submissions to all undergraduates, now abound.

If you plan to submit a paper for publication, you should first review carefully the comments received at the conference. You need not include all of the suggestions from the conference; some may not be especially useful. But many of the suggestions for additional research or refining your argument may be essential to an improved paper. After making revisions, you should consult with the professor who directed your work and seek a frank assessment. If the professor recommends additional revisions before submitting the paper, take them seriously and work diligently to make them. Engage in conversations with faculty and fellow students as you revise to encourage as much critical input as possible. Consider also any specific requirements imposed by the journal publishers and adhere to them closely. Find out what is required for submission in addition to the article itself. Is research submitted electronically or in hard copy? What materials should accompany it? Some undergraduate publications ask for verification from a faculty member indicating when the research was completed. Is a resumé required? If it is, refer to the guidelines outlined in Chapter 6. What is the expected time between submission and notification?

CONCLUSION

Once the research paper has been read and edited a final time and has been submitted, you must wait for a response from the journal. Often, you will be asked to make additional revisions before it is ready for press. At this point, the research project outlined throughout the text is concluded. The student historian has successfully defined a topic, conducted a thorough research trail, read and evaluated secondary and primary sources, written and revised the argument into a finished paper, and perhaps presented or submitted a final version to a conference or journal. The process has been intense, but the sense of personal achievement and satisfaction is exhilarating.

EXERCISES

1. Search for undergraduate conferences scheduled in the coming year, and consider applying to present.
2. Prepare an abstract to be submitted to a conference. Be prepared to explain what you have included and what you have left out.
3. Organize a poster session based upon your research paper. Be prepared to explain what you have included and what you have left out.

✳

Conclusion: The Continuing Conversation

When a piece of original research is completed, there is a sense of genuine accomplishment. The research, interpretation, and writing processes, which combined imagination and creativity with rigorous discipline, leave the researcher satisfied and likely exhausted. All of the relevant primary and secondary sources have been located and analyzed. The evidence has been used to develop a series of explanations and arguments that have added to the knowledge and appreciation of an aspect of the past. Those who read or hear the study and examine the sources critically can readily trace the structure and outline of the research, verifying the reliability of the findings.

Chapter 1 introduced the question "What is history?" and provided the tools necessary to practice it. It presented an overview of historical interpretations and approaches used by historians to study the past. By understanding these various approaches, historians better appreciate their own perspectives and theoretical foundations. In the process of studying the past, researchers add their own scholarship to the totality of historical knowledge. They have become part of an ongoing conversation about the discipline.

The second chapter presented a systematic framework for conducting historical research. The research trail offered an exhaustive approach to collecting all relevant potential sources found in standard reference works and online databases. The trail also identified specific reference works that are essential to researching any topic successfully. Following this process fully, researchers can be confident that they have found all pertinent primary and secondary evidence and are prepared to begin a thorough analysis of that evidence.

Chapters 3 and 4 discussed the interpretation and analysis of secondary and primary sources. Chapter 3 explored the steps involved in understanding historical context, historiographical interpretations, and methodological approaches. By critically reading these works, researchers learn the importance of context, that historical interpretations may change over time, and that there are various ways to interpret similar evidence. Knowledge of secondary sources enables the researcher to better engage the essence of history—primary sources. Chapter 4 examined primary sources and illustrated the ways historians evaluate them. The interpretation of secondary and especially—primary evidence provides the flesh and bones of historical analysis.

The fifth, sixth, and seventh chapters explored the writing processes, finishing the paper, and appropriate attribution of evidence. The writing chapters discussed shorter writing assignments and placed particular emphasis on the importance of drafting, proofreading, peer reviewing, editing and revising, presenting orally, and ultimately producing a written essay. They also offered instruction in grant writing and job applications. The seventh chapter described how and why historians cite evidence and offered numerous examples of how to acknowledge sources for notes and bibliographic purposes. The final chapter explored ways for researchers to extend dialogues begun in classes or seminars beyond their own campuses as they share their research with other historians.

Observing the suggestions made in the preceding chapters can transform beginning researchers into apprentice historians. The completion of the paper does not end the process; rather, it begins the next stage in an ongoing conversation about the past. It may lead to additional questions or approaches to the topic as outlined in Chapters 6 and 8. If others choose to do so, they can be guided by the work to build on or modify its conclusions. The research is a part of a continuing dialogue with other historians about the past; at this point the beginning researcher has now crossed a threshold to become an apprentice historian. Not all will continue along this path; however, learning to research, analyze, read critically, organize thoughtfully, and write effectively has benefits for citizens as well as scholars.

Appendix A

✳

A Reference Librarian's Guide to Historical Reference Works

COMPILED BY PATRICIA HARDESTY, JAMES MADISON UNIVERSITY

TABLE OF CONTENTS

FOCUS ON SECONDARY SOURCES

Guides to Reference Sources

General

[1] *ARBA Online (American Reference Books Annual)*. Westport, CT: Libraries Unlimited. 1997 to present.
(Online Library Subscription Database).
Comparable to, and in some ways superior to, the online source, *Guide to Reference* [2]. It provides better searching and browsing pathways; however, it only covers works published since 1997.

[2] *Guide to Reference*. Chicago: American Library Association. Continuously updated.
(Online Library Subscription Database).
The successor to Balay's 1996 print title, *Guide to Reference Books* [3], this online work contains over 16,000 entries describing reference sources in all formats (print or online, subscription or free). Covers all disciplines. Annotated.

[3] *Guide to Reference Books*. Edited by Robert Balay. 11th ed. Chicago: American Library Association, 1996.
(Reserves Z 1035.1 G89 1996).
The last printed edition of a classic source for locating reference books in any discipline. Emphasizes scholarly works published in the United States. The outline arrangement is finely subdivided, giving it advantages over the online *Guide* [2]. Annotated.

[4] *Reference Sources in History: An Introductory Guide*. Edited by Ronald H. Fritze, Brian E. Coutts, and Louis A. Vyhnanek. 2nd ed. Santa Barbara, CA: ABC-CLIO, 2004.
(Ready Ref D 20 F75 2004 and online).
The standard guide to history research, with comprehensive coverage of geographic areas and time periods. International in scope. Excellent annotations supplement the 930 entries, which are arranged by type of resource.

Ancient and Medieval

[5] Jenkins, Fred W. *Classical Studies: A Guide to the Reference Literature*. 2nd ed. Westport, CT: Libraries Unlimited, 2006.
(Ref PA 91 J4 2006).
Although created for the student of classical languages, this guide has useful chapters for the history student, including Primary Sources in Translation, Greek and Roman History, and Geographical Works.

North America

[6] Perrault, Anna H., and Ron Blazek. *United States History: A Multicultural, Interdisciplinary Guide to Information Sources*. Westport, CT: Libraries Unlimited, 2003.
(Ref E 178 P45 2003).
An excellent guide for American history, this updates and expands on Blazek's 1994 work, *United States History: A Selective Guide to Information Sources*. There is heavy emphasis on social, cultural, and intellectual history in this edition. Usefully annotated.

[7] Prucha, Francis P. *Handbook for Research in American History: A Guide to Bibliographies and Other Reference Works*. 2nd ed., rev. Lincoln: University of Nebraska Press, 1994.
(Ref E 178 P782 1994).
A major guide to American history research. Twenty topical chapters begin with introductions to categories such as guides to newspapers, documents of the federal government, picture sources, and oral history materials. Bibliographies, with some annotations, complete each chapter.

[8] Slavens, Thomas P. *Sources of Information for Historical Research*. New York: Neal Schuman, 1994.
(Ref D 20 S42 1994).
Over 1,100 detailed annotated entries are contained in this bibliography. Arrangement is by Library of Congress call number. The scope of this work is international. An excellent source for key books used in historical research.

Historical Encyclopedias and Dictionaries

In the early stages of researching a topic, the background information contained in encyclopedias and dictionaries is useful both to aid in identifying a topic of interest and in placing an event or topic in context. In addition, entries in these books often give lists of books and articles for further reading in a section entitled *Suggested Reading, Further Reading, Sources*, or simply *Bibliography*.

World and General History

[9] *Berkshire Encyclopedia of World History*. Edited by William H. McNeill. Great Barrington, MA: Berkshire Pub. Group, 2005. 5 vols.
(Ref D 23 B45 2005).
A scholarly work with the particular perspective of the interactions of people and events. Special emphasis on theoretical concepts. Bibliographies end the entries.

[10] *Blackwell Reference Online.* Hoboken, NJ: Wiley–Blackwell.
(Online Library Subscription Database).
The Blackwell Companions series covers a wide variety of historical subjects. In each volume, the chapters are written by scholars, often have historiographical content, and are followed by good bibliographies. The Companions are particularly strong in U.S. and British history but are wide-ranging, including *A Companion to the History of the Middle East, A Companion to Japanese History,* and *A Companion to Latin American History.* Libraries may subscribe to individual titles or bundles of titles and/or may own the Companions in print.

[11] *Encyclopedia of World Environmental History.* Edited by Shepard Krech, III, J. R. McNeill, and Carolyn Merchant. New York: Routledge, 2004. 3 vols.
(Ref GF 10 E63 2004).
Entries on the expected and the unusual, from acid rain to Protestantism to zoos. Each entry has a bibliography.

[12] *Encyclopedia of World History: Ancient, Medieval, and Modern, Chronologically Arranged.* Edited by Peter N. Stearns. 6th ed. Boston: Houghton Mifflin Company, 2001.
(Ref D 21 E578 2001).
A completely revised edition of William L. Langer's masterful encyclopedia of the same title, this one volume covers an amazing mass of material in a readable manner. The new edition covers all time periods and geographic areas, with an emphasis on social and cultural history. Arranged chronologically, it includes lists of rulers and a rich index but no bibliographies.

Ancient and Medieval

[13] *Brill's New Pauly: Encyclopaedia of the Ancient World: Antiquity.* Edited by Hubert Canick and Helmut Schneider. Leiden, The Netherlands: Brill, 2002–2010. 16 vols.
(Ref DE5 .N4813 2002).
English translation of the masterful German work, *Der Neue Pauly: Enzyklopädie der Antike,* indispensable for study of the classical world. Coverage of Greco-Roman antiquity, from the second millennium BCE to the early medieval period. Excellent bibliographies and extensive references to primary sources.

[14] *Dictionary of the Middle Ages.* Edited by Joseph R. Strayer. New York: Scribner, 1982–1989. 13 vols.
(Ref D 114 D5 1982).
The standard English-language encyclopedia on the Middle Ages. Signed articles with bibliographies.

[15] *The Oxford Classical Dictionary.* Edited by Simon Hornblower and Anthony Spawforth. Oxford, England: Oxford University Press, 2003.
(Ref DE 5 O9 2003).
The best one-volume dictionary on all aspects of the classical world. Signed articles with bibliographies.

[16] *The Oxford Dictionary of Byzantium.* Edited by Alexander P. Kazhdan. Oxford, England: Oxford University Press, 1991. 3 vols.

(Ref DF 521 .O93 1991 and online).

The best English-language encyclopedia on the Byzantine Empire. A survey of the Byzantine world, with entries often covering unexpected topics (e.g., blood, crown, beverages). Short bibliographies.

Europe (Early Modern to Present)

[17] *Encyclopedia of Eastern Europe from the Congress of Vienna to the Fall of Communism.* Edited by Richard Frucht. New York: Garland, 2000.

(Ref DJK 6 E53 2000).

There are seven lengthy articles on the countries of Poland, Hungary, Czechoslovakia, Albania, Bulgaria, Romania, and Yugoslavia. Shorter articles cover individuals, culture, geography, and trends. Bibliographies emphasize English-language works.

[18] *Encyclopedia of Russian History.* Edited by James R. Millar. New York: Macmillan Reference USA, 2004. 4 vols.

(Ref DK 14 E53 2004 and online).

Covering all aspects of Russian history and created for undergraduates, this scholarly work covers the last 1,000 years of Russian history. Bibliographies focus on works in English. Illustrated, with an helpful index.

[19] *Encyclopedia of the Holocaust.* Edited by Israel Gutman. New York: Macmillan, 1990. 4 vols.

(Ref D 804.3 .E53 1990).

Detailed treatment of the Holocaust, with excellent bibliographies that emphasize English-language publications. At end of vol. 4, glossary, chronology, tables, and index.

[20] *Encyclopedia of the Renaissance.* Edited by Paul F. Grendler. New York: Scribner's, 1999. 6 vols.

(Ref CB 361 E52 1999).

Published in association with the Renaissance Society of America, the scholarly, illustrated work covers the beginnings of the Renaissance in fourteenth-century Italy and its spread throughout Europe into the early seventeenth century. Signed entries by scholars with excellent bibliographies, containing both secondary and primary sources.

[21] *Europe 1450 to 1789: Encyclopedia of the Early Modern World.* Edited by Jonathan Dewald. New York: Scribner's, 2004. 6 vols.

(Ref D 209 .E97 2004 and online).

Important recent work. Chronology in vol. 1. Richly illustrated, with bibliographies and extensive index.

[22] *Europe Since 1945: An Encyclopedia.* Edited by Bernard Cook. New York: Garland, 2001. 2 vols.

(Ref D 1051 E873 2001).

Although arranged alphabetically, there is a subject guide at the front of vol. 1 as well as a chronology of political events. Scholarly, signed articles, but rather brief bibliographies.

[23] *Historical Dictionaries of French History*. Series published by Greenwood Press. (Various call numbers).

The books in this series are similarly organized. Signed articles, in alphabetical order, contain brief bibliographies. A chronology and index are at the back. Here are two representative titles:

Historical Dictionary of Napoleonic France, 1799–1815. Edited by Owen Connelly. Westport, CT: Greenwood Press, 1985.
(Ref DC 201 .H673 1985).

Historical Dictionary of France from the 1815 Restoration to the Second Empire. Edited by Edgar Leon Newman. New York: Greenwood Press, 1987. 2 vols.
(Ref DC 256 .H57 1987).

[24] *Historical Dictionary of Modern Spain, 1700–1988*. Edited by Robert W. Kern. New York: Greenwood Press, 1990.
(Ref DP 192 H57 1990).
Scholarly articles with bibliographies. At the end of the volume, a substantial chronology and bibliography.

[25] *World War II in Europe*. Edited by David T. Zabecki. New York: Garland, 1999. 2 vols.
(Ref D 740 .W67 1999).
Although confusing in organization, this is an excellent encyclopedia with a good index. Illustrated, with many maps and tables. The articles have up-to-date bibliographies of English-language works.

North America

[26] *The American Counties: Origins of County Names, Dates of Creation and Population Data*. Edited by Joseph Nathan Kane. 5th ed. Lanham, MD: Scarecrow Press, 2005.
(Ref E 180 K3 2005).

[27] *Dictionary of American History*. Edited by Stanley I. Kutler. 3rd ed. New York: Scribner's, 2003. 10 vols.
(Ref E 174 D52 2003).
The standard scholarly dictionary in American history. Reflecting recent historiographical trends, the new edition emphasizes social and cultural history. Long articles with illustrations and brief bibliographies. Vol. 9 contains a series of historical maps with commentary and a selection of primary source documents. Comprehensive index.

[28] *Encyclopedia of American Cultural and Intellectual History*. Edited by Mary Kupiec Cayton and Peter W. Williams. New York: Charles Scribner's Sons, 2001. 3 vols.
(Ref E 169.1 E624 2001).
A scholarly encyclopedia with signed articles and bibliographies. Arranged chronologically.

[29] *Encyclopedia of American Foreign Policy*. Edited by Alexander DeConde, Richard Dean Burns, and Fredrick Logevall. New York: Charles Scribner's Sons, 2002. 3 vols.

(Ref E183.7 E52 2002).

The lengthy articles have bibliographical essays. Comprehensive index.

[30] *Encyclopedia of American Political History: Studies of the Principal Movements and Ideas.* Edited by Jack Greene. New York: Scribner, 1984. 3 vols.
(Ref E 183 E5 1984).
About ninety topics are covered in this scholarly work. The lengthy, signed essays contain bibliographies. Useful for an understanding of basic themes and movements in American political history.

[31] *Encyclopedia of American Social History.* Edited by Mary Kupiec Cayton, Elliott J. Gorn, and Peter W. Williams. New York: Scribner, 1993. 4 vols.
(Stacks HN 57 E58 1993).
The major reference source on American social history, this encyclopedia has signed articles with bibliographies. About 180 lengthy essays. Comprehensive index.

[32] *The Encyclopedia of Southern History.* Edited by David C. Roller and Robert W. Twyman. Baton Rouge: Louisiana State University Press, 1979.
(Ref F 207.7 E52).
An outstanding collection of articles that includes biographical sketches, maps, and statistical tables. Brief bibliographies.

[33] *Encyclopedia of the American Civil War: A Political, Social, and Military History.* Edited by David S. Heidler and Jeanne T. Heidler. Santa Barbara, CA: ABC-CLIO, 2000. 5 vols.
(Ref E 468 H47 2000 and online).
An outstanding recent encyclopedia of the Civil War. Signed articles with suggestions for further reading. In vol. 5 is an extensive index, bibliography, and numerous primary documents. See also *Encyclopedia of the Confederacy* [35].

[34] *Encyclopedia of the American Presidency.* Edited by Leonard W. Levy and Louis Fisher. New York: Simon & Schuster, 1994. 4 vols.
(Ref JK 511 E53 1994).
Includes signed articles on individuals, themes, Congressional topics, and laws. Appendices include tables on the presidents with sections on personal information, cabinet and other officials, election statistics, and an index to legal cases.

[35] *Encyclopedia of the Confederacy.* Edited by Richard N. Current. New York: Simon & Schuster, 1993. 4 vols.
(Ref E 487 E55 1993).
Comprehensive coverage of the Confederacy is provided in this encyclopedia. Individuals, battles, and topics are included. Signed articles by leading scholars with bibliographies. Illustrated.

[36] *Encyclopedia of the Great Depression and the New Deal.* Edited by James Ciment. Armonk, NY: Sharpe Reference, 2001. 2 vols.
(Ref E 806 C543 2001).
Entries include thematic essays and entries on government topics, international affairs, biographies, and document texts. Bibliographies provided.

[37] *Encyclopedia of the North American Colonies*. Edited by Jacob Ernest Cooke. New York: Charles Scribner's Sons, 1993. 3 vols.

(Ref E 45 E53 1993).

The standard scholarly encyclopedia on all colonies in North America. Arranged by topic, the entries include bibliographies. A chronology is printed in vol. 1. Comprehensive index.

[38] *Encyclopedia of the United States in the Nineteenth Century*. Edited by Paul Finkelman. New York: Charles Scribner's Sons, 2001. 3 vols.

(Ref E 169.1 E626 2001).

A scholarly encyclopedia with bibliographies, alphabetically arranged.

[39] *Encyclopedia of U.S. Foreign Relations*. Edited by Bruce W. Jentleson and Thomas G. Paterson. New York: Oxford University, 1997. 4 vols.

(Ref E 183.7 E53 1997).

Scholarly encyclopedia. Vol. 4 has a chronology of foreign relations activity from 1754 to 1996, statistical tables, and a bibliography of reference works.

[40] Kammen, Carol, and Norma Prendergast. *Encyclopedia of Local History*. Walnut Creek, CA: AltaMira Press, 2000.

(Ref E 180 K25 2000).

Some bibliographies, websites, and organizations' contact information are provided. Appendices have information on ethnic groups, religious groups, state historical organizations, and National Archives facilities.

Selected Regions and Themes

[41] *Africana: The Encyclopedia of the African and African American Experience*. Edited by Kwame Anthony Appiah and Henry Louis Gates, Jr. 2nd ed. Oxford, England: Oxford University Press, 2005. 5 vols.

(Ready Ref DT 14 A37435 2005).

Unusual in scope: covers Africa and the Americas. The topical outline and the index in vol. 5 are helpful aids in finding pertinent entries. Unfortunately, only selected entries have bibliographies; broad topical bibliographies are in vol. 5.

[42] *Encyclopaedia Judaica*. Edited by Fred Skolnik. 2nd ed. Detroit, MI: Macmillan, 2007. 22 vols.

(Ref DS 102.8 E496 2007).

The standard English language encyclopedia on all aspects of Jewish studies. Approximately 25,000 signed articles with bibliographies.

[43] *Encyclopaedia of Islam*. New ed. Leiden, The Netherlands: Brill, 1954–2007. 12 vols.

(Ref DS 37 E523 1960).

The best English-language scholarly reference work on Islamic studies. Although most entry headings are foreign words transliterated according to an unusual system, the separate indexes allow for easy access to pertinent articles. A 3rd edition began in 2007.

[44] *The Encyclopedia of African-American Culture and History: The Black Experience in the Americas*. Edited by Colin A. Palmer. 2nd ed. Detroit, MI: Macmillan Reference USA, 2006. 6 vols.

(Online in Gale Virtual Reference Library).
Coverage begins in 1619 with the arrival of the first enslaved Africans in the Americas. Particularly strong in biographical entries on African Americans, the signed articles include bibliographies. Vol. 6 includes a statistical appendix.

[45] *Encyclopedia of African History*. Edited by Kevin Shillington. New York: Fitzroy Dearborn, 2005. 3 vols.
(Ref DT 20 E53 2005 and online).
Signed articles on individuals, countries, movements, and broader topics (e.g., democracy, religion), with up-to-date bibliographies.

[46] *Encyclopedia of Asian History*. Edited by Ainslie T. Embree. New York: Scribner's, 1988. 4 vols.
(Ref DS 31 E53 1988).
Entries covering Asia, broadly defined to include Central Asia, the Indian subcontinent, Indonesia, and the Philippines. Bibliographies targeted to educated nonspecialists.

[47] *Encyclopedia of Latin American History and Culture*. Edited by Barbara A. Tenenbaum. New York: Scribner's, 1996. 5 vols.
(Ref F 1406 E53 1996 is the 1st edition. The 2nd edition, 2008, is online)
Coverage of Latin America, including Brazil and all parts of the Western Hemisphere that had at one time formed part of the Spanish Empire. Bibliographies for each entry.

[48] *New Dictionary of the History of Ideas*. Edited by Maryanne Cline Horowitz. Detroit, MI: Scribner's, 2005. 6 vols.
(Ref CB 9 N49 2005 and online).
Scholarly, signed articles cover ideas from consumerism to common sense to childhood. Illustrated with good bibliographies.

[49] *The Oxford Encyclopedia of the Islamic World*. Edited by John L. Esposito. Rev. ed. Oxford, England: Oxford University Press, 2009. 6 vols.
(Ref DS 35.53 O96 2009).
Covers the beginnings of Islam up to 2008, with strong coverage of Islamic culture and movements within Islam. Bibliographies emphasize works in English.

Guides to Secondary Sources: Handbooks,
Guides, and Research Companions

Included in this section are reference works that, in addition to providing lists of useful resources (bibliographies), describe tools and strategies for researching a topic. They often include essays providing overviews of approaches to historical research.

World and General History

[50] *The American Historical Association's Guide to Historical Literature*. Edited by Mary B. Norton. 3rd ed. New York: Oxford University Press, 1995. 2 vols.

(Ready Ref D 20 A55 1995 and online).

Although dated, an excellent starting place for world history. Arranged in forty-eight topical sections, contains extensive bibliographies, mostly covering English-language publications published between 1961 and 1992. Each bibliographic section is preceded by a short historiographical essay that provides an overview of trends in scholarship.

[51] *Reader's Guide to Military History*. Edited by Charles Messenger. London: Fitzroy Dearborn, 2001.

(Ref D 25 A2 R43).

Arranged alphabetically by topic, a guide to the best secondary literature on military history. Entries range from Celtic Warfare to Strategy to Trotskii. Each topical entry lists secondary works; the entry then discusses each of these important works in relation to one another and in historiographical context. Good general index and cross-references. Other titles in this excellent series include [52], [53], [61], and [68].

[52] *Reader's Guide to the History of Science*. Edited by Arne Hessenbruch. London: Fitzroy Dearborn, 2000.

(Ref Q 125 R335 2000 and online).

See [51] for description of format.

[53] *Reader's Guide to Women's Studies*. Edited by Eleanor B. Amico. Chicago: Fitzroy Dearborn, 1998.

(Ref HQ 1180 R43 1998).

Although encompassing women's studies in a very broad way, this resource has many entries on historical topics, ranging from Marie Antoinette to the Industrial Revolution to Suffrage. See [51] for description of format.

[54] *Researching World War I: A Handbook*. Edited by Robin Higham. Westport, CT: Greenwood Press, 2003.

(Ref D 522.4 R47 2003).

Up-to-date handbook with long bibliographic essays, each by a different scholar, followed by extensive bibliographies.

[55] *Term Paper Resource Guide to Twentieth-Century World History*. Edited by Michael D. Richards. Westport, CT: Greenwood Press, 2000.

(Ref D 421 R47 2000 and online).

For one hundred key world history events of the twentieth century, the author provides an overview along with key primary and secondary sources.

[56] Webb, William H. *Sources of Information in the Social Sciences: A Guide to the Literature*. 3rd ed. Chicago: American Library Association, 1986.

(Ref H 61 W433 S64 1986).

An excellent source for an overview of history. The chapter on history is introduced by subject specialists discussing the core sources of monographic literature for major episodes in history. This is followed by sections on topics such as key reference books, bibliographies, organizations, and journals.

Ancient and Medieval

[57] Bengtson, Hermann. *Introduction to Ancient History*. Berkeley: University of California Press, 1970.
(Ref D 59 B413 1970).
Still the standard guide to ancient history. German-language works dominate the bibliographies.

[58] Crosby, Everett U. *Medieval Studies: A Bibliographical Guide*. New York: Garland, 1983.
(Ref CB 351 C76 1983).
The most current scholarly guide to medieval studies, this work contains some 9,000 entries on monographs in European languages. Entries include brief descriptive and evaluative annotations. The guide is divided into 138 geographical and topical chapters.

Europe (Early Modern to Present)

[59] *A Guide to the Sources of British Military History*. Edited by Robin D. Higham. Berkeley: University of California Press, 1971.
(Ref DA 50 G85).
Supplemented in 1988 with a work edited by Gerald Jordan (Ref DA 50 G85 supp 1988).

[60] *Modern British History: A Guide to Study and Research*. Edited by L. J. Butler. London: I. B. Tauris, 1997.
(D16.4 G7 M63 1997).

[61] *Reader's Guide to British History*. Edited by David Loades. New York: Fitzroy Dearborn, 2003. 2 vols.
(Ref DA 34 .R43 2003 and online).
Covers all time periods and all constituent parts of the British Isles. Arranged alphabetically by topic, a guide to the best secondary literature on British history, broadly defined. Entries range from Apprenticeship to Thomas Paine to the Blitz. Each topical entry lists secondary works; the entry then discusses each of these important works in relation to one another and in historiographical context. Good general index and cross-references. Other titles in this excellent series include [51], [52], [53], and [68].

North America

[62] *American Foreign Relations Since 1600*. Edited by Robert L. Beisner. Santa Barbara, CA: ABC-CLIO, 2003. 2 vols.
(Ref E 183.7 .G84 2003).
A masterful annotated bibliographic guide to the historiography of U.S. foreign relations. Each chapter has a detailed table of contents outlining the categories of bibliographic sources included; e.g., primary material, bibliographies, biography, and subtopics. Excellent indexes.

[63] Hardy, Lyda M. *Women in U.S. History: A Resource Guide*. Englewood, CO: Libraries Unlimited, 2000.
(Stacks HQ 1410 H364 2000).
First section lists sources by chronological period and by category; e.g., women's movement. Second section includes categories such as sports, work, historiography.

[64] Martin, Fenton S. *How to Research Elections*. Washington, DC: CQ Press, 2000.
(Ref JK 1976 M373 2000).
This annotated guide and bibliography offers comprehensive coverage of American elections. An introductory part lists primary sources, secondary sources, and finding tools, including Internet sources. A second part is a bibliography by topic; e.g., campaign finance, voting participation.

[65] Martin, Fenton S. *How to Research the Supreme Court*. Washington, DC: Congressional Quarterly, 1992.
(Ref KF 8741 A1 M36 1992).
This guide has major sections on primary and secondary sources, including web sources. The guide concludes with a selected bibliography on all members of the Supreme Court. Martin has a companion work entitled *The U.S. Supreme Court: A Bibliography* (1990) at Ref KF 8741 A1 M37 1990. This comprehensive, although unannotated, bibliography of over 9,400 entries (monographs, journal articles, and dissertations) looks at all areas of Supreme Court endeavor.

[66] Muccigrosso, Robert. *Term Paper Resource Guide to Twentieth-Century United States History*. Westport, CT: Greenwood Press, 1999.
(Stacks E 741 M83 1999 and online).
For one hundred events, the compilers give useful background, suggestions for a term paper, reference sources, general sources, specialized sources, audiovisual sources, Internet sources, etc.

[67] Plischke, Elmer. *U.S. Foreign Relations: a Guide to Information Sources*. Detroit, MI: Gale Research, 1980.
(Stacks JX 1407 P52 1980).
A major guide and bibliography for foreign relations. This annotated guide has sections on diplomacy and diplomats, conduct of U.S. foreign relations, official sources and resources, and memoirs and biographical material. Scholarly. See also [62].

[68] *Reader's Guide to American History*. Edited by Peter J. Parish. New York: Fitzroy Dearborn, 1997.
(Ref E 178 R43 1997).
See [61] for a description of the purpose and organization of this title. This is one in an excellent series of similarly organized guides to secondary historical literature.

Bibliographies of Bibliographies

[69] Beers, Henry P. *Bibliographies in American History, 1942–1978: Guide to Materials for Research*. Woodbridge, CT: Research, 1982. 2 vols.

(Ref E 178 B39 1982).

The standard source listing bibliographies in American history. Some 12,000 entries include monographs, book chapters, journal articles, and government documents. The 1942 edition, at the same call number, should be consulted for bibliographies published before 1942.

[70] Besterman, Theodore. *A World Bibliography of Bibliographies and of Bibliographical Catalogues, Calendars, Abstracts, Digests, Indexes, and the Like.* 4th ed. Totowa, NJ: Rowman and Littlefield, 1965–1966. 5 vols.
(Ref Z 1002 B5684).

A masterful and comprehensive bibliography containing some 117,000 entries covering all languages and the full span of human endeavor from the advent of printing. Arranged by subject with thousands of individuals included. The final volume is an index.

[71] *Bibliographic Index.* New York: H. W. Wilson, Co., 1937 to 2011.
(Storage 2 Abstract/Index).

Indexes substantial bibliographies published in monographs and journal articles, covering all subject areas and time periods.

[72] *Black Access: A Bibliography of Afro-American Bibliographies.* Compiled by Richard Newman. Westport, CT: Greenwood Press, 1984.
(Stacks E 185 N578 1984).

Including books and journal articles, this bibliography documents bibliographies created in the first decades of African American studies. Alphabetical arrangement with subject index.

[73] Coulter, Edith M. *Historical Bibliographies: A Systematic and Annotated Guide.* Berkeley: University of California Press, 1935.
(Stacks D 20 C6 1935).

Although dated, Coulter's scholarly guide has research value for early bibliographies in history.

National Bibliographies and Union Catalogs

National bibliographies are massive compilations of all items published in a given country. Union catalogs usually record the holdings of a group of research libraries. Both are standard sources for verifying citations for interlibrary loan requests. More and more of the information contained in printed national bibliographies is migrating to online library catalogs and databases.

[74] British Museum. Department of Printed Books. *General Catalogue of Printed Books to 1955.* Compact ed. New York: Readex Microprint Corporation, 1967. 27 vols.
(Biblio Z 921 B8753).

This is the British national bibliography, listing all titles held by the British Museum to 1955. Although still useful, especially for works appearing in many editions (e.g., the Bible or the works of Dickens), it is largely superseded by *The British Library Integrated Catalogue,* online at http://catalogue.bl.uk/F/?func=file&file_name=login-bl-list.

[75] *The European Library*. http://search.theeuropeanlibrary.org/portal/en/index.html.
(Public Access Database)
A portal to the national libraries of Europe.

[76] Evans, Charles. *American Bibliography: A Chronological Dictionary of All Books, Pamphlets, and Periodical Publications Printed in the United States of America from the Genesis of Printing in 1639 Down to and Including the Year 1820*. New York: P. Smith, 1941–1959. 14 vols.
(Ref Z 1215 E923 and Online Library Subscription Database).
The digital edition of all items included in the Evans bibliography is available online from Readex as *Early American Imprints, Series I: Evans, 1639–1800*. It contains some 36,000 items. Evans's *Bibliography* is continued by Shaw and Shoemaker [78]. See also [153].

[77] *The National Union Catalog Pre-1956 Imprints*. Washington, DC: Library of Congress, 1968–1980. 754 vols.
(Biblio Z 881 A1 U372).
Published by the Library of Congress, this monumental publication (known as the *NUC*) aimed to list all printed materials published before 1956 and owned by any of 700 research libraries in the United States and Canada. It lists, in author order, over 13 million books, pamphlets, maps, atlases, and pieces of music held by the Library of Congress and other libraries. The entries include variant editions and usually note the U.S. libraries that own the source. This title is especially useful for historical and literary research to verify a book's existence or to trace all editions of a work. There is no subject access to the items listed. The *NUC* has been only partially superseded by *WorldCat* [79].

[78] Shaw, Ralph R., and Richard H. Shoemaker. *American Bibliography*. New York: Scarecrow Press, 1958–1966. 22 vols.
(Ref Z 1215 .S48 and Online Library Subscription Database).
Continuing the work of Evans [76], this bibliography records all books, pamphlets, and broadsides published in the United States between 1801 and 1819. The online edition is available from Readex as *Early American Imprints, Series II: Shaw-Shoemaker, 1801–1819* [153].

[79] *WorldCat*. Dublin, OH: OCLC, 1997.
(Online Library Subscription Database).
This cooperative catalog maintained by thousands of libraries worldwide contains descriptions of over 175 million items, including books, films, manuscripts, maps, and Internet resources. This is gradually replacing the *National Union Catalog (NUC)* [77]; however, because of duplicate records and records for multiple formats of items, it can be easier to browse the printed *NUC* for research on, for example, the publishing history of a literary work.

Biographical Information

Biographical Finding Aids

Many online newspaper databases (e.g., *Proquest Historical Newspapers*, *America's Historical Newspapers* [Readex], and *Times Digital Archive* [Gale]) enable the researcher's quest for biographical material by a search limit for obituaries. This has greatly aided historians and genealogists in recent years.

[80] *Biographical Dictionaries and Related Works: An International Bibliography of More Than 16,000 Collective Biographies.* Edited by Robert B. Slocum. 2nd ed. Detroit, MI: Gale, 1986. 2 vols.
(Ref CT 104 S55 1986).
A comprehensive bibliography listing 16,000 sources. International, covering all languages and time periods. Brief annotations.

[81] *Biography and Genealogy Master Index.* Detroit, MI: Gale.
(Online Library Subscription Database).
Indexes over 1,000 publications that include biographical material, adding over half a million citations each year. Especially helpful for finding biographies of lesser known individuals, this is an essential source. Search features increase its utility, helping the student to identify, for example, every John Smith born before 1880 and alive after 1920.

Comprehensive Biographical Resources

[82] *American National Biography.* Edited by John A. Garraty and Mark C. Carnes. New York: Oxford University Press, 1999. 24 vols.
(Ref CT 213 .A68 1999 and Online Library Subscription Database).
The standard biographical dictionary for the United States, this print edition updates the *Dictionary of American Biography* [86], which did not include women or people of color. The online version is updated twice a year to add individuals who have recently died. The articles are signed and have bibliographies that include important biographical secondary sources as well as notations on where personal papers (manuscript and published) may be found.

[83] *Biography in Context.* Detroit, MI: Gale.
(Online Library Subscription Database).
A comprehensive database of biographical information on over 320,000 people from throughout history, around the world, and across all disciplines. Full text biographies are drawn from journal literature and over 150 reference titles, including the *Dictionary of American Biography* [86].

[84] *Black Biographical Dictionaries, 1790–1950.* Alexandria, VA: Chadwyck-Healey, 1991. 1,068 microfiche.
(Microforms Room)
An outstanding collection of 297 biographical sources (books, pamphlets, yearbooks, etc.) containing over 30,000 biographies of African Americans. *Black Biography, 1790–1950: A Cumulative Index* (Microforms Room E 185.96 B528 1991) edited by Randall K. Burkett,

Nancy Hall Burkett, and Henry Louis Gates, Jr., is the helpful finding aid for locating individuals on the microfiche. Vols. 1 and 2 of the index are arranged alphabetically and list place of birth, date, gender, occupation, and religion. Vol. 3 lists the source documents and indexes the individuals by facets including occupation and religion.

[85] *Current Biography Yearbook*. New York: H. W. Wilson Co. 1940 to present.
(Ref CT 100 C8).
International in coverage, and containing some 150 annual articles on persons from all walks of life.

[86] *Dictionary of American Biography (DAB)*. New York: Scribner's, 1928–1996. 20 vols. plus supplements.
(Stacks E 176 D56; also online in *Biography in Context* [83], an Online Library Subscription Database).
Until publication of the *American National Biography* [82], this had been the standard source for deceased Americans, and it remains a vital source.

[87] *Dictionary of National Biography (DNB)*. Edited by Leslie Stephen and Sidney Lee. London: Oxford University Press, 1908–1990. 28 vols. plus supplements.
(Carrier Lib Storage DA 28 D4).
Like the *Dictionary of American Biography* [86], this classic work covered people of British ancestry. The first edition in sixty-six volumes was completed in 1901. Supplements brought coverage up through 1990. For new edition, see *Oxford Dictionary of National Biography* [88].

[88] *Oxford Dictionary of National Biography*. Edited by H. C. G. Matthew and Brian Harrison. Oxford, England: Oxford University Press, 2004. 60 vols.
(Ref DA 28 .O95 2004 and Online Library Subscription Database).
Completely new edition of the *Dictionary of National Biography (DNB)* [87]. Contains biographies of over 50,000 deceased persons whose lives were connected with the British Isles.

Bibliographies, Indexing, and Abstracting Services

Note that many of the database sources listed below were originally published in print, either monthly, quarterly, or annually. They provided subject headings to allow researchers to access scholarly journal articles (sometimes also books, dissertations, and book reviews) on their topic of interest. Without these indexes, which frequently included summaries (abstracts) of the articles, the process of finding journal literature would be tedious, requiring the researcher to manually browse the table of contents for hundreds of journal issues. Indexes to popular magazines are included below in a separate section, "Popular Magazines."

Now that many of these indexes have migrated to online formats, they are much more than indexes. They often allow linking to the full text of articles, to library catalogs, and to interlibrary loan forms, vastly simplifying the research process. See also the following category, "Full-Text Journal Collections."

World and General History

[89] *Academic Search Complete.* Birmingham, AL: EBSCO, 1853 to present.
(Online Library Subscription Database).
An interdisciplinary index and source of full-text scholarly journals and popular magazines, containing over 6,300 peer-reviewed journals. Searches may be limited by peer review status, document type, publication date.

[90] *Dissertations and Theses: Full-Text.* Ann Arbor, MI: Proquest, 1861 to present.
(Online Library Subscription Database).
Lists and provides abstracts for most dissertations produced in the United States since 1861. The original research and extensive bibliographies make dissertations valuable to the undergraduate. Subscriptions often include the full text of many dissertations published since 1997.

[91] *Historical Abstracts.* Ipswich, MA: EBSCO Publishing, 1954 to present.
(Online Library Subscription Database).
Essential index with abstracts to more than 2,000 periodicals covering world history, *excluding* the United States and Canada, from the early modern period (1450) onward. This source does not index book reviews but does index review articles. Complemented by *America: History and Life* [102].

[92] *Index Islamicus.* Leiden, The Netherlands: Brill, 1905 to present.
(Online Library Subscription Database).
Indexes books, journal articles, book chapters, reviews, and proceedings in European languages. Coverage is comprehensive and scholarly, covering all countries of the world where Islam is the majority faith as well as Muslim minorities living elsewhere. Avoid using the "peer-reviewed" limit, which is inaccurate and will eliminate many scholarly articles.

[93] *OmniFile Full Text Mega.* New York: H. W. Wilson, Co., 1982 to present.
(Online Library Subscription Database).
This database pulls together the front file, from 1982 forward, of six Wilson indexes, including *Humanities Index* and *Social Sciences Index.* The interface allows the researcher to add additional indexes to an integrated search. History students should consider including the *Humanities and Social Sciences Retrospective* (1907–1984) index when searching.

Ancient and Medieval

[94] *L'Année Philologique: Bibliographie Critique et Analytique de l'Antiquité Gréco-Latine.* Paris: Société Internationale de Bibliographie Classique, 1924 to present.
(Microfiche, 1924–1973; Bound, 1983–1998, Ref Index/Abstracts).
(Online Library Subscription Database).
An index with abstracts to scholarly work (books and articles) covering all aspects of Greco-Roman antiquity from the second millennium BCE through the early middle ages (ca. 500–800 CE). Covers Greek and Latin language and linguistics, Greek and Roman history,

literature, philosophy, art, archaeology, religion, mythology, music, science, early Christian texts, numismatics, and papyrology. Absolutely essential for ancient history.

Africa

[95] *AfricaBib.org*
  (Online Public Access Database).
  Africana Periodical Literature is searchable at this website. It indexes over 500 international journals. Coverage generally begins with 1974, but coverage is much deeper for some journal titles. Maintained as a free service by the African Studies Centre in Leiden, The Netherlands.

[96] Asamani, J. O. *Index Africanus*. Stanford, CA: Hoover Institution Press, 1975.
  (Ref DT 3 A73 1975).
  Lists approximately 25,000 journal articles in Western languages published between 1885 and 1965. Following a general section, the bibliography is divided by country and then by topic.

Asia

[97] *Bibliography of Asian Studies*. Ann Arbor, MI: Association for Asian Studies, 1946 to present. Annual.
  (Stacks DS 5 B49 (1965 to 1991)).
  This is the standard bibliography on Asian studies, covering scholarship in European languages. The bibliography appeared in *Far Eastern Quarterly* between 1941 and 1956 and in the *Journal of Asian Studies* for 1956 to 1966; these titles are available in the library subscription database, *JSTOR* [119]. It appeared as a separate printed bibliography from 1965 to 1991. It is currently only available online.

Europe (Early Modern to Present)

[98] *Bibliographie Annuelle de l'Histoire de France du Cinquième Siècle à 1958*. Paris: Éditions du Centre National de la Recherche Scientifique, 1975 to present.
  (Ref DC 38 .B5).
  Covers books and articles. Has indexes by time period, subject, and author names.

[99] *Bibliography of British and Irish History (BBIH)*. Turnout, Belgium: Brepols.
  (Online Library Subscription Database).
  A partnership between the Institute of Historical Research, the Royal Historical Society, and Brepols Publishers, this database indexes scholarship on the British Isles, British Empire, and Commonwealth during all historical periods. It includes books, journal articles, and book chapters. Incorporated into the database are pre-1900 entries from a number of print sources, notably several important bibliographies published by Oxford University Press in the series *Bibliography of British History* [100].

[100] *Bibliography of British History*. Oxford, England: Clarendon Press.
  (Various editors, dates, and locations in Reference).

This excellent, though dated, series is produced under the direction of the American Historical Association and the Royal Historical Society of Great Britain. Entries from the printed works have been incorporated into *BBIH* [99]. Volumes include:

Tudor Period, 1485–1603 (Ref DA 315 .R28 1959)
Stuart Period, 1603–1714 (Ref DA 375 .D25 1970)
Eighteenth Century, 1714–1789 (Ref DA 498 .P37 1977)
1789–1851 (Ref DA 520 B75 1977)
1851–1914 (Ref DA 530 H46 1976)
1914–1989 (Ref DA 566 R62 1996)

Latin America and Caribbean

[101] *Handbook of Latin American Studies*. Gainesville: University of Florida Press, 1935 to present.
(Public Access Database for 1990 onward at http://lcweb2.loc.gov/hlas/. In Stacks and Reference at F 1408 H262).
A comprehensive and essential scholarly bibliography to all areas of Latin America. Beginning with 1964, the volumes on social sciences and humanities are published in alternate years. The online version is updated weekly. What the printed version lacks in currency it makes up for in ease of use.

North America

[102] *America: History and Life*. Santa Barbara, CA: ABC-CLIO, 1954 to present.
(Online Library Subscription Database).
Essential comprehensive index with selective abstracting of the international scholarly literature treating the history and culture of the United States and Canada in all historic periods. Covers journal articles (from over 2,400 journals), book reviews from a subset of those journals, film and video reviews, and dissertation listings. Complemented by the *Historical Abstracts* [91].

[103] Filby, P. William. *A Bibliography of American County Histories*. Baltimore, MD: Genealogical Pub. Co., 1985.
(Ref E 180 F54 1985).
Arranged by state and county, Filby's work lists significant published county histories. It also includes some regional historical studies. This should be used with the comprehensive *United States Local Histories in the Library of Congress: A Bibliography* [112].

[104] Goehlert, Robert U. *Members of Congress: A Bibliography*. Washington, DC: Congressional Quarterly, 1996.
(Stacks JK 1030 A2 G568 1996).
Books, articles, dissertations, and essays are listed in this alphabetically arranged bibliography.

[105] Griffin, Appleton P. C. *Bibliography of American Historical Societies*. Washington, DC: American Historical Association, 1907.
(Ref E 172 A60 1905 v.2).

An important bibliography for pre–twentieth century American history. Griffin indexed all major historical society periodicals up to 1905. Although the arrangement is awkward for a researcher today, the indexing and content make this a useful tool. *Writings on American History* [118] partially continues Griffin.

[106] *Harvard Guide to American History*. Edited by Frank B. Friedel. Rev. ed. Cambridge, MA: Belknap Press of Harvard University Press, 1974. 2 vols. (Ready Ref E 178 F77 1974).

Although dated, this title remains a standard bibliographic guide to American history. Topical sections cover the full range of American history. Vol. 1 covers historical sources and practice as well as historical themes (social manners, immigration, etc.); vol. 2 is arranged chronologically. Well indexed.

[107] Higginbotham, Evelyn Brooks. *Harvard Guide to African-American History*. Cambridge, MA: Harvard University Press, 2001. (Ref E 185 H326 2001 and CD-ROM).

Historiographical essays on different types of sources for African American historical research (e.g., Film and Television, Bibliography, Government Documents) are followed by extensive—but unannotated—bibliographies classified by subject area.

[108] Larned, Josephus N. *The Literature of American History: A Bibliographical Guide*. 1902. Reprint, New York: F. Ungar, 1966. (Ref E 178 L3 1966).

An important bibliography for pre–twentieth century American history. Useful for its listing of source material and the critical annotations to the citations.

[109] Miller, Gordon W. *Rockingham: An Annotated Bibliography of a Virginia County*. Harrisonburg, VA: Harrisonburg-Rockingham Historical Society, 1989. (Ref F 232 R7 M5486 1989 and in Stacks and Special Collections).

An example of a historical bibliography at the county level. Comprehensive coverage of books, articles, maps, etc. Topical arrangement. For the online supplement, go to http://www.lib.jmu.edu/rockbib/index.htm.

[110] *Reconstruction in the United States: An Annotated Bibliography*. Edited by David A. Lincove. Westport, CT: Greenwood Press, 2000. (Stacks E 668 L56 2000).

Comprehensive in its coverage, Lincove has 3,000 entries for books, essays, journal articles, theses, and doctoral dissertations.

[111] United States. Library of Congress. General Reference and Bibliography Division. *A Guide to the Study of the United States of America: Representative Books Reflecting the Development of American Life and Thought*. Washington, DC: Library of Congress, 1960. (Ref E 158 U53 1960).

A selective bibliography listing major works on American history, broadly defined. About 6,500 annotated entries cover divisions such as diplomatic, education, science, etc.

[112] United States. Library of Congress. *United States Local Histories in the Library of Congress: A Bibliography*. Edited by Marion Kaminkow. Baltimore, MD: Magna Carta Book Co., 1975–1976. 5 vols.

(Ref E 180 U59 1975).

An exhaustive bibliography of local histories. Arranged by Library of Congress call number, which places all books within a geographical hierarchy. Useful in biographical and genealogical research. See also [103].

[113] *Virginia Historical Index*. Edited by Earl G. Swem. 1934. Reprint. Roanoke, VA: Stone Printing, 1965. 4 vols.

(Ref F 221 S93 1965).

An outstanding bibliography for Virginia history, this source provides deep indexing of seven important journals and legal publications relating to Virginia. Mandatory for locating historical research on Virginia published prior to 1930.

Selected Regions and Themes

This is a *very* brief sampling of bibliographies available in the library collection.

[114] *The Gorbachev Bibliography, 1985–1991: A Listing of Books and Articles in English on Perestroika in the USSR*. Edited by Joseph L. Wieczynski. New York: Norman Ross, 1996.

(Ref DK 286 W54 1996).

This work covers English-language books and articles (primarily scholarly articles) on Gorbachev and perestroika.

[115] *The Nazi Era, 1919–1945: A Select Bibliography of Published Works from the Early Roots to 1980*. Edited by Helen Kehr. London: Mansell, 1982.

(Stacks DD 253.25 K4 1982).

[116] Work, Monroe N. *A Bibliography of the Negro in Africa and America*. New York: H. W. Wilson Co., 1928.

(Ref E 185 W67 1928).

This excellent bibliography, arranged topically, has 17,000 entries (including documents, books, articles, maps, and pamphlets).

[117] *World War II in Europe, Africa, and the Americas, with General Sources: A Handbook of Literature and Research*. Edited by Lloyd Lee. Westport, CT: Greenwood Press, 1997.

(Ref D 743.42 .W67 1997).

Signed bibliographical essays covering topics such as social change, resistance movements, economic mobilization, refugees, personal narratives, and the Mediterranean Theater are followed by lengthy bibliographies.

[118] *Writings on American History*. Washington, DC: American Historical Association, 1902–1961. Annual.

(Ref E 178 L331).

Until the publication of *America: History and Life* [102], this was the most exhaustive index to scholarly work on American history. Includes books, essays in books, dissertations, and journal articles. Chronological and subject arrangement, with an author index. A cumulative index for 1902 through 1940 is available. Not published 1904, 1905, 1941–1947.

Full-Text Journal Collections

The online resources listed above in the category "Bibliographies, Indexing, and Abstracting Services" typically allow for searching of key fields such as subject headings, titles, abstracts, and authors; the print bibliographies in that category usually offer subject categories, outlines, or indexes to assist researchers in locating resources on their topic.

Searching in the following full-text collections requires a different strategy. Since every word of every article in the collection is searched, irrelevant results may be retrieved. It is often better to begin your search in a resource such as *America: History and Life* [102] and link to the full text from there rather than launching full-text searches in one of the following resources.

[119] *JSTOR*. http://www.jstor.org.

    (Online Library Subscription Database).

    JSTOR represents the first effort to create an online archive of scholarly journals in all disciplines. Begun in 1995, it now offers access to over 1,000 titles, nearly 300 in history. Academic libraries may subscribe to sets of titles. Digital editions begin with the first issue of a journal, but the most recent three to five years is usually not available in *JSTOR* (although new features allow for linking to other platforms if the library has a current subscription). Core journals include *American Historical Review, Catholic Historical Review, Economic History Review, Traditio*, and *Annales*.

[120] *Periodicals Archive Online (PAO)* (Proquest).

    (Online Library Subscription Database).

    Digital archive of scholarly journals from the nineteenth and twentieth centuries. Libraries may subscribe to selected bundles of titles. The journals are selected from those indexed in *Periodicals Index Online*, a massive index of some 6,000 international journals. Full text content typically ends with 1995.

[121] *Project MUSE*. http://muse.jhu.edu.

    (Online Library Subscription Database).

    Originally a project of Johns Hopkins University Press, this collection has grown to encompass journals published by many academic publishers. Libraries may subscribe to individual titles or to sets of titles.

Historiography

Entries in the *Reader's Guide* series, published by Fitzroy Dearborn, often provide good historiographical context for the student (see [51], [52], [61], and [68]).

[122] *Companion to Historiography*. Edited by Michael Bentley. London: Routledge, 1997.

    (Ref D 13 C626 1997).

    Lengthy essays on the historiography of different periods and places, concentrating on trends in the recent past.

[123] *Encyclopedia of Historians and Historical Writing*. Edited by Kelly Boyd. Chicago: Fitzroy Dearborn Publishers, 1999. 2 vols.

(Ref D 14 E53 1999).

Entries on historians, study topics, and historical concepts. Each historian entry has a bibliography of principal writings; all entries include citations for further reading. An important historiographical source.

[124] *A Global Encyclopedia of Historical Writing*. Edited by D. R. Woolf. New York: Garland, 1998.

(Ref D 13 .G47 1998).

Entries include biographies of historians, surveys of national or regional historiographies, and articles on concepts.

[125] *Great Historians of the Modern Age: An International Dictionary*. Edited by Lucian Bola. New York: Greenwood Press, 1991.

(Ref D 14 G75 1991).

This source features some 700 historians from the nineteenth and twentieth centuries. Arranged by thirty-eight geographic or national areas. Has a European and male bias. Includes bibliographies.

[126] *Historiography: An Annotated Bibliography of Journal Articles, Books, and Dissertations*. Edited by Susan K. Kinnell. Santa Barbara, CA: ABC-CLIO, 1987. 2 vols.

(Ref D 13 .H58 1987).

Vol. 1 contains sections on methodologies, schools of historiography, and approaches (i.e., political economic, social history). Vol. 2 is arranged by geographical area. Both volumes have subject and author indexes.

[127] Ritter, Harry. *Dictionary of Concepts in History*. Westport, CT: Greenwood Press, 1986.

(Ref D 13 R49 1986).

Brief definitions with essays are featured in this work. Bibliographies accompany the entries. Useful for a quick understanding of a term or concept.

[128] *The Study of History: A Bibliographical Guide*. Edited by R. C. Richardson. 2nd ed. Manchester, England: Manchester University Press, 2000.

(Ref D 13 R44 2000).

A bibliography of historiography. Following an overview of general works, the bibliography is arranged by time period.

[129] Williams, Robert C. *The Historian's Toolbox: A Student's Guide to the Theory and Craft of History*. Armonk, NY: M. E. Sharpe, 2003.

(Ref D 16 W62 2003).

This reference work looks at the theory and practice of history and presents examples on researching and writing it.

Book Reviews

For the beginning historian, book reviews may provide valuable insight into the value of a specific title. How was this book received at the time of publication by the scholarly community? To what other works does the reviewer compare it? Is the book in hand supporting a mainstream argument, overturning an accepted interpretation, or opening a completely new area of study?

[130] *America: History and Life.* Santa Barbara, CA: ABC-CLIO, 1954 to present. (Online Library Subscription Database).

[131] *Book Review Digest Plus.* New York: H. W. Wilson Co., 1905 to present. (Online Library Subscription Database).

[132] *Book Review Index.* Detroit, MI: Gale, 1965 to present. (Ref Abstract/Index).

[133] *Combined Retrospective Index to Book Reviews in Scholarly Journals. 1886–1974.* Edited by Evan Ira Farber. Arlington, VA: Carrollton Press, 1979–1982. 15 vols. (Ref Abstract/Index).

JSTOR [119] and *Project MUSE* [121], large full-text collections of journals, are excellent sources for book reviews. Both allow the researcher to limit a search to reviews only.

Historical Atlases

[134] *Atlas of Early American History: The Revolutionary Era, 1760–1790.* Edited by Lester J. Cappon. Princeton: Princeton University Press, 1976. (Ref G 1201 S3 A8 1976). Great variety of maps that include colonial boundaries, cultural and economic activity, population, mail routes, and the Revolutionary War itself.

[135] *Barrington Atlas of the Greek and Roman World.* Edited by Richard J. A. Talbert. Princeton: Princeton University Press. (Ref G 1033 .B3 2000 with two supplements). A scholarly and beautifully produced atlas. The supplements provide a map-by-map directory with an introduction to each map. For each place name, there is information on the period(s) with which it is associated, its modern name, and a bibliography.

[136] Gaustad, Edwin Scott, and Philip L. Barlow. *New Historical Atlas of Religion in America.* Oxford, England: Oxford University Press, 2001. (Ref G 1201 E4 N4 2001). Excellent visual presentation of geography and statistical features of Christian denominations and Judaism in America from 1650 to 2000.

[137] *An Historical Atlas of Islam.* Edited by Hugh Kennedy. 2nd ed. Leiden, The Netherlands: Brill, 2002. (Ref G 1786 S1 H6 2002). Detailed, scholarly maps. Annotations to the maps are at the front; index to place-names and ethnic names at the back.

[138] Lathrop, J. M. *An Atlas of Rockingham County, Virginia, from Actual Surveys.* 1885. Reprint, Harrisonburg, VA: Harrisonburg-Rockingham Historical Society, 1982. (Ref G 1293 R7 L3 1982). Detailed information has value for many areas of historical research, including genealogy.

[139] Magocsi, Paul Robert. *Historical Atlas of Central Europe.* Rev. and expanded ed. Seattle: University of Washington Press, 2002.
(Ref G 2081 S1 M3 v. 1).
Excellent texts accompany the maps and tables covering the region from late antiquity to 2000. Extensive bibliography and index.

[140] *Oxford Atlas of World History.* Edited by Patrick K. O'Brien. Rev. ed. New York: Oxford University Press, 2002.
(Ref G 1030 O851 2002).
Covers the sweep of human history with attractive maps accompanied by good essays. Includes maps of trade routes, migrations, military conflicts, and population changes. Useful chronological tables, glossary, and index at the back.

[141] Paullin, Charles O. *Atlas of the Historical Geography of the United States.* Washington, DC: Carnegie Institution of Washington and the American Geographical Society of New York, 1932.
(Ref G 3701 S1 P3).
Although published in 1932, Paullin remains an important and comprehensive American historical atlas. The wide range of topics covered include environment, boundaries, exploration, society, and economy. The maps include commentary. Indexed.

[142] *We the People: An Atlas of America's Ethnic Diversity.* Edited by James P. Allen. New York: Macmillan, 1988.
(Ref G 1201 E1 A4 1988).
A scholarly work on immigration and ethnic studies. Over one hundred maps accompany the commentary and analysis.

FOCUS ON PRIMARY SOURCES

Finding Published Primary Sources in Library Catalogs

A few keys will assist the researcher in locating published primary sources in library catalogs. The history student will first want to find good keywords to describe the topic of interest—preferably words included in Library of Congress Subject Headings (LCSH), employed by most U.S. academic libraries to describe a book's contents. Secondly, by adding special subject words used by librarians to describe categories of primary sources, the researcher will be able to narrow the search to primary sources.

"Sources" is a standard subdivision for primary sources but does not always appear in the subject heading. There are other words you may try instead of "sources" to find primary documents:

Personal narratives	Interviews	Diaries
Correspondence	Registers	Speeches
Documentary films	Census	Archives

For example, this search:

Subject word:	sources	AND
Keywords:	history and Byzantine	

will retrieve primary sources related to the history of the Byzantine Empire, such as the book described here:

Author	Brubaker, Leslie
Title	Byzantium in the iconoclast era (c. 680-850) : the sources : an annotated survey / Leslie Brubaker, John Haldon
Publisher	Aldershot, Hants, England ; Burlington, VT : Ashgate, c2001
Description	xxxi, 324 p., [32] p. of plates : ill. : 24 cm
Series	Birmingham Byzantine and Ottoman monographs ; v. 7
Note	Includes bibliographical reference and index
Subject	Byzantine Empire – History – 527-1081 – Sources
Other Name	Haldon, John F
ISBN	0754604187 (acid-free paper)

Another strategy is simply to do an author search in the catalog. An author search for "Adams, Abigail" will retrieve collections of her edited correspondence and other writings.

To expand your search beyond your own library to find books you may borrow through interlibrary loan, use *WorldCat* [79]. Choose "Subject" from the drop-down box, combining keywords with one of the above subdivisions (sources, interviews, etc.). For example, to find primary sources on Winston Churchill, you might try a Subject search for "winston churchill sources." *World-Cat* will look for all three words; e.g., "Winston and Churchill and sources" in the Subject field of a record.

Many university libraries offer on-line tutorials on finding primary sources in *WorldCat*. **Note**: In a perfect world, all primary sources will show one of the designators above in the subject headings for the item described. However, since this is not always the case, you may wish to try searching for keywords or phrases such as "documents," "diary," "letters," or "documentary history" if you are not finding what you need by limiting your search to subject words.

The following three sections highlight databases (both free and subscription-based) and tangible collections that contain primary sources.

Public Access Databases (Freely Available)

[143] *American Memory*. http://memory.loc.gov/

This rich and well-organized site gives the researcher access to an ever-growing set of digitized primary source collections from the Library of

Congress and other scholarly institutions. Collections available here include the following:

- Born in Slavery: Slave Narratives from the Federal Writers' Project, 1936–1938.
- "California as I Saw It": First-Person Narratives from California's Early Years, 1949–1900.
- The Emergence of Advertising in America: 1850–1920.
- Sunday School Books: Shaping the Values of Youth in 19th Century America.
- Band Music from the Civil War Era.

[144] *The American Presidency Project.* http://www.presidency.ucsb.edu.
An archive created at the University of California at Santa Barbara, this archive contains nearly 100,000 documents related to the presidency, beginning with George Washington. A powerful search interface allows the researcher to create a refined query. Included are messages and papers of the presidents, press conferences, party platforms, oral addresses, and executive orders.

[145] *Earls Colne, Essex: Records of an English Village 1375–1854.* http://linux02.lib.cam.ac.uk/earlscolne/index.htm
A rich collection of primary documents (from the church and state) from one village in England over the course of five centuries.

[146] *The Encyclopedia of Diderot and d'Alembert.* http://www.hti.umich.edu/d/did/index.html.
A scholarly project to translate this famous eighteenth-century encyclopedia into English and to post it on the web.

[147] *EuroDocs: Primary Historical Documents from Western Europe.* http://eurodocs.lib.byu.edu.
First organized by country, then chronologically, this portal connects to European documents that are transcribed, reproduced digitally, or translated. Short annotations.

[148] *Google Books.* http://books.google.com.
Growing daily, *Google Books* includes digitized out-of-copyright books and many back runs of popular magazines such as *Popular Mechanics, Life, Jet,* and *New York Magazine.*

[149] *Internet History Sourcebooks Project.* http://www.fordham.edu/halsall/.
Fordham Professor Paul Halsall's rich website compiles and organizes collections of public domain and copy-permitted historical texts on all historic periods from antiquity to the present.

[150] *In the First Person: Index to Letters, Diaries, Oral Histories and Other Personal Narratives.* Alexandria, VA: Alexander Street Press, 2007. http://www.inthefirstperson.com/. (Public Access Database).
Search letters, diaries, oral histories, memoirs, and autobiographies (mostly in English) that are in Alexander Street Press library subscription databases, freely available on the web, or in library special collections. This tool also allows the researcher to discover repositories worldwide that have strong collections on topics of interest.

[151] *Latin American Travelogues*. http://library.brown.edu/cds/travelogues/.
> Created at Brown University, this website aims to digitize and disseminate published travel accounts in the Brown library collection.

[152] *The Making of America*. http://cdl.library.cornell.edu/moa.
> Digitized monographs and journal articles illustrating American social history from the antebellum period through reconstruction. A project of the University of Michigan.

Library Subscription Databases

[153] *Archive of Americana*. Naples, FL: Readex.
> A cluster of collections reflecting the history of the United States through its congressional publications, popular newspapers, and commercial publishing. The databases included may be searched individually or simultaneously:
>
> - American State Papers, 1789–1838. Legislative and Executive Documents.
> - U.S. Congressional Serial Set, 1817–1980. These are the reports, documents, and journals of the U.S. Congress. See also [225].
> - Early American Newspapers.
> - Early American Imprints: Evans, 1639–1800; and Shaw-Shoemaker, 1801–1819. See also [76] and [78].
> - American Broadsides and Ephemera.

[154] *Digital National Security Archive (DNSA)*. Alexandria, VA: Chadwyck-Healey.
> *DNSA* contains declassified documents—totaling more than 488,000 pages—that have been gathered through extensive use of the U.S. Freedom of Information Act (FOIA). Each collection contains a diverse range of policy documents including presidential directives, memos, diplomatic dispatches, meeting notes, independent reports, briefing papers, and White House communications.

[155] *Early Encounters in North America*. Alexandria, VA: Alexander Street Press.
> This is a series of early narratives, edited, with introductions and commentary. English-language texts include narratives from Vikings, English, French, Dutch, and Spanish writings. Coverage begins with 985 and concludes at 1708.

[156] *ECCO: Eighteenth Century Collections Online*. Detroit, MI: Gale Cengage Learning.
> Digital facsimiles of nearly all books published in Great Britain in the eighteenth century as well as important books from the Americas. Contains the full text of nearly 150,000 books printed in English and various foreign languages. Note that searching is for terms in the full text; there is no subject indexing.

[157] *Sabin Americana, 1500–1926*. Detroit, MI: Gale Cengage Learning.
> Full-text database based on Joseph Sabin's *Bibliotheca Americana, an authoritative list of books about the Americas. Coverage includes books published* worldwide between 1500 and 1926. "The Americas" broadly

includes the entire Western Hemisphere, including the Arctic, Antarctica, and West Indies. Every word of the listed books is searchable, and every page image displayable.

[158] *Smithsonian Global Sound for Libraries.* Alexandria, VA: Alexander Street Press.
A rich streaming audio collection of world music, recorded by Smithsonian Folkways Recordings. Browsing and searching by facets such as cultural group, instruments, languages, and genres.

[159] *Vanderbilt Television News Archive.* Nashville, TN: Vanderbilt University Libraries.
Includes an index to network news from ABC, CBS, CNN, and NBC. Subscribing institutions have content to streaming content for NBC from 1968 to date, and for CNN from 1995 to date.

Tangible Document Collections

This is a sampling of physical collections of primary sources; they are either in print or on microform. Call numbers are provided for printed materials. All others listed in this section are in the Microforms Room.

[160] *Africa Through Western Eyes.* Marlborough, England: Adam Matthew Publications, 1999 to present.
Online guides to the collection are available at http://www.adam-matthew-publications.co.uk/digital_guides/. These are facsimiles of collections owned by U.S. and U.K. libraries

[161] *Archives Parlementaires de 1787 à 1860: Recueil Complet des Débats Législatifs & Politiques...* Paris: Librairie Administrative de P. Dupont, 1862[?].
Records of the meetings of legislative bodies of the French Revolution.

[162] *The Aristocracy, the State, and the Local Community [1477–1828]: The Hastings Collection of Manuscripts from the Huntington Library in California.* Brighton, England: Harvester, 1986– .
This set of thirty-nine microfilm rolls has a two-volume printed guide. Content includes the correspondence of the Hastings family of Great Britain from 1477 to 1701.

[163] *Blacks in the United States Armed Forces: Basic Documents.* Edited by Morris J. MacGregor and Bernard C. Nalty. Wilmington, DE: Scholarly Resources, 1977.
Contains documents from the period of slavery up to the early 1960s.

[164] *Civil War Unit Histories: Regimental Histories and Personal Narratives.* Edited by Robert E. Lester and Gary Hoag. Bethesda, MD: University Publications of America, 1990.

[165] *Draper Manuscripts.*
Primary documents collected by Lyman Draper covering the history of the trans-Allegheny West from mid-eighteenth century into the early 1800s.

[166] *English Historical Documents.* Edited by David C. Douglass. New York: Oxford University Press, 1951–1977. 13 vols.
(DA 26 E55).
A rich collection covering England from 500 to 1914. The subject coverage is broad; documents have introductions and bibliographies. Volumes 6 and 7, covering 1559 to 1659, were never published.

[167] Great Britain. Foreign Office. *British and Foreign State Papers*. London: n.p., 1841–1934.

The standard source on British foreign relations for the period covered. Treaties, correspondence, and other documentation are included. Indexed.

[168] *Library of American Civilization or, The Microbook Library of American Civilization*. Chicago: Library Resources, 1971–1972.

This massive collection of some 20,000 titles covers American civilization up to World War I. The items in the collection have records in the library catalog. These are gradually being digitized by Google Books. Author, title, and subject indexes are available.

[169] *Major Peace Treaties of Modern History, 1648–1967*. Edited by Fred L. Israel. New York: Chelsea House, 1967–80. 5 vols.

(Ref JX 121 .I8).

Begins with the Treaty of Westphalia in 1648. Commentaries included.

[170] *Records of Ante-Bellum Southern Plantations from the Revolution to the Civil War. Series L. Selections from the Earl Gregg Swem Library, the College of William and Mary. Part 1: Carter Papers, 1667–1862*. Edited by Kenneth Stampp. Bethesda, MD: University Publications of America, 1994.

[171] *Records of the Confederate States of America*. Washington, DC: Library of Congress Photoduplication Service, 1967.

[172] *Schomburg Center Clipping File*. Alexandria, VA: Chadwick Healey, 1989.

Over 14,000 microfiche covering the twentieth-century African American experience, primarily through newspaper and magazine clippings. A print guide is available.

[173] *Southern Historical Society Papers*. Millwood, NY: Kraus Reprint, 1977. 52 vols.

(Ref E 483.7 S76 1977).

This collection includes reminiscences, memoirs, battle reports, and Confederate government minutes. Indispensable for serious Civil War research. The index, *An Index-Guide to the Southern Historical Society Papers, 1876–1959* is at Ref E 483.7 1977 index.

[174] *Southern Women and Their Families in the 19th Century, Papers and Diaries*. Bethesda, MD: University Publications of America, 1991.

Copies of records held at UNC (Chapel Hill) and at William & Mary.

[175] *Vietnam National Security Council Histories*. Edited by Paul Kesaris. Frederick, MD: University Publications of America, 1981.

The guide to the collection is entitled *A Guide to the War in Vietnam*.

[176] *Voices from Ellis Island*. Frederick, MD: University Publications of America, 1987.

An oral history of American immigration. This series consists of 185 microfiche with a printed guide.

[177] *Women's Journals, 1919–1968: From Franchise to Feminism. Part 1. Eve, 1919–1929*. Marlborough, England: Adam Matthew, 1997– .

An early British women's magazine with articles for the "new woman."

Newspapers

Until recently, only a few newspapers had subject indexes to aid the researcher. Among those titles, only a handful (e.g., *The New York Times* or *The Times* [London]) had indexes that covered content in any depth. Tedious scanning of newspapers (often on microfilm) was a common occupation of historians. Now that many digital editions of historical newspapers are available, newspaper research is often simplified and more widely available to the undergraduate student. The following guides and union lists are helpful for identifying key titles for a research project. Your librarian will be able to assist you in finding out what newspapers are accessible at your library or online. It is often possible for interlibrary loan departments to borrow reels of microfilmed newspapers from libraries that hold them.

[178] *American Newspapers 1821–1936: A Union List of Files Available in the United States and Canada*. Edited by Winifred Gregory. 1937. Reprint, New York: Kraus, 1967.
(Ref PN 4855 A53 1967).
Originally published in 1937, this comprehensive directory predates microfilming of newspapers. Arranged by state and city, the available issues are keyed to holding libraries.

[179] Brigham, Clarence S. *History and Bibliography of American Newspapers 1690–1820*. Westport, CT: Greenwood, 1975. 2 vols.
(Ref PN 4861 B86 1976).
Brigham's work covers the early years and is used as a predecessor to *American Newspapers*[178]. Over 2,000 newspapers are identified. Brigham has lengthy descriptions of the newspapers, noting editors and publishers.

[180] Cappon, Lester J. *Virginia Newspapers 1821–1935: A Bibliography with Historical Introduction and Notes*. Charlottesville, VA: Institute for Research in the Social Sciences, 1936.
(Ref F 230 C28 1936).
A union list of newspapers published in Virginia. Includes dates of publication and information on holding libraries. Cappon notes publishers by date and includes bibliographical notes on his sources.

[181] *Chronicling America: Historic American Newspapers*. http://chroniclingamerica.loc.gov.
(Public Access Database).
Indispensable website for research on American newspapers, sponsored by the National Endowment for the Humanities and the Library of Congress. It contains a directory of newspapers published from 1690 to the present, searchable by state, county, city, dates of publication, ethnicity, and language. In addition, libraries holding the print editions or microfilms are listed.
   Also at this website is a growing archive of completely digitized and searchable newspapers, now stretching from 1836 up to 1922. This is an outgrowth of the U.S. Newspaper Project, which began as a cooperative program to locate, catalog, and preserve, on microfilm, all newspapers published in the United States.

[182] *New Serial Titles: A Union List of Serials Commencing Publication After December 31, 1949.* Washington, DC: Joint Committee on the Union List of Serials, Library of Congress, 1953–1999.
(Biblio Z 6945 U5 S42).
Periodicals beginning since 1950 are listed in this comprehensive source. International in coverage.

[183] *Printed U.S. Newspaper Indexes in the Newspaper and Current Periodical Reading Room, Library of Congress.* http://www.loc.gov/rr/news/newsind.html.
(Public Access Database).
Very helpful tool for determining if a printed newspaper index is available.

[184] *Ulrichsweb.com. Ulrich's International Periodicals Directory.* New Providence, NJ: Bowker.
(Online Library Subscription Database).
A major source for current periodicals published worldwide. Over 125,000 titles are listed. Includes some brief reviews, publisher contact information, available formats, and pricing.

[185] *Union List of Serials in Libraries of the United States and Canada.* Edited by Edna Brown Titus. 3rd ed. New York: H. W. Wilson, 1965. 5 vols.
(Biblio Z 6945 U45 1965).
The print source lists periodicals published prior to 1950 and held in 950 libraries. Coverage is international and comprehensive. Continued by *New Serial Titles* [182]. Complemented and updated online by *WorldCat* [79], which contains records describing most serial publications, including those in the printed *Union List*.

Popular Magazines

General interest magazines, while usually of less regional interest than newspapers, are useful primary sources for the researcher. Guides and indexes to magazines are listed here. As with newspapers, digitized collections are becoming more accessible.

[186] *American Mass-Market Magazines.* Edited by Alan Nourie and Barbara Nourie. New York, Greenwood, 1990.
Profiles of historical and recent American magazines with circulation over 100,000. Includes publishing histories and bibliographies.

[187] Mott, Frank Luther. *A History of American Magazines.* Cambridge: Harvard University Press, 1938–1968. 5 vols.
Covering magazines published from 1741 to 1930, a rich historical record of magazine publishing.

[188] Poole, William Frederick. *Poole's Index to Periodical Literature, 1802–1906.* New York: Peter Smith, 1938.
(Online Library Subscription Database included in *C19: The Nineteenth Century Index;* also in print, Ref Abstract/Index).
Similar in scope to *Readers' Guide Retrospective* [189], this resource indexes popular magazines of the nineteenth century from the United States and Britain.

[189] *Readers' Guide Retrospective.* New York: Wilson, 1890–1982.
(Online Library Subscription Database).
Excellent subject indexing for popular magazines of the twentieth century. This is the place to discover how America reacted to *Sputnik*'s launch in 1957 or the discovery of King Tut's tomb in 1922. *OmniFile Full Text Mega* [93] will bring coverage up to the present time.

Archives and Manuscript Collections

Access to the Internet has revolutionized the task of discovering where special archival and manuscript collections may be found. Guides to specific collections and in-depth finding aids are often freely available to any researcher with an Internet connection. Increasingly, the rare documents are also being digitized. It is still often essential that the researcher visit the repository where the original documents are preserved.

Guides to Specific Collections or Topics

[190] *Black History: A Guide to Civilian Records in the National Archives.* Compiled by Debra L. Newman. Washington, DC: GPO, 1984.
(Ref E 185 N576 1984).

[191] Bond, Maurice F. *Guide to the Records of Parliament.* London: HMSO, 1971.
(Ref CD 1063 B63).
Very useful guide to British parliamentary records from the fifteenth century up to 1970.

[192] *Labor History Archives in the United States: A Guide for Researching and Teaching.* Edited by Daniel J. Leab. Detroit, MI: Wayne State University Press, 1992.
(Stacks HD 8066 L22 1992).
Description of the labor holdings of forty libraries, archives, and historical societies. Published sources and manuscript holdings are noted.

[193] *The National Archives, In-Depth Research Guides.* http://www.nationalarchives.gov.uk/records/research-guide-listing.htm.
(Public Access Database).
The National Archives is the United Kingdom's official archive, and it is hard at work digitizing documents. At this page, the researcher will find a detailed A to Z listing, with links, to in-depth guides to the collections, and, in some cases, to digitized archives.

[194] Neagles, James C. *Confederate Research Sources: A Guide to Archives Collections.* Salt Lake City, UT: Ancestry, 1986.
(Ref E 487 N3 1986).
A scholarly presentation of the Confederacy and the records it produced.

[195] Neagles, James C. *The Library of Congress: a Guide to Genealogical and Historical Research.* Salt Lake City, UT: Ancestry, 1990.
(Ref E 180 N4 1990).
A comprehensive guide, with annotated bibliography, to the historical collections at the Library of Congress (LC), although many sources

listed are also available outside of the LC. Arranged by topic and geographical area.

[196] *Records of the Presidency: Presidential Papers and Libraries from Washington to Reagan.* Edited by Frank L. Schick. Phoenix, AZ: Onyx Press, 1989.
(Ref CD 3029.82 S35 1989).
An excellent guide to researching the presidency and individual presidents. The first section details agencies that work with presidential records. Additional sections look at presidential papers at the Library of Congress, papers in historical societies and special libraries, and the presidential libraries administered by the National Archives. Scholarly.

[197] United States. Library of Congress. *Special Collections in the Library of Congress: A Selective Guide.* Edited by Annette Melville. Washington, DC: GPO, 1980.
(Stacks Z 733 U58 U54 1980).
A guide to over 250 major collections at the Library of Congress. Scope and contents of each collection described. Scholarly.

[198] United States. National Archives and Records Administration. *Guide to Federal Records in the National Archives of the United States.* Compiled by Robert B. Machette and Anne B. Eales. Washington, DC: GPO, 1995. 3 vols.
(Ref CD 3026 1995; regularly updated online at National Archives website, http://www.archives.gov)
A very useful introduction to National Archives collections. Contains information on the scope of holdings of various government agencies, and assists the researcher in determining the Record Group number for pertinent records.

[199] United States. National Archives and Records Administration. *Guide to Records in the National Archives of the United States Relating to American Indians.* Compiled by Edward E. Hill. Washington, DC: GPO, 1981.
(Ref E 93 H642 1981).

[200] Vandercook, Sharon. *A Guide to British Documents and Records in the University of Virginia Library.* Charlottesville, VA: Reference Department, University of Virginia Library, 1972.
(Ref CD 1042 V363 1972).
University of Virginia has extensive holdings of British documents, especially for the nineteenth and twentieth centuries.

[201] Wigdor, Alexandra K. *The Personal Papers of Supreme Court Justices: Descriptive Guide.* New York: Garland, 1986.
(Stacks KF 8744 W55 1986).
Alphabetical arrangement by justice. Information includes location, size, access restrictions, provenance, and description of the collection.

[202] *The WPA Historical Records Survey: A Guide to the Unpublished Inventories, Indexes, and Transcripts.* Compiled by Loretta Hefner. Chicago: Society of American Archivists, 1980.
(Ref E 173 H43 1980).
Arranged by state; contains listings of the holdings of each repository.

Directories and Indexes

[203] *Articles Describing Archives and Manuscript Collections in the United States: An Annotated Bibliography.* Compiled by Donald L. DeWitt. Westport, CT: Greenwood, 1997.
(Ref CE 3022 A2 D478 1997).
The initial arrangement is by broad subject category. The final two categories list foreign repositories holding U.S.-related records and U.S. repositories holding foreign records. Entries are annotated.

[204] *Directory of American Libraries with Genealogy or Local History Collections.* Compiled by P. W. Filby. Wilmington, DE: Scholarly Resources, 1988.
(Ref CS 47 F56 1988).
A directory of libraries in the United States and Canada with outstanding local history collections. Entries include collection strengths, interlibrary loan possibilities, and contact information. Over 1,300 libraries are featured.

[205] *Directory of Historical Societies and Agencies in the United States and Canada.* 15th ed. Madison, WI: American Association for State and Local History, 2002.
(Ref E 172 A538 2002).
A comprehensive directory arranged by state or province and then by city or town. Entries include contact information, publications, major programs, and collection features.

[206] *The National Union Catalog of Manuscript Collections.* Washington, DC: Library of Congress, 1959/1961–1993.
(Biblio Z 6620 U5 N3 and Public Access Database at http://www.loc .gov/coll/nucmc/).
The most comprehensive guide to United States manuscript collections. All types and forms of manuscript materials are listed. Entries include a description of the collection, the donor(s), the repository, years of coverage, the collection size, and any finding aids. Cumulative indexes are available. The online database at the Library of Congress provides free searching of the manuscript subset of records in *WorldCat* [79] for records added since 1986.

[207] *Oral History Index: An International Directory of Oral History Interviews.* Edited by Ellen S. Wasserman. Westport, CT: Meckler, 1990.
(Ref D16.14 .O74 1990).
Organized by name of interviewee, this volume directs the researcher to the repository that holds the transcript of the original interview. Covers oral history centers in the United States, Canada, Great Britain, and Israel.

[208] *Repositories of Primary Sources.* http://www.uiweb.uidaho.edu/special-collections/ Other.Repositories.html.
(Public Access Database).
A listing of worldwide repositories of manuscripts, archives, and special collections websites, organized geographically. Compiled by Terry Abraham at the University of Idaho.

[209] *Researcher's Guide to Archives and Regional History Sources.* Edited by John C. Larsen. Hamden, CT: Library Professional Publications, 1988.

(Stacks CD 3021 R47 1988).

In fourteen topical chapters, Larsen presents issues important to regional research; contains some bibliographic sources. Chapters cover, e.g., oral history, cartographic sources, and business records.

[210] Smith, Allen. *Directory of Oral History Collections*. Phoenix, AZ: Oryx Press, 1988. (Ref D 16.14 S54 1988).

Organized by state, this guide describes the oral history holdings of various U.S. repositories. A subject index allows the researcher to identify potential libraries and archives by subject.

[211] *Subject Collections: A Guide to Special Book Collections and Subject Emphases as Reported by University, College, Public, and Special Libraries and Museums in the United States and Canada*. Compiled by Lee Ash. 7th ed. New Providence, NJ: Bowker, 1993. 2 vols. (Ref Z 688 Z2 A8 1993).

A comprehensive directory to libraries having special collections. Arranged by subject. Entries give an account of their collections, their size, and outside availability.

Diaries

[212] Arksey, Laura, Nancy Pries, and Marcia Reed. *American Diaries: An Annotated Bibliography of Published American Diaries and Journals*. Detroit, MI: Gale Research, 1983. 2 vols. (Ref CT 214 A73 1983).

The standard bibliography to American diaries, it supersedes William Matthews' *American Diaries*, published in 1945. Annotations to some 6,000 published diaries, arranged chronologically by the year in which the diary began, from 1492 to 1980. Author, subject, and geographic indexes.

[213] Havlice, Patricia Pate. *And So to Bed: A Bibliography of Diaries Published in English*. Metuchen, NJ: Scarecrow, 1987. (Ref CT 25 H38 1987).

This bibliography lists diaries published as books, chapters in books, journal articles, dissertations, or microforms. It is particularly helpful for finding diaries that have been translated into English from other languages. It is organized chronologically and covers all historical periods. Generally, it *does not* duplicate items listed in Matthews, *British Diaries* [214], but contains an index of those persons as well as those listed in Matthews' *Canadian Diaries*. There are indexes to diarists as well as a general index that includes places and occupations.

[214] Matthews, William. *British Diaries: An Annotated Bibliography of British Diaries Written Between 1442 and 1942*. 1950. Reprint, Gloucester, MA: P. Smith, 1967. (Stacks PR 1330 .M38 1967).

This bibliography lists both published and unpublished journals and diaries. Front matter includes a list of all diaries that extend for at least ten years. Generally omits travel accounts, minutes, and ships' logs. Organized by year diary begins, with an index to diarists.

U.S. Government Information

Guides

[215] Morehead, Joe. *Introduction to United States Government Information Sources*. Englewood, CO: Libraries Unlimited, 1999.

(Ref Z 1223 Z7 M67 1999).

The best current introduction to using government documents. Arranged generally by agency, Morehead includes sections on the Government Printing Office, statistical sources, historical background, etc. For advanced information on government documents see also Schmeckebier [216].

[216] Schmeckebier, Laurence F. *Government Publications and Their Use*. 2nd rev. ed. Washington, DC: Brookings Institution, 1969.

(Stacks Z 1223 A7 S3 1969).

Although published over forty years ago, this guide remains the standard for a detailed understanding of how to use government documents from a historical perspective. See the entries under Morehead [215] and Sears [217] for current guides to government documents.

[217] Sears, Jean L., and Marilyn K. Moody. *Using Government Information Sources: Electronic and Print*. 3rd ed. Phoenix, AZ: Onyx Press, 2001.

(Ref Z 1223 .Z7 S4 2001).

A practical guide that deals with specific types of government research searches; for example, subject, agency, statistical. Includes special techniques section, which includes legislative history and treaties.

Indexes and Full-Text Databases by Coverage Dates

1774 to 1881

[218] Poore, Benjamin P. *A Descriptive Catalogue of the Government Publications of the United States, September 5, 1774–March 4, 1881*. 1885. Reprint. New York: Johnson Reprint, 1962. 2 vols.

(Ref Z 1223 A1885d).

This is the earliest effort to publish a guide to government documents. Although difficult to use, it lists the majority of documents printed up to 1881. The bulk of the work is a chronological listing of publications with short descriptions, followed by an index of names and subjects.

1789 to 1909

[219] United States. Superintendent of Documents. *Checklist of United States Public Documents 1789–1909, Congressional...* 3rd ed., rev. and enl. Washington, DC: GPO, 1911.

(Ref Z 1223 A113).

This source indexes documents by agency. It allows the researcher to determine the series that were published by departmental agency. Useful for its providing of *Serial Set* (see [225]) numbers and historical data on the agencies. A second (index) volume was never published.

1881 to 1893

[220] Ames, John G. *Comprehensive Index to the Publications of the United States Government, 1881–1893.* 1905. Reprint, New York: Johnson Reprint Corp., 1970. 2 vols. (Ref Z 1223 A 1970).

A continuation of the work by Poore [218] but organized alphabetically by subject. It first appeared as House Document 754 (in 2 parts) and is available in the online library subscription database, *U.S. Congressional Serial Set* [225].

1893 to 1940

[221] United States. Superintendent of Documents. *Catalog of the Public Documents of the Congress and of All Departments of the Government of the United States...* Washington, DC: GPO, 1893–1940.

(Ref Z 1223 A13).

For the years of coverage this index is the most complete recording of government documents ever published. Subject arrangement with complete cataloging information. Known as the *Document Catalog.*

1940 to Present

[222] *Catalog of U.S. Government Publications (CGP).* http://catalog.gpo.gov/F. (Public Access Database).

This is the standard finding aid for government documents published since 1976, although earlier documents are also indexed. The Government Printing Office plans to expand indexing retrospectively to include documents published since the late 1800s.

[223] *FDsys: GPO's Federal Digital System.* http://www.gpo.gov/fdsys/. (Public Access Database).

The successor to the *CGP* [222], this database goes beyond indexing to include the digitized government documents. Excellent searching and browsing capabilities.

[224] *Monthly Catalog of United States Government Publications.* Washington, DC: GPO, 1940 to present.

(Gov Docs GP 3.8).

This is the standard print indexing tool since 1940.

[225] *U.S. Congressional Serial Set Digital Edition (Readex).*

(Online Library Subscription Database).

A rich collection of primary source material on all aspects of government interest, originating from Congress and federal agencies. Covers commerce, exploration, science, military, environment, health, economics, and social issues. Diverse document types include reports, journals, letters, treaties, illustrations, official records, hearings, eyewitness accounts, statistics, and maps. Along with *American State Papers, 1789–1838* (Readex) [153], this database covers 1789 to 1980.

U.S. Law and Legislation

[226] *Black's Law Dictionary.* Edited by Bryan A. Garner. St. Paul, MN: West, 2009. (Carrier Ready Ref KF156 B53 2009).

The best reference work for legal terminology.

[227] *A Century of Lawmaking for a New Nation: U.S. Congressional Documents and Debates, 1774–1875.* http://memory.loc.gov/ammem/amlaw/
(Public Access Database).
From the *American Memory* [143] web, this site brings together records and acts of Congress through the 43rd Congress and includes Journals, Debates, and Statutes.

[228] *Congressional Quarterly Almanac.* Annual. Washington, DC: Congressional Quarterly, 1961 to present.
(Ref JK 1 C66).
An outstanding source for United States government information, especially useful for tracing Congressional activity during a given year. Data includes all recorded votes in Congress.

[229] *Congressional Research* (Proquest).
(Online Library Subscription Database).
Searchable full text for congressional publications and legislation. Includes abstracts and indexing for congressional publications, legislative histories, member biographies, committee assignments, voting records, financial data, and the full text of key regulatory and statutory resources. Most titles (includes Congressional Committee Prints, House & Senate Documents and Reports, Hearings, and Legislative Histories) are online from 1970 to present.

[230] *Thomas.* http://thomas.loc.gov.
(Public Access Database).
"In the spirit of Thomas Jefferson," the Library of Congress offers legislative information through this portal. Coverage varies; bill summaries and public laws covered from the 93rd (1973) through current Congress; bill text search available from 101st (1989) Congress through present.

[231] *United States Statutes at Large.* Washington, DC: U.S. Government Printing Office.
(Ref KF50 U52 and in Microforms for 1789–1972).
This work compiles all laws enacted by Congress. At the American Memory [143] website, the full text of the Statutes is available online for 1789 through 1875 (1st through 43rd Congress). An individual statute is often referred to by Public Law number; e.g., PL 94-142. This denotes a law (the 142nd law) passed during the 94th Congress.

Treaties

United States

[232] *Treaties and Other International Agreements of the United States of America, 1776–1949.* Edited by Charles I. Bevans. Washington, DC: Government Printing Office, 1968–1976. 13 vols.
(Ref JX 231 A32).
Contains texts of all U.S. treaties through 1949. Vol. 13 is a general index. Often referred to as *Bevans.* See also *U.S. Congressional Serial Set Digital Edition* [225]. Continued by *TIAS* [234].

[233] U.S. Department of State. *Treaties in Force: A List of Treaties and Other International Agreements of the United States on January 1, ...* Annual.

(Most recent edition is online at State Department: http://www.state .gov/s/l/treaty/tif/).

Compiled as of 1 January of each year, this finding aid has bilateral agreements of the United States listed by country (or organization) and subject, and multilateral agreements listed by subject.

[234] U.S. Department of State. *United States Treaties and Other International Acts Series.* Washington, DC: Government Printing Office, 1950 to present.

(Stacks JX 231 .A34; online since mid-1990s at http://www.state.gov/ s/l/treaty/tias/).

This source is often abbreviated *TIAS.* It publishes the full texts of all U.S. agreements.

Multilateral and World

[235] *FLARE Index to Treaties.* http://ials.sas.ac.uk/library/flag/introtreaties.htm.

(Public Access Database).

Searchable index that focuses on treaties between three or more parties. Maintained by Institute of Advanced Legal Studies at the University of London.

[236] *Multilaterals Project of The Fletcher School.* http://fletcher.tufts.edu/Multilaterals/.

(Public Access Database).

Tufts University maintains this website, which contains the full text of many international conventions since 1945, with subject and chronological access. Important historical treaties are also included. Has links to helpful guides for researching treaties as well as websites of organizations and countries where treaties are found.

Public Opinion Sources

Many organizations that conduct or sponsor polls make the results freely available online. These include the Pew Research Center, the World Values Survey Association, and the Association of Religion Data Archives (ARDA). Cornell University maintains a webpage linking to many of these sources for public opinion data at http://ciser.cornell.edu/info/polls.shtml.

[237] *iPOLL: Public Opinion Archives.* Roper Center, University of Connecticut.

(Online Library Subscription Database).

Results of polling in the United States by all major public opinion survey firms, with earliest coverage for the 1935 Gallup Poll.

Speeches

[238] *American Rhetoric Online Speech Bank.* http://americanrhetoric.com.

(Public Access Database).

Maintained by a professor of communication at the University of Texas (Tyler), this website offers a large number of speeches in text, audio, and video formats. Be aware that the audio versions of some speeches, e.g., *The Gettysburg Address*, are recorded by actors, which is plainly stated. As a dot-com, the website contains ads, but it remains a quality tool.

[239] *Speech Index: An Index to 259 Collections of World Famous Orations and Speeches for Various Occasions.* Edited by Roberta Briggs Sutton. 4th rev. ed. 1966. New York: Scarecrow Press, 1966. Supplements continue coverage up to 1980. (Stacks AI 3 S85).
Coverage is for all time periods and geographic areas.

[240] *Vital Speeches of the Day.* New York: The City News, 1934 to present. (Periodical) (Online Library Subscription Database, print, and microform).
Indexing and PDF documents are available online from 1934 in *Academic Search Complete* [89]. Limit your search to the journal *Vital Speeches of the Day.* An excellent source for speeches worldwide (translated into English, if in another language) since 1934.

Statistical Sources

United States

[241] *America Votes.* Washington, DC: Governmental Affairs Institute, Congressional Quarterly, 1956 to present. Biennial.
(Ref JK 1967 A8).
The standard source for detailed voting statistics since 1956. Contains presidential, gubernatorial, senatorial, and congressional statistics. A standard Library of Congress Subject Heading to search in library catalogs is Elections—United States—Statistics. Additional election sources include:

- *Presidential Elections Since 1789.* 5th ed. Washington, DC: Congressional Quarterly, 1991. (JK 524 C65 1991).

- *America at the Polls: A Handbook of American Presidential Election Statistics.* Edited by Alice V. McGillivray and Richard M. Scammon. Washington, DC: Congressional Quarterly, 1994. (Ref JK 524 A73 1994). Vol. 1 covers 1920 to 1956; vol. 2, 1960 to 1992.

[242] *Historical Census Browser.* http://fisher.lib.virginia.edu/collections/stats/histcensus/. (Public Access Database).
Detailed U.S. census information to the state and county level from 1790 to 1960. Permits selection of single or multiple variables to construct data lists.

[243] *Historical Statistics of the United States: Earliest Times to the Present.* Edited by Susan B. Carter. Cambridge: Cambridge University Press, 2006. 5 vols.
(Ref HA 202 H57 2006 and Online Library Subscription Database).
Covers the complete time period of American history. The 2006 edition is a new compilation of statistical information on the United States and colonial America. The online database contains all of the data from the print edition but also allows the researcher to create tables for manipulation in statistical software programs. The *Statistical Abstract of the United States* [245] provides more recent data.

[244] *ICPSR.*

(Online Library Subscription Database).

The Inter-University Consortium for Political and Social Research is a finding aid and repository for datasets of social science research in areas such as criminal justice, aging, demographics, and health. Both U.S. and international sources are available.

[245] *Statistical Abstract of the United States.* U.S. Census Bureau. Annual. http://www .census.gov/compendia/statab/past_years.html.

(Public Access Database, also in print, HA 202 A35, and on microfiche).

Now fully digitized as PDF files, this has long been the standard, detailed source for U.S. statistics. Most tables contain citations that refer the researcher to the original source of the information.

[246] *Vital Statistics on American Politics 2009–2010.* CQ Press Online Editions.

(Online Library Subscription Database).

Despite the dates in the title, this resource contains tables of historical statistics on many aspects of politics, including media, the judiciary, military conflicts, education, and foreign aid.

Selected Regions and Themes

[247] *British Historical Statistics.* Edited by B. R. Mitchell. Cambridge: Cambridge University Press, 1988.

(Ref HA 1134 M58 1988).

[248] Clodfelter, Micheal. *Warfare and Armed Conflicts: A Statistical Reference to Casualty and Other Figures, 1500–2000.* 2nd ed. Jefferson, NC: McFarland, 2002.

(Ref D 214 C54 2002).

Very useful volume, containing descriptions of wars, rebellions, and individual battles (when possible) for the modern period. Includes estimates of numbers of combatants and casualties.

[249] Great Britain. Central Statistical Office. *Statistical Digest of the War.* London: HMSO, 1951.

(Ref HA 1125 .A53).

Statistics for Great Britain during World War II.

[250] *International Historical Statistics: Africa, Asia & Oceania, 1750–2005.* Edited by B. R. Mitchell. Houndmills, Basingstoke, Hampshire: Palgrave Macmillan, 2007.

(Ref HA 4675 M552 2007).

[251] *International Historical Statistics: Europe, 1750–2005.* Edited by B. R. Mitchell. Houndmills, Basingstoke, Hampshire: Palgrave Macmillan, 2007.

(Ref HA 1107 M5 2003).

[252] *International Historical Statistics: The Americas, 1750–2005.* Edited by B. R. Mitchell. Houndmills, Basingstoke, Hampshire: Palgrave Macmillan, 2007.

(Ref HA 175 .M55 2003).

Appendix B

✳

Guilty until Proven Innocent

PAUL MCDOWELL

They had been found innocent. After six months of uncertainty, the jury had finally awarded the defendants their freedom. Tomorrow, they would go back to their families and celebrate the birthday of King Umberto I[1] with singing, dancing, and feasting. Life would return to normal. They would go back to working on the docks, along the streets, or in the stores. The nine Sicilians accused of murdering New Orleans Police Chief David Hennessy went to sleep on March 13, 1891, with freedom in their minds and hope in their hearts. Unfortunately, seven of those nine would never experience their freedom. The next morning, thousands of New Orleans residents stormed the Parish Prison and brutally executed eleven Italians locked inside, claiming to bring justice when the American courts failed to do so. Newspapers around the United States quickly seized the opportunity, using the event to display anti-immigrant sentiments. Many newspapers favored the extreme measure to which the upper-class New Orleans residents had carried out justice upon the devious Sicilians, and only a few factions of the American press condemned such rash action. Despite different political and social reasoning, most newspapers from all around the United States shared the same underlying anti-Italian sentiment in their reports of the 1891 lynching of eleven Sicilians in New Orleans.[2]

---

1. Italian monarch during the late nineteenth century.

2. Any in-depth research on the results of immigration into the United States begins with John D. Buekner and Lorman A. Ratner, *Multiculturalism in the United States: A Comparative Guide to Acculturation and Ethnicity* (New York: Greenwood Press, 2005). John Higham, *Strangers in the Land: Patterns of American Nativism, 1860–1925* (New Brunswick: Rutgers University Press, 1955), and Desmond Humphrey Joseph, *The APA Movement* (New York: Arno Press, 1969), which provide excellent overviews and analyses of general American nativism around the turn of the nineteenth century. Alexander DeConde, *Half Bitter, Half Sweet: An Excursion into Italian-American History* (New York: Scribner, 1971), provides a good introduction to the overall Italian-American experience during the height of Italian immigration. Edwin Fenton, *Immigrants and Unions, a Case Study: Italians and American Labor, 1870–1920* (New York: Arno Press, 1957), and Donna Gabaccia, *Militants and Migrants: Rural Sicilians Become American Workers* (New Brunswick: Rutgers University Press, 1988), adequately describe Italian-Americans and their roles in the American labor system throughout different parts of the United States around the turn of the twentieth century. For information on the city of New Orleans itself during the 1890s, Joy J. Jackson, *New Orleans in the Gilded Age: Politics and Urban Progress, 1880–1896* (Baton Rouge: Louisiana State University Press, 1969), and her, "Crime and the Conscience of a City," *Louisiana History* 24, no. 4 (Summer 1968): 229–244, analyze the general background of New Orleans around the time of the 1891 lynching. To discover detailed reports of other lynchings of Sicilians in the South, see Clive Webb, "The Lynching of Sicilian Immigrants in the American South, 1886–1910," *American Nineteenth Century History* 3, no. 1 (Spring 2002): 45–77. For a combination of extended

American nativism and extreme xenophobia plagued the entire United States around the turn of the twentieth century. Not all of this nativism, however, attacked one common ethnicity; northerners despised immigrants from southern and eastern Europe, while westerners in California loathed immigrants from eastern Asia. Residents of the South held fewer anti-immigrant convictions than most other Americans simply because immigrants were not streaming into the southern states at the same rate as they were in the North and the West. Southerners still demonstrated a strong distaste for minorities, however, and ostracized and ridiculed most people without Anglo-Saxon blood during the last half of the nineteenth century. Much of this hatred throughout the southern states and the rest of the country proved completely groundless, as few minorities posed a direct threat to a white majority; in fact, many minorities and most immigrants actually assured white Americans a continued social dominance. The immigrants arrived in all parts of the United States very eager for employment, and this hunger for labor forced the immigrants to work for incredibly low wages. The rapidly increasing immigrant population, which offered its labor for miniscule wages, single-handedly drove down the cost of employment for white business owners, ensuring that the owners could make more products for less.[3]

Italians worked just as hard and for just as little as other immigrants of the late nineteenth century. Yet the American population still foolishly stereotyped the Italians as lazy, dirty, and devious workers who could not be relied upon despite their tendency to work for lower wages than other laborers and their offering to replace striking workers. Residents of New Orleans held this anti-Italian belief just as strongly as other Americans, if not more so. While immigrants refrained from entering most southern states for one reason or another, Louisiana proved a monstrous exception. As a large maritime port between the Mississippi River and the Gulf of Mexico, New Orleans had attracted many seafaring immigrants throughout its history. By 1860, 38 percent of New Orleans' entire population was foreign-born, and rural Sicilians were beginning to

---

narrative and in-depth analysis on the events surrounding the actual lynching on 14 March 1891, see Richard Gambino, *Vendetta: A True Story of the Worst Lynching in America, the Mass Murder of Italian-Americans in New Orleans in 1891, the Vicious Motivations Behind It, and the Tragic Repercussions that Linger to this Day* (Garden City, NY: Doubleday and Co., 1977); Joseph Gentile, *The Innocent Lynched: The Story of Eleven Italians Lynched in New Orleans* (New York: Writer's Showcase Press, 2000); Tom Smith, *The Crescent City Lynchings: The Murder of Chief Hennessy, the New Orleans 'Mafia' Trials, and the Parish Prison Mob* (Guilford, CT: The Lyons Press, 2007); Humbert S. Nelli, "The Hennessy Murder and the Mafia in New Orleans," *Italian Quarterly* 19, no. 75 (1975): 77–95. Other works focus on different aspects of the event: J. Alexander Karlin, "New Orleans Lynchings of 1891 and the American Press," *Louisiana Historical Quarterly* 24, no.1 (January 1941): 187–204, examines the nationwide media's reaction to the event. Barbara Botein, "The Hennessy Case: An Episode of Anti-Italian Nativism," *Louisiana History* 20, no. 3 (1979): 261–279, discusses how the trial and lynching were cases of extreme nativism during a time of heightened xenophobia. For contemporary reports on the lynching, the most trustworthy works include "Correspondence in Relation to the Killing of Prisoners in New Orleans on March 14, 1891," Harvard University Library Virtual Collections, http://pds.lib.harvard.edu/pds/view/4987805 (accessed 15 February 2009); *New York Times; Washington Post; Harper's Weekly*; and the *New Orleans Daily Picayune*.

3. Gentile, 63–73.

represent a large part of that number.[4] By 1880, the foreign-born population had dropped to 19 percent, but most of those foreign-born residents were now Italians. Contrary to the assumptions of most upper-class residents, however, most Italians arrived in New Orleans without the intention of establishing permanent residence. Many Italian immigrants planned to return to their homeland once they had made a sufficient amount of money, and a long-term stay in the United States was usually not part of the picture.[5]

Nevertheless, many southerners still disliked the growing number of Italian immigrants throughout southern Louisiana. Some southerners, especially those with a strong Protestant faith, saw the influx of the Italians as a dangerous religious coup. They denounced the Italians' Roman Catholicism, labeling it an imminent threat to the long-standing Protestant tradition in the South. Some even called the Catholic religion the "antichrist," suspecting all the Italians of being under direct control of the Papacy. The preachers who warned of a Catholic takeover, however, were ignoring a major rift between the Italian population and the Catholic Church at the time, as many Italians of the late nineteenth century held a very weak relationship with the Papacy.[6]

Some native southerners disliked the Italians because of their close ties with the black community. Aligning with the Populist Party,[7] disagreeing with discrimination practices against blacks, and participating with former slaves or slave descendents in commercial ventures, the Italians opened themselves to glaring judgments of white southerners, many of whom had a direct association with the former Confederacy. The Italians were buying and trading from blacks around New Orleans, but they were also doing so with incredible success. Several Italian trading families in New Orleans blossomed into major businesses during this time, and many members of the southern aristocracy envied the immediate success of these Italian productions. By 1890, the famous French Quarter and French Market had been unofficially renamed "Little Palermo," as the Italian immigrants won control of many businesses

---

4. While Italians are most known for immigrating to major northern cities, such as New York, Boston, and Chicago, a number of Italians also immigrated to New Orleans. Louisiana held the largest Italian population prior to the Civil War, and Italians did not begin their miss migrations to northern cities until the 1880s. The Italian immigrants in the northern United States tended to hail from northern and mainland Italy, but the immigrants who arrived in New Orleans were chiefly Sicilians. While no single cause has been found to explain why Sicilians left for New Orleans in particular, most scholars agree that the similar climates of New Orleans and Sicily and the resemblances between the Gulf of Mexico and the Mediterranean Sea played a big role.

5. Gentile, 8; U.S. Bureau of the Census, *Population of the United States in 1860: Compiled from the Original Returns of the Eighth Census under the Direction of the Secretary of the Interior*, xxxii; U.S. Bureau of the Census, *Statistics of the Population of the United States at the Tenth Census (June 1, 1880): Embracing Extended Tables of the Population of State, Counties and Minor Civil Divisions, with Distinction of Race, Sex, Age, Nativity, and Occupations*, compiled by Joseph C. G. Kennedy, Superintendent of the Census (Washington, DC: Government Printing Office, 1883), 1: 538–541.

6. The Catholic Church of the late nineteenth century routinely impeded the political unification of Italy, which greatly frustrated many Italians. Patrick J. Gallo, *Old Bread, New Wine: A Portrait of the Italian Americans* (Chicago: Nelson, Hall, 1981), 121–122; Gentile, 12; "Our Italians," *New York Times*, 9 December 1884.

7. The Populist Party was a major political rival to the Democratic Party of the late nineteenth century. Most southerners were members with the Democratic Party, so the fact that the Italians joined the Populist Party would not have won them many friends in the South. Gentile, 7.

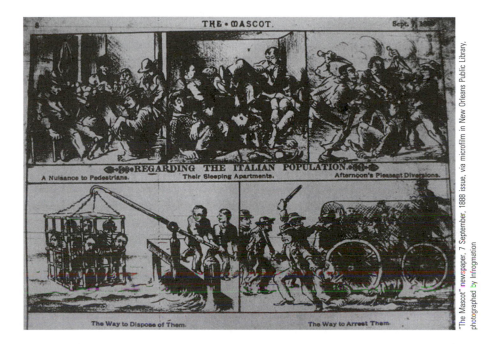

"The Mascot" newspaper, 7 September, 1888 issue, via microfilm in New Orleans Public Library, photographed by Infrogmation

around the heart of the city. Unfortunately for the Italians, the white citizens of New Orleans did not appreciate this newfound success. As the Italians became wealthier and continued to go against the social norms of nineteenth-century New Orleans, the native residents of the city became even more infuriated with the uncooperative and incredibly successful immigrants.[8]

The picture above, featured in *The Mascot*,[9] a popular journal in New Orleans during the last half of the nineteenth century, illustrated mainstream New Orleans' views towards the Italian population. The upper-left part of the cartoon first labeled the Italians "a nuisance to pedestrians," showing the Italians unproductively lying around the streets. The next description showed the Italians' living spaces, where they were all crammed into a tiny closet like sardines. Mocking them as "afternoon's pleasant diversions" in the next illustration, the author of the cartoon showed the Italians, almost resembling monkeys, brawling in the middle of the street. The final two portions of the cartoon displayed the white residents dragging the Italians off and then dropping them in the Mississippi River, as if the Italians were incontrollable savage beasts who required

---

8. Gentile, 8.

9. "Regarding the Italian Population," *The Mascot, An Independent Journal of the Day*, 7 September 1888.

immediate disposal. This cartoon demonstrated the flagrant anti-Italianism in New Orleans and exemplified most New Orleanians' perspective towards Italians.[10]

Contrary to the widespread belief that Italians were lazy and dangerous beasts, both the Provenzano and the Matranga families controlled two of the most successful businesses in New Orleans during this time. These Italian families came to dominate the lower strata of New Orleans just before the turn of the twentieth century, and they soon began to compete for control of the docks. Ultimately the Matranga family won control, and soon after the change of command, the Provenzanos responded with several violent attacks upon their rival workforce. After nearly two years of skirmishes between the two Italian factions, the rough-and-tumble Police Chief David Hennessy[11] and his police force finally arrested the Provenzano leaders. Discrepancies, however, marred the trial against the Provenzanos. Nearly all of the police testimonies supported the Provenzano faction, while every other testimonial, mostly given by people connected with the Matranga faction, accused the Provenzanos of malicious intent. Some people began to suspect the possibility of an underground Italian society and mulled its possible deals with the police department or the witnesses. After a grand jury declared a mistrial, a new trial was set for 22 October 1890.[12]

David Hennessy would not live to see that trial. On the foggy, rainy night of 15 October, exactly one week before he was to testify, David Hennessy walked into an ambush. As he headed back to his house from the police headquarters late at night, several dark figures came out of nowhere and riddled him with bullets. The assassins scattered, dropping their weapons in the process. David Hennessy lived on for nearly nine more hours, during which he repeatedly denied knowing who had attacked him. Despite his consistent denial, however, fellow police officer William O'Connor, who was the first to find Hennessy following the attack, declared that Hennessy had indeed told him who had committed the assassination. According to O'Connor,[13] "the Dagos did it."[14] The police force quickly rounded up scores of Italian males, while

---

10. "Regarding the Italian Population," *The Mascot, An Independent Journal of the Day*, 7 September 1888.

11. David Hennessy's past remains somewhat of a mystery, but it is widely believed that he was both corrupt and ruthless. According to Dr. Patrick Gallo of New York University, Hennessy was "what we nowadays call a 'gangster,' if he had not happened to line up on the side of law and order." Gallo, 121–122.

12. Gentile, 14–21; Smith, 120–124.

13. O'Connor, Hennessy's police partner and close friend, claimed that Hennessy had told him that "the Dagos did it" when he first found Hennessy following the assault. Hennessy, however, repeatedly denied ever knowing the identity of attackers during the nine hours between the attack and his final death. Once Hennessy was dead, it was merely assumed that O'Connor was telling the truth, and the New Orleans newspapers instantly began constructing explanations for why the Italians would have committed the murder. "Assassinated, Superintendent of Police David C. Hennessy Victim of the Vendetta," *New Orleans Daily Picayune*, 16 October 1890; "Shot Down at His Door," *New York Times*, 17 October 1890; Gentile, 14–21.

14. *Dago* is an offensive term for an Italian. The root of the term traces to the name "Diego," and it was once used as a demeaning term for Italians, Spaniards, or Portuguese. Gentile, 15; "Assassination of the Chief of Police," *New Orleans Daily Picayune*, 16 October 1890; "The Slain Chieftain," *New Orleans Daily Picayune*, 17 October 1890.

the Provenzanos quickly accused the Matranga faction of the murder. The New Orleans police chose to believe the Provenzanos' declaration and released any Italian affiliated to the Provenzanos. After deliberation, the police indicted nine suspects for the murder of David Hennessy, and a trial was set for 28 February 1891.[15]

The prosecution had absolutely no evidence that the suspects had committed the murder. All of the accused Italians were able to provide alibis, and the prosecution's reliance on witness testimonies collapsed when cross-examination of the witnesses revealed that the night of the murder was too clouded with fog and rain for anyone to clearly distinguish any individual more than five feet away. On 13 March 1891, the jury announced their verdict: the defendants were found not guilty.[16]

Residents of New Orleans exploded with outrage. The Italians had murdered the beloved David Hennessy, and they were now going to walk away unscathed. Many citizens believed someone had fixed the jury, and the jury members instantly became the most hated residents in the entire state of Louisiana. Local politicians immediately began pointing fingers at Dominick O'Malley, a local private detective who had been previously arrested in Cleveland for perjury and bribery. The Sicilians had appointed O'Malley as their agent and associate in previous court hearings, and many citizens of New Orleans held that O'Malley had been a "deadly enemy" of David Hennessy, who had been chosen over O'Malley for the New Orleans police chief position. For William S. Parkerson, a local politician and the mayor's right-hand man, only one thing could be done: justice. The following morning, the biggest papers in New Orleans ran the same headline: "All good citizens are invited to attend a mass meeting on Saturday, March 14 at 10 o'clock A.M., at Clay Statue to take steps to remedy the failure of justice in the Hennessy case." In the last four words, the most prominent citizens of New Orleans declared their dire objective: "Come prepared for action."[17]

The Saturday morning meeting quickly became a boisterous mob. Following a brief rally at Clay Statue, several local politicians led thousands of citizens to the Parish Prison, picking up Winchester rifles from a warehouse along the way. Some of the mob broke off in an attempt to capture Jacob M. Seligman, a successful jeweler and the foreman of the jury. The mob found Seligman as he attempted to flee the city, but the police quickly rescued him. Several of his associates were able to conceal him until he could escape to Cincinnati the following day, but he soon lost his business and never quite recovered.[18]

---

15. Gentile, 14–21.

16. "NONE GUILTY!, The Jury in the Hennessy Case Deliver Their Verdict," *New Orleans Daily Picayune*, 14 March 1891; "The Hennessy Case," *New Orleans Daily Picayune*, 14 March 1891; Gentile, 32–40.

17. "NONE GUILTY!, The Jury in the Hennessy Case Deliver Their Verdict," *New Orleans Daily Picayune*, 14 March 1891; "Chief Hennessy Avenged; Eleven of His Italian Assassins Lynched by a Mob," *New York Times*, 15 March 1891; "The Massacre at the Parish Prison," *Harper's Weekly*, 28 March 1891; Gentile, 34–36.

18. "Chief Hennessy Avenged; Eleven of His Italian Assassins Lynched by a Mob," *New York Times*, 15 March 1891; "The Mafia and What Led to the Lynching," *Harper's Weekly*, 28 March 1891; Gentile, 34–35.

The main part of the mob proceeded toward the prison. Upon hearing about the incoming mass of angry citizens, the warden of Parish Prison unlocked the Italians from their cells and frantically told them to hide on the women's side of the jail. The mob stormed towards the locked front door of the Parish Prison. As they began battering the door with a gigantic wooden beam, some citizens remembered a side door to the cells. A group of men armed with shotguns and pistols charged inside and began hunting for their prey. Soon after the men had entered the side door, the front door was bashed open and the leading participants of the mob busted inside the prison.[19]

The non-Italian prisoners, fearing for their own lives if things got out of hand, told the attackers that the Italians had fled to the women's side of the jail. Upon reaching the women's section, an elderly African American woman told them to look upstairs. The Italians above the women's corridor stood no chance; four of the accused and two non-related Italians were gunned down instantly, as each assassin fired at point-blank range. Another part of the mob found three others in a nearby corridor and quickly riddled them with bullets. One was shot an implausible forty-two times.[20]

One of the innocent, Manuel Polizzi, was dragged outside and hanged on a gaslight as he howled for mercy. As men pulled on the rope, raising his body higher, the rope snapped and Polizzi came crashing to the ground. Someone found a clothesline, and Polizzi was raised again. Yet Polizzi would still not cooperate; he grabbed the line and pulled on it, gasping for air. Agitated, the mob put him down one last time and tied his hands. As he rose a third time, several people in the crowd shot the helpless Polizzi, finally killing him. Minutes later, Antonio Bagnetto would hang as well. Unlike Polizzi, however, Bagnetto was lucky enough to be dead before he was hanged. Several of the prisoners were able to escape the mob's wrath, yet by the time the citizens of New Orleans sat down to lunch, eleven Italians had been slain, four of whom had nothing to do with the Hennessy trial. Nonetheless, not one Italian in the entire prison ever admitted to knowing who killed Police Chief David Hennessy, even with guns pointed at their heads. The mystery remained: "Who killa de chief?"[21]

That night the newspapers feasted. As the Italian government exploded with anger, newspapers from all around the country jumped on the event, from Tacoma, Washington, to New Haven, Connecticut. Most reports supported the event, celebrating the lynching as a victory for Americans everywhere. Some newspapers, however, questioned the act and mocked the chaotic way in which the New Orleans citizens had responded to the verdict. Either way, the

---

19. "The Massacre at the Parish Prison," *Harper's Weekly*, 28 March 1891; "Chief Hennessy Avenged; Eleven of His Italian Assassins Lynched by a Mob," *New York Times*, 15 March 1891; Gentile, 28–29; Smith, 220–223.

20. "Chief Hennessy Avenged; Eleven of His Italian Assassins Lynched by a Mob," *New York Times*, 15 March 1891; "The Last Rites, Burial of the Victims of Popular Vengeance," *New Orleans Daily Picayune*, 16 March 1891; "The Massacre at the Parish Prison," *Harper's Weekly*, 28 March 1891; Gentile, 28; Smith, 224–230.

21. "The Last Rites, Burial of the Victims of Popular Vengeance," *New Orleans Daily Picayune*, 16 March 1891; "Chief Hennessy Avenged; Eleven of His Italian Assassins Lynched by a Mob," *New York Times*, 15 March 1891; "The Massacre at the Parish Prison," *Harper's Weekly*, 28 March 1891; Gentile, 28–30; Smith, 225–227.

violent lynching of eleven Italians on 14 March 1891 brought great upheaval to newspapers around the country and allowed many reporters to demonstrate their anti–immigrant feelings through their writings.[22]

Most of the papers around New Orleans reacted in similar fashion. They aligned with the New Orleans mob, celebrating the lynching and the triumph of American justice. The newspapers treated the mob-leading politicians as heroes who had bravely stood up for their country. The *New Orleans Daily Picayune* proclaimed that "when the ministers of the law fail," such forceful action was required. The New Orleans papers emphasized the jury's suspicious failure to convict the Italians and the moral need to right the wrong. The newspapers belittled the violence against the Italians and highlighted how few Italians the mob had attacked throughout the whole debacle. According to the local papers, death had only been given to the ones who had deserved such a fate. In a state with one of the largest Italian immigrant populations at the time, this reaction in and around New Orleans does not prove peculiar. The lynching sent a clear warning to any future Italian immigrants to New Orleans, and the majority of white citizens were glad that such an opportunity for a warning arose.[23]

Despite not having even remotely similar immigrant situations, many other southern newspapers also supported the actions of the mob. Much of the support drew upon a basic allegiance to fellow southerners. Less than thirty years since the Confederacy's fall, many white southerners still held a sense of genuine brotherhood with their fellow southerners. The widespread Democratic Party, which controlled much of the South and many of its major newspapers, also contributed far-reaching support for the mob's actions. Like their Republican rivals, the southern Democrats disliked all minorities and magnified their ill effects upon American society whenever they had the chance. The *Knoxville Journal* called the event a "work of vindication," while the report in the *Dallas Morning News* boasted that New Orleans "rose in its might" and "wreaked vengeance upon the Sicilian assassins who relentlessly slew David C. Hennessy." The front headline of the *Macon Telegraph* boldly proclaimed "Justice Satisfied!" Most southern papers treated the mob as a procession of saints instead of a riot of merciless murderers. The *Knoxville Journal* described the storming of the Parish Prison as an "orderly" occurrence, and noted how the people "dispersed quietly" once the measures had been taken. Likewise, the *Dallas Morning News* noted that the storming mob was "not an unruly midnight mob," and the citizens of New Orleans were merely ensuring the preservation of justice. In a completely contradictory statement, the *Macon Telegraph* noted how a "mob of cool-headed men, lawyers, doctors … quietly decided that some action must be taken …

---

22. "Administering Popular Justice," *New Orleans Daily Picayune*, 15 March 1891; "Weakness of the Authorities," *New Orleans Daily Picayune*, 15 March 1891; "Outside Opinion Not to Be Feared," *New Orleans Daily Picayune*, 15 March 1891; "Eleven Lynched, Citizens Break into New Orleans Jail," *Tacoma Daily News*, 14 March 1891; "Hennessy Avenged, Eleven of His Alleged Assassins Lynched," *New Haven Register*, 14 March 1891; "Chief Hennessy Avenged; Eleven of His Italian Assassins Lynched by a Mob," *New York Times*, 15 March 1891; "The Mafia," *Harper's Weekly*, 28 March 1891.

23. "The Last Rites, Burial of the Victims of Popular Vengeance," *New Orleans Daily Picayune*, 16 March; "When the Ministers of the Law Fail," *New Orleans Daily Picayune*, 15 March 1891; Gentile, 8–9, 74–81.

swiftly and surely visited." No city in the South had experienced the same immigration issues as New Orleans, and yet many of the major southern newspapers still celebrated the lynching of the eleven Sicilians.[24]

Most of these southern papers attempted to focus on the legal need for the lynchings. The journalists in the South emphasized the ineffectiveness of the jury and the presence of underground Italian deals rather than highlight the treachery committed by the mob. Nevertheless, the anti-immigrant fervor that existed around the country underlay the entire event. Had anti-Italianism not existed in New Orleans and William O'Connor not conjured up the idea that "the Dagos did it," the Italians would not have been imprisoned, tried, and subsequently lynched. Although they maintained few immigrant problems themselves, the southern states and their newspapers still chose to join the wealthy citizens of New Orleans in slandering the Italians and accusing them of having secret societies. While not openly denouncing immigrants, the newspapers of the South still sent a clear message to all immigrants: stay out, or else.[25]

Not all southern papers celebrated the lynchings, however. The *Charlotte News* differed from its fellow southern newspapers, citing the crowd for "murderous work," during which the "officers of the law … cheered the mob." The *Charlotte News* never once defined the mob participants as citizens, as did nearly every other newspaper around the country. The *Daily Register* of Mobile, Alabama, claimed that the event was "a terrible tragedy" and there was "no good reason for the lynching," and that it would "increase the spirit of lawlessness." It added that the actions "must be deplored by every well-wisher to the Crescent City, as well as by every upholder of law and order." Similarly, the *Houston Post* reported that the event was a "monstrous tragedy." The reports largely mocked the attackers, construing the event as a chaotic free-for-all brought upon by savage animals bent on murdering helpless victims. Despite these few exceptions, however, most of the South took pride in the mob's actions.[26]

Like many reports in the South, the northern newspapers also emphasized the failure of the jury rather than focusing on the transgressions against the Italians. From Chicago to New York, northern journalists criticized the trial results, although they expressed far more reluctance to celebrate the mob's work than most southern newspapers. Italian immigrants, numbering over one million by 1900, had a much larger presence throughout the North, so any rash report that openly celebrated the mob's actions would have been an unwise political and personal move. Nevertheless, northerners held some of the

---

24. "Their Nemesis, The Avenger Overtakes the New Orleans Assassins," *Knoxville Journal*, 15 March 1891; "Hennessy Avenged, And Eleven Sicilians are Stark in Death in New Orleans," *Dallas Morning News*, 15 March 1891; "Justice Satisfied!, The Sentence of the People Promptly Executed," *Macon Telegraph*, 15 March 1891.

25. Gentile, 87–100; "Chief Hennessy Avenged," *New York Times*, 15 March 1891.

26. "The People a Mob, Slaughter of the Italians in New Orleans," *Charlotte News*, 16 March 1891; "A Ridiculous Ending, The Hennessy Assassination Case in New Orleans," *Daily Register* (Mobile, AL), 14 March 1891; "Swift Vengeance, The People of New Orleans Make and Execute Their Verdict," *Daily Register* (Mobile, AL), 15 March 1891; "Lynch Law in New Orleans," *Daily Register* (Mobile, AL), 15 March 1891; "The New Orleans Riot," *Houston Post*, 15 March 1891; "Reign of the Commune at New Orleans," *Houston Post*, 15 March 1891. The *Houston Post* devoted the entire front page to this story.

most extreme anti-immigrant feelings in the entire country. As numerous migrants from southern and eastern Europe began flocking to the United States during the late nineteenth century, many Americans began to worry about the incredible rate of immigration. Unlike the South, which experienced declining numbers of foreign-born residents during the late nineteenth century, the North began to experience a large new wave of immigrants, mostly hailing from Italy, Poland, Austria-Hungary, and Russia. New York's immigrant population rose more than 300 percent between 1860 and 1900, from 383,717 to 1,270,080. With proportionally similar increases in many other northern cities such as Chicago and Philadelphia, many Americans began to worry about their country's future. Most native-born Americans and many older Irish and German immigrants saw the new immigrants as dirty sleazebags who were quickly taking all the blue-collar jobs away and polluting American society. Citizens began protesting against the constant immigration, calling for new laws to stop the endless flow of "inferior" ethnicities into their nation. When the government did not respond immediately, some Americans took matters into their own hands and began practicing incredibly intense discrimination against the newcomers. Since Italians marked a large proportion of the immigrant population around the turn of the twentieth century, Americans were eager to treat Italians as harshly as any other ethnic group.[27] Northern journalists proved little exception to the widespread anti-Italianism throughout the region, and this intrinsic prejudice clearly marred their reports of the 1891 lynching in New Orleans.[28]

Nevertheless, the immigrant-heavy environment in which the northern newspapers resided duly affected their treatment of the event. As the reporters in the North began composing their own reports of the incident, Italians in many major cities held mass gatherings and collected money to send to the victims' families in New Orleans. These gatherings drafted petitions and openly condemned the mob's actions in New Orleans, and the potential for a massive Italian riot prevented any northern newspapers, especially those located around a large Italian population, from candidly supporting the lynchings. Any northern journalist who valued his job or his life did not completely endorse the series of events in New Orleans; instead, he celebrated subliminally.[29]

On the surface, most northern newspapers eased up on the Italian victims. The *Washington Post* mocked the lack of protection given to the Italians by the

---

27. One example of the drastic anti-Italian xenophobia occurred in Buffalo in 1888. After one Italian killed another, the police superintendent arrested 325 Italians, virtually all the Italian males in the entire city. After thorough searches, only two were found with weapons. When asked why he had arrested so many Italians, the superintendent merely stated that Italians routinely carried concealed weapons and the public had demanded such drastic measures. Luciano J. Iorizzo and Salvatore Mondello, *The Italian Americans* (Boston: Twayne Publishers, 1980), 81–82.

28. Gentile, 4–8; U.S. Bureau of the Census, *Twelfth Consensus of the United States Taken in the Year 1900*, compiled by Joseph C. G. Kennedy (Washington, DC: Government Printing Office, 1901) 1, Pt. 1, lxix, cix.

29. "Chief Hennessy Avenged; Eleven of His Italian Assassins Lynched by a Mob," *New York Times*, 15 March 1891; Gentile, 89–92.

Parish Prison authorities, stating that "no material resistance was offered by the police or sheriff to the work of the citizens." *Frank Leslie's Illustrated Newspaper* also criticized the New Orleans authorities, noting how the mob was "openly encouraged by the police, and met with no serious resistance at the prison." The paper also offered a full page drawing of the incident on the front page. The *Inter Ocean*, a large Republican newspaper in Chicago,[30] sympathized with the Italians despite still exhibiting a strong anti-Italian sentiment. The report vividly described the event as a "massacre," brought upon by a "savage mob;" yet the headline still called the Italians "murderers" and "slayers" despite no proof that they committed the murder. Both the *Philadelphia Inquirer* and the *Baltimore Sun* also put down the mob while degrading the victims at the same time, labeling the Italians as deadly "assassins." Even though they had been found not guilty and no sufficient evidence had linked them with the murder of David Hennessy, the northern papers still accused the Italians of committing the murder. Thus, while not actively encouraging the act of the lynchings, several major northern newspapers made a conscious effort not to free the Italians of their murderous label.[31]

This murderous label demonstrated the North's double standard for the event, which led to confusing contradictions. While depicting the mob as a violent slaughtering machine, the northern papers nevertheless provided thorough rationale for the mob's actions. The *Philadelphia Inquirer* boasted how the mob went to the Parish Prison to "slay [the Italians] in their cells without mercy," eliciting images of a violent butchering, yet noted how "the acquittal of the accused yesterday came like a thunder clap from a clear sky." *Frank Leslie's Illustrated Newspaper,* a very popular national publication based in New York, even published John C. Wickliffe's[32] justification for the event on 4 April 1891.[33] Several other newspapers followed suit, and soon the memory of a violent mob disappeared as Wickliffe's rationalization began to circulate around the country. Using his background in politicking and his uncanny ability to appeal to the

---

30. Almost all of the leading politicians and citizens of New Orleans belonged to the Democratic Party, so Republican newspapers that dominated the North, such as the *Inter Ocean*, would have denounced the lynching if only because its political rivals caused and supported the event.

31. "No Mercy Was Shown, Vengeance Wreaked on the Cruel Slayers of Chief Hennessy," *Washington Post*, 15 March 1891; "Crimes of the Mafia: Record of the New Orleans Branch of an Assassin Band," *Washington Post*, 15 March 1891; "The New Orleans Outbreak," *Frank Leslie's Illustrated Newspaper*, 28 March 1891; "Lawlessness in New Orleans – The Mob Breaking Down the Doors of the Parish Prison," *Frank Leslie's Illustrated Newspaper*, 28 March 1891; "Massacre of the Mafia," *Chicago Inter Ocean*, 15 March 1891; "Lynchers' Vengeance, Citizens Kill Eleven of the Mafia Assassins in New Orleans," *Philadelphia Inquirer*, 15 March 1891; "War on La Mafia, Eleven Sicilians Killed by a Mob in New Orleans," *Baltimore Sun*, 16 March 1891; "Details of the Massacre, The Meeting, Speeches, March to Prison, Execution and Dispersal," *Baltimore Sun*, 16 March 1891; "The Dread Mafia: How the Members Wreck Vengeance on Their Betrayers," *Baltimore Sun*, 16 March 1891; "The Mafia," *Harper's Weekly*, 28 March 1891.

32. John C. Wickliffe, whose father was the governor of Louisiana from 1856 to 1860, was a leader in the lynching. Appointed by the mayor of New Orleans to the Committee of Fifty (a group of leading citizens given the power to decide what to do with the accused Italians), Wickliffe proved instrumental in the decision to storm the Parish Prison. Gentile, 74.

33. The published interview occurred three long weeks after the event, so Wickliffe had undoubtedly been able to prepare his exact words for this interview.

common citizen, Wickliffe swiftly and effectively rationalized the lynching by citing the constitutional need to correct the government when it failed to perform its duty.[34] He bragged that the people had "executed the law upon the men found guilty," ignoring the fact that every Italian had clearly been found not guilty by the jury.[35]

As Wickliffe defended himself in *Frank Leslie's Illustrated Newspaper*, William S. Parkerson[36] found a similar opportunity to announce his own rationalization when the *Illustrated American*, another popular periodical of the time, interviewed him in the weeks following the event. While not as overtly racist as Wickliffe, Parkerson nevertheless defended his actions and expressed no regret. As these interviews circulated around the United States, the American people gradually forgot about the brutal violence instigated by the mob and began to approve of their fellow countrymen's effective response. The northern newspapers initially reported the event with delicacy and precaution, but within a few short weeks the papers began endorsing the mob's justifications, circulating them around the rest of the country.[37]

Even the newspapers throughout the West held underlying prejudices against the Italians. Although most of the western reports gave a fairly objective account of the event for that time period, they still erroneously accused the Italians of being members of the Mafia and labeled them as merciless killers. The *San Francisco Bulletin* clearly reported that the jury found the accused not guilty yet hastily called the Italians "Sicilian assassins" who had murdered David Hennessy. The *Idaho Statesman* emphasized the role of the Mafia in its report despite the fact that there was no valid proof of the Mafia's existence at that time. The initial wire from the *San Jose Mercury* reported that the Italian victims were "alleged murderers," providing much more defense for the lynched victims than most other newspapers. Yet the very next sentence of the report stated that the jury had "failed" to convict the eleven "members of Lamafia," clearly demonstrating the writer's underlying belief that the victims were truly guilty. The *Tacoma Daily News* of Washington provided an almost southern-like perspective, blindly citing the Italians as "members of the Mafia society, a lawless organization

---

34. While the United States Constitution does state that the people must correct the government when it goes awry, no proof of jury tampering had ever been found. In this case, the thought that the governmental system did not fulfill its duty proved merely an opinion, not a fact, and Wickliffe's justification is therefore groundless. During this time of heightened xenophobia, however, many people would have readily assumed Wickliffe's opinion as a hard fact.

35. "Quiet in New Orleans, Funerals of All the Victims of the Mob's Summary Vengeance," *Philadelphia Inquirer*, 16 March 1891; "A Jury of Twenty Thousand," *Frank Leslie's Illustrated Newspaper*, 4 April 1891.

36. Parkerson was another member of the Committee of Fifty and a leading participant in the lynching. His interview was published on the same day as Wickliffe's interview, so he also had three long weeks to prepare his justification for the media.

37. "New Orleans' War on the Mafia, The Court of Lynch Law and Its Judges," *Illustrated American*, 4 April 1891, 319–323; Gentile, 74–86. The publication also ran a multipage "supplement" to its 28 March 1891 issue that described the Mafia from its origins in Italy to the incident in New Orleans. "Exterminating the Mafia, Pictorial Account of the Work of Judge Lynch in New Orleans," *Illustrated American*, 28 March 1891, Supplement to No. 58, 1–20. The magazine claimed in an editorial that if its warning about the Mafia threat had been "heeded in time, the massacre at New Orleans would never have taken place." "How the New Orleans Massacre Might Have Been Avoided—Warning of 'The Illustrated American,'" *Illustrated American*, 4 April 1891, 314.

of Italians." The Tacoma paper even resorted to manufacturing its own truths, declaring that the Mafia "had decreed the assassination of several [other] prominent citizens," a statement that had not been reported anywhere else, even in New Orleans.[38]

The western newspapers proved the kindest to the Italians for various reasons. While Italian immigrants numbered in the thousands in California, Italians elsewhere in the West were few and far between. The West's mixed reaction to the event reflected the fact that most westerners simply did not have to deal with the European immigration influx that the North did. Americans of the western United States still demonstrated incredible nativism, however, but they directed most of their nativism towards the Asian population, which accounted for most of the immigration to the western part of the country. More often than not, American westerners held any kind of European, no matter the exact cultural background, in higher esteem than most Asians, who were infiltrating the West during this time in vast numbers. The westerners treated Asians like the New Orleanians treated Italians, with jealousy and spite, for many of the same envious reasons.[39] Fortunately for European immigrants, they more closely resembled the Americans physically, and the western Americans subsequently treated the European immigrants better than most Asian newcomers.[40]

In their own newspapers, Italian Americans called the debacle an outrage, even calling for revenge. This call for retribution only made matters worse, however, as it provided the American people with another reason to suspect the Italians of underlying violence. Most of the outside world abhorred the mob's actions. The *Post* in London famously called the event a "deplorable page in American history," and the newspapers in Berlin insisted that the United States government should hunt for the murderers and justify the victims' deaths. The newspapers in Italy were unsurprisingly furious and cried for swift punishment upon the American people. The Italian government even threatened war if the United States government did not issue an apology and offer some sort of financial reimbursement for the deaths of its citizens. Unfortunately for the Italians, however, many Congressmen applauded the efforts of the New Orleans citizens, and even President Benjamin Harrison hesitated to issue an apology. Theodore Roosevelt, who would lead the country ten years later, cheerfully called the event a "rather good thing." For a brief time, the United States and Italy braced for conflict, waiting for the other to make the first move. As an unpopular

---

38. "Latest Telegraph, A Violent Uprising in New Orleans," *San Francisco Bulletin*, 14 March 1891; "The Mafia Case," *Idaho Statesman* (Boise), 14 March 1891; "A Crime Revenged, Eleven Mafia Assassins Are Killed in New Orleans," *Idaho Statesman* (Boise), 15 March 1891; "Lynched, A Mob in New Orleans This Morning," *San Jose Mercury News*, 14 March 1891; "Eleven Lynched, Citizens Break into New Orleans Jail," *Tacoma Daily News*, 14 March 1891; "Mafia Murderers, The Crimes for Which They Were Executed," *Tacoma Daily News*, 16 March 1891; "The New Orleans Mob," *Tacoma Daily News*, 16 March 1891.

39. Like the Italians in New Orleans, some Asians in the West became successful businessmen and made as much if not more money than many whites of the area.

40. Gentile, 63–73.

president nearing reelections, Harrison desperately needed to regain the support of many American voters. Southerners especially disliked their current president, a northern Republican, and Harrison needed some way to rekindle his relationship with the white southern voters. He tried to please his potential electors by waiting a considerable time to denounce the lynching, but the possibility of conflict with Italy ultimately forced him to put the fate of his country before the fate of his presidency. Finally, nine months after the lynching, President Harrison realized the Italians were serious and gave into the Italian demands, issuing a lukewarm apology along with $25,000 to the families of the three Italian citizens who had been murdered.[41]

While most newspapers across the country provided rationale for the mob's actions, even more newspapers accused the Mafia of undermining the legal process in New Orleans. Virtually every newspaper in the United States, no matter the regional location, agreed that the Mafia tampered with the jury and deeply influenced the verdict. The invention and spread of the term *Mafia* proved the most basic example of anti-Italian sentiment. Before 1890, the Mafia was known to exist only in Italy and Sicily, where it provided underground protection when the government failed to do so.[42] The *padrone* system, not the Mafia, existed in New Orleans and many other American cities, and this padrone system did not resemble the Italian Mafia organization. While the Italian *padroni*, or bosses, provided Italians with labor opportunities and effectively took care of their people's well-being in the United States, they also exploited their Italian brethren for financial advancement and personal gain. Unlike the Mafia, the padrone system existed only for the benefit of a few select people rather than for the good of many Italians. Nevertheless, most American newspapers, looking for a catchy term that would increase their own profits, modified the perception of the *padrone* system and claimed that the Mafia lay behind the scandal. The confusion between the *padrone* system and the true Mafia organization proved a costly error on behalf of the Italians, as the American people began fearing the potential dangers of such a crooked underground society.[43]

---

41. Many contemporaries agreed that Italy's navy was superior to that of the United States during this time, a belief that helped steer Harrison away from conflict with Italy. Several naval officers also used this incident as an excuse to reinvest in the United States Navy, and seven years later, American naval powers were able to fight and defeat Spain in the Spanish-American War. "Views of the London Press: The Occurrence Will Form a Dark Blot in American History," *Washington Post*, 16 March 1891; "Instructions from Rome: Haron de Fava Directed to Protest Against the Outrage at New Orleans," *Washington Post*, 16 March 1891; "Its International Aspect," *Washington Post*, 16 March 1891; "The New Orleans Riot: Minister Rudini Instructs Baron Fava to Enter a Protest," *Washington Post*, 16 March 1891; "Blaine Acts," *New Orleans Daily Picayune*, 16 March 1891; "Italy Acts," *New Orleans Daily Picayune*, 16 March 1891; Gentile, *The Innocent Lynched*, 92–93; Gambino, 118; "Italians Want Indemnity," *New York Times*, 17 March 1891; "New Orleans Threatened: Italians Who Insist on Government 'Reparation' or Revenge," *New York Times*, 17 March 1891; "Lynch Law and the Mafia," *New York Times*, 17 March 1891; "Italy's 'Crispinade,'" *Harper's Weekly*, 11 April 1891.

42. Esposito, an infamous outlaw in Sicily and New Orleans during the 1870s and 1880s, was credited with bringing the Mafia to New Orleans and the rest of the United States. Most scholars now agree that Esposito was not a member of the Mafia, however, and that he more resembled a bandit or common outlaw than a member of the Mafia system. The *New York Times* in 1881 called him "a genuine Italian … black-eyed, swarthy, and wicked," and this description has been credited as the first widely publicized anti-Italian defamation in the United States. Gentile, 50–54; "An Italian Bandit Captured," *New York Times*, 9 July 1881.

43. Gentile, 11, 49–53, 59–62.

At a time when anti-Italianism abounded throughout the nation, Americans unsurprisingly accepted the Mafia idea. For many newspapers and their readers, the Mafia proved the only plausible reason for such a failure in the American court system. Some people claimed to have evidence for the existence of the Mafia in the United States, but virtually all of those claims proved groundless. Both the Provenzano faction and David Hennessy claimed to have evidence of a Mafia in New Orleans, but this evidence was never brought forth in either the Provenzano or Matranga trial. If the Mafia did indeed exist, it would never have resorted to the extent of legality that the Italians in New Orleans did. A true Mafia organization would not bring another faction to court, as happened with the Provenzano case when the Matranga faction testified against the Provenzanos. Yet the police and press continued to publicize the Mafia concept around the time of the Hennessy trial, and these constant warnings of secret Italian societies undoubtedly affected many opinions on the matter. As the New Orleans newspapers began to publish the concept of a Mafia, more newspapers around the country followed suit. Within a matter of days, the press had invented the Mafia in the United States.[44]

Italians all around the country quickly denounced any relations to the Mafia in a variety of public ways. Secrecy and a code of silence trademarked the Italian Mafia throughout its history, so any open denouncement of the Mafia clearly went against the common Mafia principles. From New York to California, hundreds of thousands of Italians publicly denied any connections with the Mafia, making the existence of such an apparently widespread organization implausible at best.[45]

While not all newspapers openly celebrated the 1891 lynching of eleven Sicilians in New Orleans, every single one exhibited anti-Italian prejudice in one way or another. From San Francisco to New York, the entire country believed that the victims were guilty. Even the newspapers that eased up on the eleven lynched Sicilians demonstrated clear prejudice against the Italian people. The same anti-Italian fervor that plagued the Hennessy case lasted well into the twentieth century, and the belief in the Mafia's existence in the United States never disappeared. The trial of those accused David Hennessy's murder and the subsequent lynching of eleven Sicilians soon became lost in history,[46] but the event nevertheless altered the American outlook towards Italians for many years afterward.[47]

---

44. "The Last Rites, Burial of the Victims of Popular Vengeance," *New Orleans Daily Picayune*, 16 March 1891; "Chief Hennessy Avenged; Eleven of His Italian Assassins Lynched by a Mob," *New York Times*, 15 March 1891; "The Mafia," *Harper's Weekly*, 28 March 1891; "The Mafia and What Led to the Lynching," *Harper's Weekly*, 28 March 1891; Gentile, 58–62, 89–91.

45. Gentile, 58–62, 89–91.

46. Edward Holmes, a native New Orleanian born in 1922, never recalled having heard of the Hennessy trial or the lynching of eleven Sicilians just a few decades prior. "I've never heard of anything like that," he commented, "but people didn't like Italians, that was for sure." Almost forty years after the incident, the event had been discarded, even in New Orleans, yet the legacy of anti-Italianism clearly kept on chugging.

47. Gentile, 107–115.

ANNOTATED BIBLIOGRAPHY

I. Primary Sources

Baltimore Sun, 1891.
> Located in Maryland, this newspaper held similar beliefs as other northern papers and reported the lynching in a similar way to the *New York Times* and *Philadelphia Enquirer*, reluctant to overtly praise the mob's actions but subliminally doing so nonetheless.

Charlotte News, 1891.
> Although located in the South, this newspaper displayed much more rational thinking about the incident, especially considering the time period. Unlike most other southern papers, the *Charlotte News* did not express any reluctance to criticize the mob's actions.

Chicago Inter Ocean, 1891.
> Republican-run newspaper. Chicago held one of the largest Italian populations just before the turn of the twentieth century, so the Republicans, although firmly against immigration, had to be cautious with word choice when reporting the event.

"Correspondence in Relation to the Killing of Prisoners in New Orleans on March 14, 1891." Harvard University Virtual Collections. http://pds.lib.harvard.edu/pds/view/4987805 (accessed 15 February 2009).
> This collection of correspondence contains letters written between Italian and American officials that dealt directly with the incident. The Italians quickly blamed the United States officials, while the United States officials tried to talk their way out of the blame.

Daily Register (Mobile, AL), 1891.
> Based in Alabama, this newspaper did not share other southerners' opinions about the lynching but largely accused the mob and adopted a surprisingly critical tone towards the entire event.

Dallas Morning News, 1891.
> Texas had few Italian immigrants, yet this newspaper still openly praised the mob's actions. Texas's bordering on and having a similar political background to Louisiana contributed to the Dallas newspaper's treatment of the event.

Frank Leslie's Illustrated Newspaper, 1891.
> Published in New York City, this illustrated newspaper covered many popular topics in the given time. This journal was the first to publish one of the mob leader's justifications, clearly demonstrating its underlying support for the mob.

Harper's Weekly, 1891.
> New York-based national journal that covered many social affairs in the United States. It provided much more defense for the Italian victims than most other northern newspapers of the time.

Houston Post, 1891.
> Located relatively close to New Orleans but did not share the same enthusiasm for the mob as other southern newspapers. It proved largely critical of the entire debacle and defended the Italians fairly well in a time of heightened xenophobia.

Idaho Statesman (Boise), 1891.

Based in Boise, this newspaper largely followed trends in other larger newspapers in the West, expressing gentler opinions about the event than most eastern and southern reports due to lack of experience with Italian and other European immigrants.

Knoxville Journal, 1891.

Large Tennessee newspaper that exhibited sincere approval of the mob's actions and rashly accused the jury and the Mafia, following the pattern of most southern newspapers then dominated by both the Democratic Party and their Confederate backgrounds.

London Post, 1891.

Popular newspaper in London that publicly criticized the lynchings. Its was not too keen on American behaviors in this event and made no effort to conceal its critique.

Macon Telegraph Georgia, 1891.

Southern paper that shared similar sentiments as the *Dallas Morning News, Knoxville Journal*, and most other southern newspapers. It praised the mob's actions and slandered the jury and the Italian victims.

New Haven Register, 1891.

Connecticut newspaper dominated by the Republican Party, this paper did not encourage the mob but subtly praised it nonetheless, displaying the anti-immigrant beliefs that the Republican Party held. It attempted to straddle the fence, just in case of Italian backlash.

New Orleans Daily Picayune, 1890–1891.

One of several major newspapers in New Orleans, the *Picayune* exhibited the same anti-Italian sentiment that populated mainstream New Orleans during this time, attempting to appeal to the common New Orleanian and make some profit in the process.

New York Times, 1881, 1884, 1890–1891.

One of the most popular and important newspapers during the late nineteenth century, this paper expressed superficial uncertainty about the event but consistently slandered Italians and Italian Americans in a very quiet way.

Philadelphia Inquirer, 1891.

Like most other northern papers, this newspaper externally questioned the mob's actions but actually expressed strong anti-Italian sentiment in between the lines.

San Francisco Bulletin, 1891.

Western newspaper that held kinder words for the Italians involved in the event. This paper showed minimal racism towards the victims, but this was because most of the *Bulletin*'s racism was saved for the Asian immigrants.

San Jose Mercury News, 1891.

Like the *San Francisco Bulletin*, this newspaper held fewer anti-Italian beliefs than most other newspapers around the country because it did not have experience with European immigrants to the degree that the eastern coast did.

Tacoma Daily News, 1891.

This Washington-based newspaper demonstrated fairly overt racism for a western newspaper, manufacturing its own myths about the Mafia. It held far more anti-Italian sentiments than most other newspapers around the West.

The Illustrated American New York, 1891.
  A popular national magazine that supplied the public with one of the mob leaders' rationalizations for the event, subsequently expressing its underlying support for the lynching.

The Mascot, an Independent Journal of the Day (New Orleans), 1888.
  A local journal based in New Orleans, this magazine commented on popular social issues in the Crescent City. It expressed strong anti-Italian sentiments just like its other periodical counterparts around New Orleans.

U.S. Bureau of the Census, *Population of the United States in 1860: Compiled from the Original Returns of the Eighth Census under the Direction of the Secretary of the Interior* (Washington, DC: Government Printing Office, 1861).
  This report compiled by the U.S. Bureau of the Census provided the numbers of native and immigrant population during the year 1860.

———. *Statistics of the Population of the United States at the Tenth Census* (Washington, DC: Government Printing Office, 1883).
  This census report, tallied in 1880 but not completely compiled until 1883, reported the native and immigrant population throughout the United States of the time.

———. *Twelfth Census of the United States Taken in the Year 1900* (Washington, DC: Government Printing Office, 1901).
  Tally of the census in 1900 that reported the population in the United States with a reasonable amount of accuracy.

Washington Post, 1891.
  A major newspaper in the United States that expressed fewer anti-Italian sentiments than most of the country, but only because of its proximity to the United States government and foreign ambassadors.

II. Secondary Sources

Botein, Barbara. "The Hennessy Case: An Episode of Anti-Italian Nativism." *Louisiana History* 20, no. 3 (1979): 261–279.
  Botein focuses on the anti-Italianism sentiments in New Orleans and how such feelings of resentment led to the accusation of Italian suspects, the trial of the nine Italians, and their subsequent lynchings.

Buekner, John D., and Lorman A. Ratner. *Multiculturalism in the United States: A Comparative Guide to Acculturation and Ethnicity*. New York: Greenwood Press, 2005.
  This dense work provides a very general background to immigration and its effects on the United States, encompassing the country's entire ethnic history. With such a vast topic, however, the authors are not able to focus too much on one specific ethnicity.

DeConde, Alexander. *Half Bitter, Half Sweet: An Excursion into Italian-American History*. New York: Scribner, 1971.
  The author of this work provides a well-developed introduction to the overall Italian American experiences during the height of Italian immigration, highlighting both the positive and negative effects of the mass migration to the United States.

Fenton, Edwin. *Immigrants and Unions, a Case Study: Italians and American Labor, 1870–1920*. New Brunswick: Rutgers University Press, 1988.

Fenton examines Italian immigrants and their roles in American labor around the turn of the twentieth century. The author focuses on immigrant labor organizations and the effects of these organizations on American labor around the country.

Gallo, Patrick J. *Old Bread, New Wine: A Portrait of the Italian Americans.* Chicago: Nelson, Hall, 1981.
Like the work above, this book provides a general overview of the Italian American experience. The author also proves critical of the American response to Italian immigration, especially around the turn of the twentieth century.

Gambino, Richard. *Vendetta: A True Story of the Worst Lynching in America, the Mass Murder of Italian-Americans in New Orleans in 1891, the Vicious Motivations Behind It, and the Tragic Repercussions that Linger to this Day.* Garden City, NY: Doubleday and Co., 1977.
Gambino provides the best overview and analysis of the 1891 lynching, although the author proves slightly biased towards the Italians. Excellent presentation of the information and very detailed comments on the event as a whole.

Gentile, Joseph. *The Innocent Lynched: The Story of Eleven Italians Lynched in New Orleans.* Lincoln, NE: iUniverse.com, 2000.
Gentile provides basic descriptions of the events surrounding the lynchings, providing a firm presentation of the hard facts. The author does not supply too much analysis and leaves much of the conclusion up to the reader.

Higham, John. *Strangers in the Land: Patterns of American Nativism, 1860–1925.* New Brunswick: Rutgers University Press, 1955.
Higham effectively analyzes the constant anti-immigrant sentiments that plagued the United States around the turn of the twentieth century, providing examples of nativism exhibited against many different ethnicities.

Iorizzo, Luciano J., and Salvatore Mondello. *The Italian Americans.* Boston: Twayne Publishers, 1980.
This work provides a very broad overview of Italian Americans and their experiences and lifestyles since coming to the United States. The authors critique the long-standing American negativity towards Italians.

Jackson, Joy J. "Crime and Conscience of a City." *Louisiana History* 24, no. 4 (Summer 1968): 229–244.
Jackson focuses on the underground world in New Orleans during the turn of the twentieth century, including the alleged existence of the Mafia and the infamous Committee of Fifty. A fair amount of focus is given to the 1891 lynching.

———. *New Orleans in the Gilded Age: Politics and Urban Progress, 1880–1896.* Baton Rouge: Louisiana State University Press, 1969.
The author analyzes New Orleans just before the twentieth century, focusing more on the political and social world than the 1891 tragedy. She severely downplays anti-Italian sentiments in New Orleans when referring to the lynching.

Joseph, Desmond Humphrey. *The APA Movement.* New York: Arno Press, 1969.
Joseph describes the revitalization of nativism in the United States in the late nineteenth century, focusing specifically on the American Protective Association, which focused most of its negative sentiments towards new Catholic immigrants.

Karlin, Alexander J. "New Orleans Lynchings of 1891 and the American Press." *Louisiana Historical Quarterly* 24, no. 1 (January 1941): 187–204.

Karlin focuses on the press' reaction to the lynching in 1891. The author captures most areas of the United States and effectively analyzes some of the possible causes for the reactions across the country.

Nelli, Humbert S. "The Hennessy Murder and the Mafia in New Orleans." *Italian Quarterly* 19, no. 75 (1975): 77–95.
  The author adequately depicts the events surrounding the murder of Police Chief David Hennessy but with more emphasis on the actual ambush and possibility of the Mafia's involvement than the actual court case and subsequent lynching.

Smith, Tom. *The Crescent City Lynchings: The Murder of Chief Hennessy, the New Orleans "Mafia" Trials, and the Parish Prison Mob.* Guilford, CT: Lyons Press, 2007.
  Smith draws upon nearly all other works concerning the 1891 lynching. He provides an incredibly detailed narrative and presents the event as a well-written story. This work provides more stories, however, than actual analysis.

Webb, Clive. "The Lynching of Sicilian Immigrants in the American South, 1886–1910." *American Nineteenth Century History* 3, no. 1 (Spring 2002): 45–77.
  The author describes and explains a multitude of violent acts committed against Sicilians around the South around the turn of the twentieth century, including, but not limited to, the 1891 lynching in New Orleans.

Appendix C

＊

CourseReader Assignments

This appendix includes some additional assignments to supplement the assignments and sample writing in Chapter 6, "Writing the Short Essay." The assignments link out to a collection of secondary and primary sources contained in the online supplement, *CourseReader for Doing History*. If your instructor has opted to use CourseReader, your book will come packaged with CourseReader passkey information. To access the readings, you will need to log in to the CourseReader collection at http://login.cengagebrain.com. Have your access code handy when you log in, along with the Reader Enrollment Code from your instructor.

Detailed instructions for each assignment using the selections in *CourseReader: Doing History* are provided below.

COURSEREADER ASSIGNMENT 1: SUMMARY

Read the newspaper article entitled "Europe in Arms." Summarize the article by first listing the main points in bullet format. Using only the points listed, write no more than 200 words that capture your bullet points. Reread the newspaper article and compare what you have written in your summary to the original. Revise until you are comfortable with the results.

COURSEREADER ASSIGNMENT 2: ANALYSIS

Historians have grappled with this complex question since the events unfolded nearly a century ago. Students can try their hand by consulting the same kinds of evidence. Refer to the "Outbreak of World War I: Did Germany Cause

World War I?" selection in your CourseReader collection. This selection first appeared in a 2004 edition of *History in Dispute*.[1]

First read and summarize a few of the secondary accounts to get a sense as to what historians have written about this event. What are the basic facts they describe? Where do they agree? Disagree? How do they differ in their interpretations? What is the relationship between these points of agreement and disagreement that enable one to offer an interpretation based upon the weight of the evidence? How serious are the disagreements? Do the historians seem to be using the same evidence? Consult pages 40–53 for guidance on critical reading of secondary sources as well as pages 104–105 for some elements of secondary source analysis.

After reading some of the secondary sources, proceed to test the validity of each historical argument against some primary sources. For this exercise, apply the following questions to the following primary accounts in your CourseReader collection: What are the main points?

- Who is the author?
- Who is the intended audience?
- What is the purpose?
- What is the bias?
- Which is the most reliable source? Why?
- Which of these is the most problematic source? Why?

Primary Accounts:

- "Bylaws of the Organization: Union or Death"[2]
- Images: French postcard, 1914. "Je suis prêt"! (I am ready!)[3]
- "Europe in Arms, *Times*, 1 August 1914.[4]
- "Dual Alliance Between Austria-Hungary and Germany—October 7, 1879"[5]
- "General Friedrich von Bernhardi, The Next War"[6]

---

1. "Outbreak of World War I: Did Germany Cause World War I?" *History in Dispute*, ed. Paul du Quenoy, Vol. 16: *Twentieth-Century European Social and Political Movements* (Detroit: St. James Press, 2004): 192–98. *World History in Context*, http://ic.galegroup.com/ic/whic/?userGroupName=tlearn_trl (accessed 4 February 2012).

2. Black Hand, "Bylaws of the Organization: Union or Death," *Terrorism: Essential Primary Sources*, ed. K. Lee Lerner and Brenda Wilmoth Lerner (Detroit: Gale, 2006): 110–12. *World History In Context*, http://ic.galegroup.com/ic/whic/?userGroupName=tlearn_trl (accessed4 February 2012).

3. "French postcard, 1914. The phrase Je suis prêt! (I am ready!) reflects the optimism of the...," *Europe Since 1914: Encyclopedia of the Age of War and Reconstruction*, ed. John Merriman and Jay Winter, vol. 1 (Detroit: Charles Scribner's Sons, 2006). *World History in Context*, http://ic.galegroup.com/ic/whic/?userGroupName=tlearn_trl (accessed 4 February 2012).

4. "Europe in Arms," *Times* (London, England), 1 August 1914. *The Times Digital Archive*, http://ic.galegroup.com/ic/whic/?userGroupName=tlearn_trl (accessed 4 February 2012).

5. "The Dual Alliance between Austria-Hungary and Germany—October 7, 1879," *The Avalon Project: Documents in Law, History and Diplomacy*, Yale Law School, Lillian Goldman Law Library, http://avalon.law.yale.edu/19th_century/dualalli.asp (accessed 4 February 2012).

6. Friedrich von Bernhardi, *Germany and the Next War*, trans. Allen H. Powles (New York: Longmans, Green and Company, 1914), 16–20, 85–105, 114, 167–82. *The World War I Document Archive*, http://h-net.org/~german/gtext/kaiserreich/bernhardi.html (accessed 4 February 2012).

After reading the sources, in what ways do they support one another? Note in particular the brief statement in the *Times* that precedes the article "Europe in Arms." What does it reveal about perceptions at that paper on 1 August 1914? What major events are corroborated by more than one account? Where do the sources conflict? Why? Can you reconcile such conflicting pieces of evidence?

COURSEREADER ASSIGNMENT 3: ESSAY

After reading, summarizing, and analyzing the evidence found in your Course-Readercollection, write a five-paragraph essay that answers the question "Did Germany Cause World War I?" Be sure to use the primary evidence to support your case. You may wish to consult pages 105–106 for some guidance in writing this assignment.

ADDITIONAL COURSEREADER ASSIGNMENTS

Find two or more secondary sources in the *CourseReader: Doing History* collection on the same topic. Read them and note the interpretations of the scholars.

Find primary sources in the CourseReader collection that relate to the secondary sources you found above. For each one, first perform external and internal criticism on the documents. Second, using the secondary sources as context, write an essay in which you use the primary sources to answer the question posed in assignment number 2.

Index